NEGATIVE LIBERTY

NEGATIVE LIBERTY

PUBLIC OPINION AND THE TERRORIST ATTACKS ON AMERICA

DARREN W. DAVIS

Russell Sage Foundation • New York

The Russell Sage Foundation

The Russell Sage Foundation, one of the oldest of America's general purpose foundations, was established in 1907 by Mrs. Margaret Olivia Sage for "the improvement of social and living conditions in the United States." The Foundation seeks to fulfill this mandate by fostering the development and dissemination of knowledge about the country's political, social, and economic problems. While the Foundation endeavors to assure the accuracy and objectivity of each book it publishes, the conclusions and interpretations in Russell Sage Foundation publications are those of the authors and not of the Foundation, its Trustees, or its staff. Publication by Russell Sage, therefore, does not imply Foundation endorsement.

BOARD OF TRUSTEES
Thomas D. Cook, Chair

Kenneth D. Brody	Jennifer L. Hochschild	Cora B. Marrett
Robert E. Denham	Kathleen Hall Jamieson	Richard H. Thaler
Christopher Edley Jr.	Melvin J. Konner	Eric Wanner
John A. Ferejohn	Alan B. Krueger	Mary C. Waters
Larry V. Hedges		

Library of Congress Cataloging-in-Publication Data

Davis, Darren W.
   Negative liberty : public opinion and the terrorist attacks on America / by Darren W. Davis.
     p. cm.
   Includes bibliographical references and index.
   ISBN-13: 978-0-87154-322-6
   ISBN-10: 0-87154-322-2
  1. Civil rights—United States. 2. National security—United States. I. Title.
   JC599.U5D285   2006
   323.0973—dc22   2006027800

Copyright © 2007 by Russell Sage Foundation. All rights reserved. Printed in the United States of America. No part of this publication may be reproduced, stored in a retrieval system, or transmitted in any form or by any means, electronic, mechanical, photocopying, recording, or otherwise, without the prior written permission of the publisher.

Reproduction by the United States Government in whole or in part is permitted for any purpose.

The paper used in this publication meets the minimum requirements of American National Standard for Information Sciences—Permanence of Paper for Printed Library Materials. ANSI Z39.48-1992.

Text design by Suzanne Nichols.

RUSSELL SAGE FOUNDATION
112 East 64th Street, New York, New York 10021
10 9 8 7 6 5 4 3 2 1

To Karen, Peyton, and Quinn

Contents

	About the Author	ix
	Preface	xi
	Acknowledgments	xv
Chapter 1	Introduction: A Climate of Threat and Vulnerability	1
Chapter 2	Context: The Promise of 72 Virgins	16
Chapter 3	Value Conflict: Civil Liberties Versus National Security	31
Chapter 4	Explaining the Support for Civil Liberties	59
Chapter 5	Acceptable Consequences	87
Chapter 6	Civil Liberties in an Evolving Context	113
Chapter 7	Spiral of Silence: Partisan Orientations in a Climate of Threat	138
Chapter 8	Racial Reactions	164
Chapter 9	Social Group Affect, Intolerance, and Threat	192
Chapter 10	Conclusion	218
Appendix A	Terror Event Timeline	225
Appendix B	Data and Research Design	228
Appendix C	Survey Questions	231
	Notes	245
	References	253
	Index	267

About the Author

Darren W. Davis is professor of political science at Michigan State University.

Preface

AMERICAN CITIZENS are likely to remember where they were and what they were doing when they first learned that America was under attack on the morning of September 11, 2001. I was in my office when a colleague, who had been listening to the radio, mentioned that the first airplane had crashed into the World Trade Center. By the time of the second crash, I was home glued to the television in disbelief. In addition to the terrible images of airplanes flying into buildings, which to this day are difficult to watch, I suspected immediately, as many others did, that the American way of life would change and that the freedoms we enjoyed would be challenged not only by terrorists, but also by the government. Before the collapse of the World Trade Center buildings, many questions were beginning to form in my mind about how individual citizens would respond to the attacks and to government efforts to provide for their safety and security. I have always believed that democracies are more likely to fail as a consequence of a crisis than over deliberative thought. There was much speculation about how life as we knew it would change, but my curiosity would be satisfied only through systematic research, which would involve writing a grant and soliciting financial support, constructing reliable and valid instruments to measure individual reactions, marshaling the instrument through human subjects review, executing the research, and, finally, analyzing the data. It would take more than three years, and repeated interviewing of survey respondents, to understand the individual reactions to the attacks. Time was important in understanding how the context shaped individual attitudes, but I imagine that as more time passes and events unfold we will continue to learn about how the September 11 attacks shaped our political development.

One of the basic arguments of this book is that the heightened sense of threat and vulnerability that arose from the attacks was a new experience for most Americans. That a small group of foreign terrorists from the other side of the globe was able to exploit the openness of American society to perpetrate the most heinous and horrific attack against innocent citizens on American soil was incomprehensible and terrifying. The U.S.

government with arguably the most powerful military was said to be caught off guard, but now, with its defenses up and a desire to prevent further attacks, questions were raised concerning the new adjustments and tolerances citizens would have to endure in the post-September 11 America. This led to what I consider an intriguing set of questions that go to the foundation of democratic society: With a newfound sense of anxiety and vulnerability, how far would American citizens be willing to go to maintain their sense of security and freedom? If American citizens were willing to acquiesce to political authorities, even those many believed had been elected illegally just several months prior to the attacks, would individual concessions become permanent or would they reflect only a temporary reaction to an emotional event? In addition, how would the rise in patriotism, trust in the political authorities, psychological insecurity, and cultural factors like race influence the willingness to compromise civil liberties for security? Basically, where do American citizens draw the line between liberty and order when these two conflict?

From a liberal democratic theory perspective, my curiosity might seem misplaced, because order and security have not been deemed mutually exclusive where the delight in one means the sacrifice of the other. It was only through order and security that individuals could enjoy liberty and freedom. If such values did collide, the political authorities were considered to have failed in their fundamental duties and individuals had the right to start over. The reality, however, is that democratic values frequently clash with each other and security. When they do, it is important, even necessary, to understand the compromises between civil liberties and security individuals are willing to make and where they are willing to draw the line. As tragic and horrible as the attacks of September 11 were, they created a phenomenal context in which to study the commitment to democratic norms. American citizens have faced few situations in which they believed that their sense of security came at the expense of their liberty and freedom. Most of what we know about the support for civil liberties derive either from simulated and hypothetical perceptions of threat or from social and political contexts in which the support for democracy and security have no real consequences. This book examines the theoretical foundations of the individual support for democratic rights, but it uses the context of the September 11 attacks as a counterweight to democracy. Like others before me—Samuel Stouffer, Jim Gibson, and Paul Sniderman—I argue that it is one thing to study the support for abstract democratic principles, but an entirely different story to examine the trade-off between civil liberties and security when there are tangible consequences to one's decision. The support for democracy is certainly situational, and there is no better test of America's democratic resolve than the events surrounding the attacks.

There are several important themes in this book, but perhaps the most important is that democracy requires some give and take. Individual citizens seem to understand that absolute adherence to democratic rights yields untenable consequences. Following the attacks, a heightened sense of threat and vulnerability compelled many people to lower the bar on democratic rights, but not as low as they would have without any threat of terrorism. Given the heightened sense of threat in the immediate aftermath, citizens were willing to acquiesce to political authorities and accept some of the antidemocratic consequences. Such concessions were temporary, however. Citizens were willing to acquiesce to political authorities because they trusted them, but, as trust in political authorities diminished over time, support for democratic values reappeared. American citizens have shown remarkable patience and resiliency.

Acknowledgments

MANY PEOPLE have contributed to this research project. Without the generous support of the Russell Sage Foundation and an initial grant from the Law and Society Program of the National Science Foundation this research would not have been possible. I feel especially indebted to Paul Wahlbeck, program officer at the time, and Frank Scioli, political science program director, for their enthusiastic support of this research. I would also like to acknowledge the initial support of Marietta Baba, dean of the College of Social and Behavioral Sciences at Michigan State University.

This research project began as a collaborative effort with Brian Silver at Michigan State University. Brian's seminal contribution to the project was invaluable. Throughout the book, I draw on several published and unpublished papers we wrote together and countless hours of conversations. Several people were very gracious with their time and patience in reading drafts of the manuscript. Jim Gibson, first and foremost, was an incredible friend and source of inspiration. He is owed a special thanks because his research on public opinion and political tolerance paved the way for this project. I am also indebted to Paul Sniderman for always being available and for his insight on earlier drafts. Bob Erikson, Jack Citrin, Paul Abramson, Melinda Hall, Christopher Parker, and Christian Davenport provided helpful comments on earlier drafts of the book. Colleagues such as Dave Rhode, Jerry Weinberger, Bill Allen, Mike Bratton, and Reggie Roberts were incredible resources and provided insightful reactions to many of my thoughts. There is nothing like having good friends and colleagues who can help you get rid of bad ideas quickly. Sarah Corp and Sasha Miller were invaluable research assistants throughout the project. Larry Hembroff and Karen Clark in the Office of Survey Research in the Institute for Public Policy and Social Research at Michigan State University did a fine job with the data collection.

Chapter 1

Introduction: A Climate of Threat and Vulnerability

THE SEPTEMBER 11 attacks transformed a nation that had been absorbed in the contentious 2000 presidential election, Republican-proposed tax cuts, shark attacks off the California coast, and Barry Bonds's pace to break Mark McGwire's single-season home run record into a nation contemplating its own mortality and the threat of terrorism. Previous controversies, social conflicts, and esoteric concerns became infinitesimal compared to the newfound sense of fear and vulnerability American citizens suddenly faced. Time literally stood still as the images of that day were replayed in a never-ending loop: passenger airliners exploding into buildings, people leaping from the top floors of the World Trade Center towers, the collapse of the towers onto both office and rescue workers, and the smoldering Pentagon. This came at the hands of foreign terrorists, who used America's openness to carry out a massive and heinous attack against innocent citizens. Perhaps indicative of an increasingly self-absorbed and complacent culture that viewed international affairs as remote and inconsequential, it was simply unimaginable that nineteen men with box cutters from one of the more desolate regions in the world could organize an attack that could kill thousands of American citizens and, in the process, compel American society and political authorities to reassess its security and freedom. In coming to terms with their new sense of vulnerability, American citizens had to confront the fact that they were part of a larger community of nations, in which their happiness and security were increasingly attached to the happiness of others around the world.

Although America had been attacked before—by Japan in 1941, by foreign terrorists, also on the World Trade Center, in 1993, and by domestic terrorists on the Federal Building in Oklahoma City in 1995—most Americans had neither experienced nor understood what it was like to live under the threat of terror. For much of its existence, America has been a stable and relatively orderly society. Citizens largely have had little to fear, and the things they feared the most were usually small and vicarious. Most other societies had already experienced the ravages of war and uncertainty, but Americans had been, for the most part, exempt from direct threats and feelings of vulnerability. Fear that another attack was waiting to happen weakened many previous convictions and governed how Americans interacted with each other and perceived political authorities.

American citizens have also had to adjust to restrictions on their civil liberties and personal freedoms. Political authorities framed and widely promoted the notion that individual citizens would have to accept constraints on some of their freedom and civil liberties if those responsible were to be brought to justice and other attacks thought to be imminent were to be prevented. That citizens' rights should be protected from the government has been a fundamental tenet of American democracy: swapping liberty for greater security, even in the face of an external enemy, meant shifting the balance of procedural rights away from the individual and toward the government—another uncertain and frightening endeavor. Of course, many citizens seemed to tolerate the infringement on their civil rights and liberties as a necessary trade-off, given the threat of terrorism, but many others were also justifiably troubled by the constraints.

The conflict between national security and civil liberties in American society can be placed in a broader historical context. For instance, in 1798, with the threat of war with France and growing criticism of President John Adams's Federalist foreign policy by Thomas Jefferson's Republican Party, American citizens faced imprisonment or deportation for criticizing the government. Intended to silence the opposing Republican Party, the Alien and Sedition Acts could have nullified the First Amendment guarantees of freedom of speech and an independent press. In 1861, during the Civil War, President Abraham Lincoln suspended the writ of habeas corpus and restricted the freedoms of speech and the press for acts that discouraged enlistment or engaged in disloyal practices. World War I ushered in a number of laws and practices intended to crush dissent and leftist activities. Foreigners, generally viewed as suspicious or undesirable, were prohibited from working certain jobs and living in certain areas. With the Palmer Raids of the 1920s, suspected communists and socialists could be arrested or deported. In 1942, President Franklin D. Roosevelt, fearing internal sabotage and attacks, ordered the forcible internment of Japanese Americans, detaining more than 120,000 citizens in prison camps for as long as three years. During this period, the Smith Act was passed, mandating the fingerprinting and registration of aliens in the United States. The 1950s witnessed McCarthyism and the suppression of First Amendment rights of suspected communists. In the

1960s, during the Vietnam War, military and CIA spies targeted war protestors, and President Richard Nixon attempted to stifle criticism from the press. From 1956 to 1971, the Federal Bureau of Investigation's (FBI) Counter Intelligence Program (COINTELPRO) prevented the exercise of the First Amendment rights of speech and association, and engaged in physical violence and false imprisonments, on the theory that preventing the growth of radical and dangerous groups, such as the Black Panther Party and the Southern Christian Leadership Conference, protected national security.

With the September 11 terrorist attacks, American citizens experienced more extensive challenges to their freedom and liberty. Although many of the increased powers of law enforcement were unilateral, resulting from executive orders or rule changes quietly announced in the Federal Register, some of the restrictions of civil liberties were approved by Congress as part of the USA Patriot Act. Many of the freedoms and civil liberties frequently claimed to be under attack conflicted with law enforcement efforts to investigate and prevent terrorist attacks. American citizens were forced to weigh the balance between their personal freedoms and government efforts to provide for their personal security. This time, it was not only foreigners or perceived radicals who came under suspicion, but ordinary American citizens as well. Vice President Dick Cheney explained shortly after the attacks,

> We're going to have to take steps, and are taking steps, that'll become a permanent part of the way we live. In terms of security, in terms of the way we deal with travel and airlines, all of those measures that we end up having to adopt in order to sort of harden the target; make it tougher for terrorists to get at us. And I think those will become permanent features in our kind of way of life. ("Cheney Says War Against Terror 'May Never End.'" *Washington Post*, October 21, 2001)

Purpose of the Book

If American society is now at a new stage in its political development, in which citizens perceive greater tension between freedom and security, understanding how exposure to events like the September 11 attacks shapes such decisions is critical. Democracies are not likely to fail in response to reflective thought but rather in response to crisis events in which citizens become more accepting of anti-democratic measures and political authorities who, during such periods, are more likely to act on anti-democratic impulses. Passions, expected to be held in check during quiet times, become excitable in context. As a result, theoretically grounded and systematic analyses of individual attitudes are required to delineate how the overwhelming feelings of threat and vulnerability influence trade-offs between civil liberties and security. With original data from a national public opinion survey conducted shortly after September 11, and subsequent follow-up interviews, this book provides such an analysis. Its goal is to examine individual citizens' attitudes toward civil liberties in the face of incredible threat and vulnerability. As tragic as the terrorist attacks were, the context provides an incredible and unique opportunity to study the commitment to democratic principles. Never before has liberty clashed with other important values like security, and never before have scholars been prepared to examine the nature of the trade-off. Studying the support for democratic principles in abstract and hypothetical situations has been important, and provides the basis for theoretical expectations, but it is a totally different matter to study the support for democratic values in context, where they clash with other important values and have tangible consequences. Abstract support for democracy and civil liberties usually garner overwhelming support, but in applied contexts where citizens have to practice what they preach, democracy likely suffers. To begin to unravel the viability of liberal democratic principles and where America citizens draw the line, it is critical to examine those rights when they conflict with other values. A person who supports the rights against unreasonable searches and seizure, the right against self-incrimination, jury trials, and the right to privacy might interpret such rights differently when they protect terrorists and constrain political authorities from protecting society. Whereas such values can be perceived in detached terms, they take on different meaning and urgency in context. Hence, this book is about understanding the reactions to the terrorist attacks as much as it is about advancing and challenging various theoretical literatures, though I do not view either as mutually exclusive.

As I mentioned earlier, before the attacks, American citizens probably felt that they had little to fear and little reason to relinquish any of their civil liberties. The stability and orderliness of the American political system, evidenced by the peaceful resolution of the highly contentious 2000 presidential elections, made it inconceivable that security and liberty could conflict in such a way that citizens would be asked to choose between them. Until the democratic resolve of American society was challenged by a heightened sense of vulnerability and governmental policies intended to provide for greater security, most citizens had been spared such discomfort and distress. Under the threat of terrorism, however, individuals were compelled to make that choice and the outcome was attached to substantive consequences. Americans were no longer innocent and dispassionate bystanders in an easily dismissed drama being played out on the other side of the globe. Fear and uncertainty involved in the trade-offs were at their doorstep.

Security trade-offs are not easy. Although it is probably true that "we live almost our entire lives making judgments about security" (Schneier

2003, 7), individual citizens, operating from a heightened sense of fear, patriotism, and renewed faith in government, appeared to give the government the latitude to prevent future attacks and apprehend terrorists. People may have particular difficulty reconciling their desire to conform to democratic values with their fears about terrorism and governmental policies intended to make them safe and secure. To refuse to compromise, even on important civil libertarian values, would have been considered imprudent and unpatriotic, given the threat individual citizens faced. As reflected by the level of fear and threat of future terrorist attacks, Americans were also expected to acquiesce to government under the logic that they themselves were law abiding citizens who had nothing to hide and that increased monitoring and surveillance without prior court approval was not terribly harmful. But the nature and extent of such concessions, and individual perceptions of the proper balance between freedom and security, were open questions. From an academic standpoint, much has been written about the uneasy task of balancing civil liberties and national security in times of crises (Chang 2002; Cole and Dempsey 2002; Leone and Anrig 2003; Rehnquist 1998), but little is known about individual reactions to system norms and principles when the society is attacked and when it is easy to cave in to anti-democratic passions. The attacks created new and unexpected experiences across American society, some of which we are now only beginning to understand.

The questions I find most intriguing and important involve the situational components of liberty and freedom. There are limits to the amount of freedom and liberty civil society can enjoy before it reverts to the state of nature, and the context of the September 11 terrorist attacks takes us closer to understanding the parameters of individual acceptance. The idea of negative liberty captures the essence of the dilemma over the trade-off between liberty and security. Negative liberty is a philosophical concept dating back to classical philosophers such as Hobbes and Rousseau, but promoted more recently by Isaiah Berlin. As he defined it, negative liberty pertains to the idea that there should be a minimum area of personal freedom or a set of rights that are free from external interference or coercion by others and the government. There might be individual rights that are beyond the interference of others, such as the ability to be punished under retroactive law or to being declared guilty without a trial (Berlin 1958, 211), but individual liberty is not considered unequivocal, because it is not the only goal. People may place high values on other goals, such as justice or happiness, or culture, or security, or varying degrees of equality (Berlin 1958, 171). And, because "men are largely interdependent, and no man's activity is so completely private as never to obstruct the lives of others in any way," the clash of values must be weighed against each other and a compromised sought (Berlin 1958, 171).

6   Negative Liberty

Understanding the parameters of negative liberty—freedom from external interference or coercion—troubled many American citizens after September 11. Just where should they draw the line between their desire for individual liberty and their need for security? Fitting as the title, negative liberty sums up nicely the debate over individual rights and conveys a basic theme of the book: individual liberty and civil rights are not absolute.

Within an area of negative liberty, American citizens are probably somewhere between the two unfathomable extremes of complete freedom (that is, a state of nature) and complete government control, but it is unclear where individual citizens are willing to draw the line. Questions of particular relevance include: What does it take to transform a staunch supporter of civil liberties into their most ardent antagonist, and what does it take to sustain this decision? How does the context affect the willingness to trade civil liberties for security? What happens to the traditional standard-bearers of democratic rights, such as political liberals, Democratic Party supporters, the young, the highly educated, and African Americans, when they are exposed to anxiety and threat? Can democracy survive if support for civil liberties is situational? These are some of the broader questions I hope to address in this book, but such questions are best addressed incrementally, one puzzle piece at a time.

Understanding how context influences the development of political and social attitudes has become increasingly important (Huckfeldt 1984; MacKuen and Brown 1987), but nowhere more so than in the political tolerance and democratic norms literature (Gibson 1987a, 1992; Gibson and Bingham 1985; Stouffer 1955). Applying democratic principles, unlike many political and social attitudes, hinges on if and how they clash with other important values in real contexts, and research on political tolerance and support for democratic norms has deep roots in studying individual commitment to civil liberties contextually. As Paul Sniderman and his colleagues (1996, 62) observed, "arguments over rights are arguments embedded in a context." The strength of individual commitments to democratic norms may be best understood when people have to tolerate and live with the consequences of their democratic beliefs. According to Herbert McClosky and Alida Brill (1983), "often the question we must face is not whether to grant or to deny freedom, but whether to honor it in a context in which conflicting values and goals are also present" (431).

This book is about the public's reactions to trading off civil liberties for security as political authorities and the media framed it. Using the term *trade-off* to describe the relation is intended to reflect this framing, because the media and authorities in turn shaped how individuals eventually thought about it. Such a disclaimer is necessary because the clash of rights and the eventual politicization of the civil liberties and security decision assumes such values are mutually exclusive, and though this

Hobbesian and Lockean framing of liberty and security as opposites simplifies the issue for individuals with little information to go on, liberty and security traditionally have not been thought of as contradictory. Thomas Hobbes believed that the individual impulses of fear of death and desire for power, if left unchecked, would result in brutish and solitary lives. To keep these impulses in order, individuals would have to cede all authority and sovereignty to a single authority in exchange for security from each other and foreign threats. Through brute force, the sovereign power would control the violent and selfish impulses of individual members of society. They would lose liberty, but they would gain security and community.

Rousseau, however, pointed out that positing freedom and security as inimical was fundamentally flawed. The social contract, for Rousseau, reflected a similar concession of authority to the general will in exchange for safety. However, individuals did not have to be protected from their impulses, but rather from political authority that did not seek to maximize individual liberty while preserving order. Through security and order, individuals gained equality and freedom. Following this line of thought, liberal democratic theory rests on the idea that individuals have certain rights, and that they surrender their liberty to the promise that civil society will protect their rights. Moving from the state of nature, in which there is complete liberty but no security, the purpose of civil society is to protect citizens from each other and from the government. Without security, one cannot enjoy liberty or freedom. John Locke suggested in the *Second Treatise of Government* that "the great and chief end, therefore, of men's uniting into common-wealths, and putting themselves under government, is the preservation of their property," meaning liberty (1690/1980, 66).

American citizens were not asked to make trade-off decisions in a formal sense. Many of the challenges to civil liberties were unnoticeable. The trade-off decisions I refer to involve the decision to protect civil liberties in the face of tangible consequences.

Political Acquiescence and Threat

At the end of the day, American citizens had tangible reasons to remain fearful and discreet in their reactions to efforts to provide for their security. Many traditional defenders of civil rights and liberties, such as the Democratic Party, were notoriously silent on the trade-off decision. Expressing disapproval or disagreement required incredible courage. Individuals appeared to give up their liberty and freedom easily and without regret. Elisabeth Noelle-Neumann suggests that such silence on civil liberties in context should not be confused with agreement (1993). Reflecting an aspect of the pressure to acquiesce to popular opinion, the terrorist attacks created a climate in which there could be no counterargument to the restrictions on civil liberties proposed by the Bush administration to combat terrorism. According to Noelle-Neumann, individuals, using a "quasi-statistical sense" of their environment based on their exposure to media messages, are extremely sensitive to how their opinions match the climate of opinion in different situations. If the current climate is seen as hostile to their own opinions, individuals avoid speaking out and isolating themselves. They are more willing to express their views publicly if they find them to be prevalent or on the rise. People who perceive popular sentiment as consistent with their preferences are more willing to express them than people who see prevailing sentiment as discordant with their preferences.

The paucity of debate on issues that would have otherwise been extremely controversial reflects the core component of Noelle-Neumann's spiral of silence. Perhaps the minimal discussion on the balance of civil liberties and security should not have been too surprising, given the sense of threat and vulnerability among Americans, but people who would normally be expected to counter the challenges to civil liberties were cautious in their criticism. Thinking ahead and to their future accountability, few wanted to be labeled as unpatriotic, anti-American, or weak if they were not willing to acquiesce to the policies and viewpoints of the Bush administration. This meant supporting media reports concerning the continued threat of terrorism, but also accepting restrictions on civil liberties. For Noelle-Neumann (1993), the media play a critical role in political acquiescence. Because the mass media are the primary source of information for most citizens, they become the principal mechanism by which political authorities communicate with citizens and citizens become aware of popular sentiment. To the extent that the mass media reflect the sentiments of political authorities when following national crises, they could account for the continued heightened sense of vulnerability and political acquiescence.

Several scholars have noted how the mass media promote fear and anxiety during quiescent periods. David Altheide (2002) argues that even when there is nothing objectively to fear, the media convey to individuals that they are not safe. This is attributed to an overemphasis on negative and problem-oriented news that promotes a sense of vulnerability, exacerbated by the media's entertainment format. The media use of the word *fear* in headlines, and text has dramatically increased to the point where "it becomes part of the take-for-granted word of 'how things are,' and one consequence is that it begins to influence how we perceive and talk about everyday life" (Altheide 2003, 38). Similarly, Barry Glassner (1999) argues that the mass media stoke societal fear by overemphasizing negative and violent images. He suggests that using anecdotal stories in place of scientific evidence, misusing statistics to convey trends, and using expert opinions legitimize and exacerbate feelings of vulnerability.

Recent studies on the mass media following the September 11 attacks portray a media that tended to promote the preferences of political authorities in the Bush administration. Analyzing the content of stories in *Time* and *Newsweek* following the attacks, John Hutcheson and his colleagues (2004) find that topics related to national identity paralleled the perspectives of U.S. government and military sources rather than other U.S. elites and citizens. By reflecting the sentiment of political authorities, news stories tended to affirm core American values and demonize the enemy, directing blame away from U.S. policies. With most of the information sources created by government officials and used by the media following the attacks (Li and Izard 2003), the mass media was seen as complicit in mobilizing citizens to accept the worldview of the Bush administration. Similarly, content analyses of the editorials in the *New York Times* following the attacks seem to mirror political leaders, urging citizens to prepare for greater sacrifices (Lule 2002). Moreover, according to Brigitte Nacos,

> by dwelling endlessly on the outburst of patriotism and the idea of national unity without paying attention to other important matters in the political realm, the media helped to create an atmosphere in which criticism of the various crisis-related policy initiatives in Washington was mostly absent from the mass-mediated public debate. (2002, 195)

Robert Entman (2004, 107) goes considerably further in asserting that "in the wake of September 11, 2001, the government propound a line designed to revive habits of patriotic deference, to dampen elite dissent, dominate media texts, and reduce the threat of negative public reaction—to work just as the Cold War paradigm once did." Because the Democrats were basically compliant, as one might expect, the media found it especially difficult to challenge the administration, as top officials brought pressure on media personnel and organizations to reflect their worldview and to toe the White House line.

All of this supports Noelle-Neuman's point about the critical role of the media in fostering a silent public. Not only were American citizens likely to develop a keen sense of the risks and acceptable positions that would produce political acquiescence or silence, but they also had every right to believe that another attack was imminent, because they were being told as much. The climate was not conducive to debate or to understanding the implications of surrendering certain liberties and freedoms. However, such a silence, I hope to uncover, was only temporary acquiescence, as opposed to substantive support. American citizens were likely under a different source of threat.

In addition to highlighting a different manifestation of threat, this body of research makes it possible to respond to a common observation made following the attacks of September 11, 2001. There was a belief that the emotional response and feelings of vulnerability among American citizens were irrational and overblown. Commentators pointed out that the chance of dying from a terrorist attack was so small that anyone concerned about another attack was somehow deranged or overemotional. I completely disagree.

Although it is probably true that the likelihood of death from a terrorist attack is small because there have been so few terrorist attacks on American soil, Americans believed they had a great deal to fear because they were continuously being shown horrifying images, and how politicians and the media framed the issues contributed to that fear. That there might be a discrepancy between an actual and perceived threat does not make the fear of it any less relevant. Unlike other fears that have gripped the nation, the terrorist attacks involved an actual event, coupled with the images and language by the media and political leaders. I submit that Americans were anxious and fearful because they were being told that they needed to be extra vigilant, that other attacks were likely, that they would have to adjust to this new way of life, and because they were being shown images supporting why they should be fearful. The Terror Alert System only exacerbated the anxiety by reminding people that there were terrorists out there trying to hurt them, drawing attention to a threatening situation without an appropriate plan. Of course, this was not the system's intention (though many would probably disagree).

The bottom line is that emotions of despair, anger, and threat are likely ingrained in the consciousness of American citizens and can be recalled with relative ease. Memories of the attacks and associated feelings of vulnerability do not just fade away, but instead become a part of what will define Americans collectively, much like the memories of the assassinations of President John F. Kennedy and the Reverend Martin Luther King, Jr. and the Challenger disaster. The significance of these events is captured in what are considered flashbulb memories (Brown and Kulik 1977). These are distinctively vivid and lasting recollections of the personal circumstances surrounding the discovery of terrifying events. New and significant events cause people to respond with heightened emotional arousal, leading to the encoding of the circumstances. People are likely to remember in detail the context in which they first heard about the news, such as where they were and what they were doing. The degree of emotional arousal causes people to engage in overt rehearsal (conversations about what happened) and covert rehearsal (thinking about the event). Talking about the event and being exposed to pervasive media information can only, it is fair to expect, increase the memories and sustain the associated emotions (Finkenauer, Gisle, and Luminet 1997).

It is only a matter of time before memory researchers show the significance of the September 11 attacks. With the remarkable amount of media attention focused on the event, and the highly disturbing images of airplanes exploding and buildings collapsing, Americans will not be able to escape the emotional underpinnings of the events. A direct measure of this ingrained event was shown in a 2006 Pew Research Center survey, that indicated 95 percent of respondents remembered exactly where they were and what they were doing the moment they heard the news about the attacks. It is clear from this high percent that memories and emotions of the attacks are highly accessible and, therefore, likely to influence political decisions for a long time to come. Though we can expect the accessibility of such memories to diminish with more time, the process of generational replacement will probably have to occur to diminish the effects of September 11, assuming no future attacks occur. The question I consider incredibly important is whether the consequence of sustained memories will lead to support for further restrictions on civil liberties. Although a heightened sense of vulnerability and the willingness to concede liberties for security are expected immediately following attacks, what happens over time to the trade-off of civil liberties for security as the attacks recede into the past and no others occur on American soil? I hope to describe a "new normal" within American society and how it pertains to support for civil liberties. Can the level of threat that was instrumental in influencing the willingness to concede civil liberties for security be sustained when the political context changes?

Theoretical Importance

Although there is a practical element to examining the trade-off between civil liberties and security in the context of the terrorist attacks, there is also an equally important theoretical element. The theoretical significance of this book centers on how individual citizens think about their democratic rights and respond to the perceptions of threat and vulnerability. We know from the theoretical literature on political tolerance that the support for civil liberties is situational. Some situations require individuals to be flexible with their commitment and, for the most part, American citizens have been. Staunch defenders of democracy in one situation can be made to moderate their beliefs while democratic antagonists can be made to soften their beliefs. But, this type of situation has usually involved the conflict between individuals or groups. It has been certainly true that the exercise of civil liberties and rights of a person or a group can translate into negative liberty for others, and the literature has done a superb job at detailing the parameters of this form of social conflict or where individuals draw the line. What we know about the support for civil liberties and the commitment to democratic principles is based on the willingness to tolerate the behavior of others. However, the clash of individual rights does not just occur between groups. Political authorities and the government often require incredible forbearance among citizens to tolerate restrictions on their civil liberties and rights. I therefore examine a different form of tolerance, not so much the traditional focus on the willingness to tolerate the behavior of others as on the tolerance for government intrusion on civil liberties. Although the clash over rights frequently occurs between individual citizens, the literature has failed to consider what happens when political authorities and the government want to take away one's rights. This type of trade-off can be expected to involve a different calculus because the government is thought to protect individual rights and liberties. As I will show, how individuals think about government will be an important factor in the willingness to trade civil liberties for security.

Another problem with understanding where individuals might draw the line between democratic beliefs and concerns about security is that the value trade-off has been tied mostly to hypothetical situations. In this book, threat and perceptions of vulnerability are no longer hypothetical. Rather, perceptions of threat and vulnerability are part of the context of the attacks. Because the traditional focus in the study of democratic principles has centered on group behavior and the extent to which a group appeared menacing or threatening, perception of threat has been somewhat of a simulated concept. In the measure of the conflict between values, survey respondents have traditionally been asked to tolerate the behavior of their most "disliked" groups. This was an important approach in considering the nature of the conflict between groups during the early 1950s. Taking a step back from this approach raises questions about the nature of the value conflict between democratic values and threat. Perceptions of threat, the most important factor in determining whether a person is willing to concede support for democratic rights, are taken as the degree to which a person dislikes a certain group. Despite several important attempts to make threat less abstract by studying tolerance in context, threat has remained primarily hypothetical and simulated. We still do not completely understand the nature of threat and how it works. By linking the study of the commitment to democratic principles to the most frightening attacks on innocent American citizens, I consider threat as a direct function of personal reactions to the terrorist attacks.

In short, the major theoretical advancement of this book lies in the two most important aspects of support for democracy: a different and more explicit form of value conflict and the study within the context of a tangible rather than hypothetical threat. With this approach, many of the findings of the political tolerance literature are supported, but at the same time, many also require additional thought.

Data

This approach would not be possible without appropriate data. I will incorporate a variety of public opinion data in this analysis, but the primary data come from the National Civil Liberties Survey conducted by the Office of Survey Research of IPSIR at Michigan State University. Shortly after September 11, Brian Silver and I, with generous support from the National Science Foundation, the Russell Sage Foundation, and Michigan State University, were able to field a national survey on the reactions to the attacks. The first survey was conducted between November 15 and December 12, 2001. With African American and Latino oversamples, this survey focused on the basic trade-offs between civil liberties and security, reactions to different social groups in society, political trust, patriotism, dogmatism, and perceptions of the root causes of terrorism.

Fearing that more terrorist attacks were likely to occur, just like everyone else, two panel waves were initially planned. The intent was to use the first survey as a baseline against which to compare reactions to subsequent attacks. However, when no further attacks did occur, we waited a year to conduct the second survey (January 21 to May 28, 2003) and still another to conduct the third survey (July 20 to November 5, 2004). Many of the questions were repeated across the panels, but we also considered new issues that came up between panel waves. The analysis for this book draws most heavily from the first wave of the data, with the understanding one must first thoroughly appreciate initial reactions to explore change. Nevertheless, because it contextualizes the initial reactions, change is also important.

Plan of the Book

I examine the support for civil liberties in the highly charged and emotional atmosphere following the 9/11 attacks across several chapters. Each is a puzzle piece; each question I address has a special role toward an ultimately larger argument. I develop different aspects of public perceptions and reactions to the terrorist attacks, the government, civic culture, democratic norms, and other citizens.

Chapter 2 focuses attention on the context of the terrorist attacks and related events. I am interested in showing the significance of the attacks and what it meant for American citizens. However, context is more than the acts of terror themselves. As far as I am concerned, it also encompasses the reactions to government behavior that had the likely consequence of exacerbating concerns about vulnerability.

In chapter 3, I develop the concept of trading off civil liberties for security, fit it into the appropriate theoretical context, and attempt to measure it. Drawing heavily on political tolerance literature, I look at the public support for civil liberties as a process of trade-off reasoning. Because of the social desirability aspects involved in measuring support for democratic norms, and the risk of confounding related preferences, conceptualizing and measuring support for civil liberties involves more of an implicit consideration of competing preferences than of other political attitudes and beliefs. My approach, following the framing of the media and political authorities, is to make the trade-off decision more explicit. This approach is weighed against the existing literature.

In chapter 4, I disentangle the explanations for the support of civil liberties in the immediate aftermath of the attacks. Relying on eclectic bodies of literature, I develop and test a theoretical model of support for civil liberties. Though my main focus is on the various aspects of threat and vulnerability on the trade-off decision, I consider other relevant aspects of the context, such as the role of political trust, patriotism, political ideology, dogmatism, and sociodemographic factors. The model I develop here is the basic one I use throughout my analyses. It is clear from this chapter that freedom and liberty, unlike certain approaches to issues such as abortion and affirmative action, are not absolutes, because people who are protectors of liberty can become ardent antagonists of liberty.

Chapter 5 relies on several experiments embedded in the National Civil Liberties Survey to assess the extent to which individuals are capable of defending their choices regarding civil liberties and security. I assume here that initial choices reflect an opening bid, with the full range of consequences of individual preferences, either way, not fully appreciated. I challenged respondents' initial preferences confrontationally with the consequences of their choice. How do respondents react when presented with the consequences of their initial attitudes about the trade-off? What this approach reveals is remarkable. People under a heightened sense of threat did not consider the full consequences of their democratic concessions and were willing to go quite far in supporting political authorities.

In chapter 6, I turn to the panel aspects of the National Civil Liberties Survey to consider how support for civil liberties and its associated predictors have changed over a two-year period. Many observers have remarked that American society was changed forever by the attacks of September 11, and that individual citizens would have to develop new ways of thinking about their security and rights. This so-called new normalcy was to usher in new thoughts about vulnerability and weakness in support for civil liberties. I address these questions directly, with an interest in how changes in the political context (that is, decreasing political trust and increasing vulnerability) shape the willingness to trade civil liberties for security.

In chapter 7, I consider the extent of political acquiescence involved in the decision regarding civil liberties and security. A remarkable consequence of the heightened sense of vulnerability after the terrorist attacks seems to be people's adopting preferences they would not ordinarily support. Political partisans, specifically Democratic identifiers, had to accept restrictions on civil liberties—values they have traditionally protected. Given the extent of ideological and partisan polarization in American society, this required amazing forbearance on the part of Democrats.

Using partisanship, I examine the process of depolarization and silence in the context of the terrorist attacks.

Chapter 8 explores in greater detail the role of race and ethnicity in the support for civil liberties. I show that race is one of the most important explanations for supporting civil liberties following the attacks. African American support for civil liberties reflects not only a history of commitment to democratic norms, but also a certain sense of distrust and alienation. The protection of civil liberties among African Americans is not accidental, but it reflects a general support for the political system and its underlying principles.

Chapter 9 considers a different aspect of political tolerance by examining social group affect. American citizens were observed to have a renewed faith in each other after the attacks, but at the same time, social groups perceived as sympathetic to foreign terrorists were targets of violence and harassment. I consider the extent to which social group affect toward Islamic fundamentalists, Middle Easterners, African Americans, Jews, Latinos, whites, and Christian fundamentalists was influenced by feelings of vulnerability. Of particular interest is the extent to which a sense of threat and vulnerability places other groups, which are perceived to not conform to an American identity, at risk of intolerance.

In the final chapter, I step back to interpret the influence of the terrorist attacks on public opinion and the support for civil liberties.

Chapter 2

Context: The Promise of 72 Virgins

CONTEXTUALIZING THE value trade-offs citizens faced after September 11 and taking a hard look at the major events following the attacks, I hope to give some insight into individual perceptions during the period. My primary goal is to define the social and political context, how it may have shifted over time, and the events that impinge on the decisions among individual citizens. The context I refer to throughout involves more than simply exposure to the horrific events surrounding the September 11 attacks. Such events are a major component of the context and, as I mentioned in the opening chapter, they will not likely to be forgotten (see appendix A for a timeline of the attacks and related events). The context also pertains to subsequent activities by the government and political authorities, which also influenced individual perceptions of vulnerability.

I will admit, however, that it is rather difficult to interpret statistical results without thoroughly understanding the context within which decisions are made and people interact. I hope to make clear that my conceptualization of context is, first and foremost, the climate of fear and threat created by the attacks. I will argue that this initial threat was very powerful and intensely capable of upsetting many previously held convictions about democracy and many other beliefs. As the government began to respond to the attacks, this climate was exacerbated to the point where feelings of vulnerability were connected to government behavior and media framing. Over time it is nearly impossible to separate the threat generated by the terrorist and that generated by government actions.

The Terrorist Attacks on America

What will be regarded as one of the most important and defining moments in American history began at 8:46 on a Tuesday morning, when the hijacked American Airlines Flight 11 flew into the north tower of the

World Trade Center and exploded. Seventeen minutes later, another hijacked passenger airliner, American Airlines Flight 175, crashed into the south tower. Live television captured the graphic images of the planes and the skyscrapers—symbols of U.S. dominance in the world economy—ablaze. It was unimaginable to most Americans. However, others, who saw the World Trade Center as a symbol of economic exploitation and repression, reacted differently, and with a sense of gratification. Unfortunately, the attacks on the World Trade Center, though powerful enough for citizens to begin questioning how vulnerable they were, were only the beginning. Forty minutes after the second attack, another hijacked airplane, American Airlines Flight 77, crashed into the Pentagon in Arlington, Virginia. Because the Pentagon is the headquarters for the U.S. Department of Defense, representing the power and security of the military, an attack on it was also a powerful symbolic message to both America and the international community. The U.S. government and its citizens were not as invincible as previously believed. It was possible to reach Americans on their own soil. Less than an hour after the World Trade Center was attacked, the south tower collapsed, sending millions of tons of steel and glass crashing down on emergency response personnel and workers. More horrific images were captured as people trapped in the higher floors of the north tower began leaping out of the windows to escape the fire. Twenty-eight minutes later, the north tower also collapsed, spreading debris and ash over lower Manhattan visible to the naked eyes of astronauts orbiting 240 miles above in the International Space Station. The fires from the debris of the collapsed buildings smoldered for ninety-nine days, and would take nine months to clean up, at an estimated cost of $600 million. Though somewhat difficult to ascertain because of the magnitude of the destruction, the official death toll was estimated at 2,752 for the World Trade Center alone ("Not Found or Not Existing, 40 names to leave WTC Death Toll," *USA Today*, October 29, 2003). Another 189 people were killed in the attack on the Pentagon. The eventual cost of reconstructing the Pentagon was $700 million ("Pentagon Repairs to Cost $700 Million." *USA Today*, January 1, 2002). A fourth hijacked passenger airliner, United Airlines Flight 93, believed to be headed for the U.S. Capitol, the White House, or Camp David, crashed in the Pennsylvania countryside. All forty-five passengers on board were killed but were also credited—in having attempted to regain control of the flight—with diverting what would have been a fourth attack.

That the terrorists had spent years planning this attack by attending flight schools in the United States and had agreed to sacrifice their own lives for the promise of seventy-two virgins in paradise seemed to intensify Americans' sense of vulnerability. The attacks were planned like a precise military exercise. They required substantial financial support.

All of this had to go undetected. Many questioned not only why it happened, but also how. This led to the creation of the National Commission on Terrorist Attacks Upon the United States, more commonly known as the 9/11 Commission, designed to investigate the circumstances surrounding the attacks. The commission report would reveal that U.S. intelligence missed important signals that might have thwarted the attacks.

To make matters worse, the threat of bioterrorism added to the anxiety less than a month later. On October 5, 2001, a photo editor of the Florida-based tabloid *Sun* was the first to die from anthrax inhaled from a mailed letter. Letters tainted with anthrax were also discovered at NBC offices, Senate offices (prompting evacuations and closings), Governor Pataki's office in New York City, postal facilities in Florida, and offices of the *New York Post*. Postal workers in Washington, D.C., were hospitalized after inhaling anthrax. Small amounts of the substance were also discovered at CIA headquarters. In all, five people died and thirteen others were hospitalized. For many American citizens, the anthrax incidents raised the issue of other potential bioterrorist threats, such as smallpox, and ecoterrorism, such as food and water contamination. The threat of smallpox was given special media attention because it was considered one of the most effective biological weapons, and one to which the United States was particularly vulnerable. There was talk that smallpox vaccinations, which had ended in the 1970s, should be resumed.

Protecting America from Terrorism

The Bush administration's initial response sought to prevent further attacks, to protect the president and vice president, to maintain a functioning government, and to begin investigating the events. All flights in U.S. airspace were grounded, stranding passengers for several days; military fighter jets patrolled the airspace of large metropolitan areas, prepared to shoot down suspicious passenger aircraft. Stricter rules governing airport security would also be implemented. Potential targets—federal offices, monuments, and other symbols of American identity, such as the Sears Tower in Chicago and the Empire State Building—were closed. Bridges, tunnels, power plants, and petro-chemical refineries, all of which could result in a devastating loss of life if destroyed, were on alert and under heavy security. More than 18,000 law enforcement agencies around the nation were placed on the highest level of alert and cautioned to notify the FBI of any unusual or suspicious activity immediately. Airplanes flying within a ten-mile radius of nuclear power plants could be shot down.

Because of the fear that large gatherings of people and crowds would be vulnerable to a terrorist attack, many athletic events were postponed, such as college football, professional golf, and professional car racing events. For the first time since 1944 (D-day), major league baseball teams postponed fifteen games. After almost a week of consecutive cancelled games, which had not occurred since 1918 (World War I), they resumed under greater security. Fans ran a security gauntlet of metal detectors before entering stadiums. Under surveillance planes flying miles overhead and with the military patrolling the streets, the Winter Olympics in Salt Lake City occurred without incident.

From an individual perspective, American citizens had to tolerate restrictions on civil liberties and personal freedoms, and the democratic laws they enjoyed made it almost impossible to detect terrorists and their operatives. Suddenly, there was a real risk that a person could be pulled out of bed in the middle of the night, detained in a secret location, refused legal representation, and denied judicial supervision. Although American society as a whole was subject to extra scrutiny by security and law enforcement, people of Middle Eastern descent, with Middle Eastern sounding names, or who "looked" Middle Eastern were subject to markedly more. Just before the attacks, racial profiling of African Americans in New Jersey was heavily criticized; yet after the attacks, profiling those perceived as Middle Eastern was deemed acceptable and necessary to combat terrorism. Because interrogating everyone and checking everyone's background is an impossible task, profiling was considered a more efficient screening process because it relied on factors that correlated with terrorism. Based on looks, dress, name, or accent, a person could be interrogated and imprisoned. Although there were many accounts of citizens being strip-searched, interrogated, and detained, the most significant aspect of racial profiling involved Attorney General John Ashcroft's request for assistance from local law enforcement to interview 5,000 men of Arab descent across the country. Many police departments refused to participate in the dragnet, but a number of the detainees were held for months with no evidence of wrongdoing, and others were deported or detained indefinitely on the basis of minor visa violations. Ashcroft subsequently ordered that all legal visitors and immigrants from the Middle East and South Asia be registered and fingerprinted on their arrival in the United States. In a well-publicized case, racial profiling hit close to home for President Bush when an Arab American member of his secret service detail was removed from an American Airlines flight ("Abusive Behavior, Or Racial Profiling?" *Washington Post*, January 4, 2002). The pilot presumably feared having an armed Arab on his plane, despite assurances that the agent had the right to be armed. It was reported that President Bush said he was "madder than heck," but this emotional reaction did not seem to halt a practice that the government thought was useful in its attempt to make American citizens safe and secure.

Material witness warrants became an important government tool in subverting future attacks and investigations, but such a powerful statute involved serious repercussions for individual rights. Many people were arrested and detained under federal material witness statutes. By labeling suspects as material witnesses in an ongoing investigation of terrorism, federal agents could legally detain them indefinitely without formally charging them with a crime—circumventing the need to establish probable cause and secure an arrest warrant from a judge. Material witnesses in terrorism investigations are not generally afforded the rights granted under routine arrests, such as the right to see documents related to their detention and the right to legal representation (or at least one provided by the government). Supporters of the material witness statutes argued that the statutes allowed the government to effectively disrupt ongoing terrorist plots without having to gather solid evidence of illegal conduct. More than 1,200 individuals were reportedly detained under material witness statues, and the statutes were critical in apprehending Zacarias Moussaoui, who was believed to be a member of al Qaeda and the so-called twentieth hijacker.

Dissent and criticism of political authorities and the tactics they used to respond to attacks, normally considered an exercise of democratic rights, were considered anti-American after the attacks. Dissent appeared in various forms. Shortly after the attacks, the American Council of Trustees and Alumni (ACTA), an academic watchdog group founded by Lynne Cheney, released a report titled *Defending Civilization: How Our Universities Are Failing America and What Can Be Done About It*. This report declared that "college and university faculty have been the weak link in America's response" to terrorism and listed the names of 117 students and professors who had, it claimed, made anti-American statements. The report also claimed that university faculty undermined the fight against terrorism and that they blamed the United States for the 9/11 attacks. Because ACTA named names in the report, released it over the Internet, and threatened to send the list to the trustees of more than 3,000 universities, the report was viewed as an attempt to stifle dissent and publicly vilify individuals who openly criticized the president and U.S. foreign policy. Accusations of anti-Americanism were also leveled against those who produced unflattering artistic depictions of the president. Federal agents, for example, interrogated the owner of a Houston art museum about an exhibit called "Secret Wars" that included a drawing of President Bush tangled in barbed wire, a drawing the agents considered unpatriotic and un-American.

Government surveillance of citizens by telephone and digital wiretapping, email tracing, and wireless eavesdropping began almost immediately. Two days after 9/11, the Senate amended the House Appropriations Bill H.R. 2500 to expand the surveillance authority of law enforcement. The measure, called the Combating Terrorism Act of 2001, granted law enforcement almost unlimited power to track, record, and scrutinize citizen behavior. Unlike traditional telephone wiretapping systems, which attempt to isolate individuals, the new technology gave law enforcement warrantless surveillance authority over citizens. It also enabled the FBI to initiate its electronic online surveillance system, CARNIVORE, which could comb through millions of emails every second. The surveillance net was cast broadly, scrutinizing innocent citizens with no connection to terrorists or terrorist organizations. Although interest in expanding this law led to the crafting of the Patriot Act, many people saw the law (as they would see the Patriot Act) as an encroachment on basic civil rights and liberties.

Ashcroft also initiated a series of immigration programs to disrupt terrorist activities in the United States. Immigration and Naturalization Services (INS) agents, working with the FBI, began arresting individuals for immigration violations under "special interest." Eventually, 768 so-called special interest aliens were detained, not granted bonds, and held until the FBI and other agencies cleared them of terrorist connections. The number of visas given to individuals from countries with significant Muslim populations was reduced. Justice Department proposals included freezing all visas, suspending visas to nationals from selected countries, and requiring FBI and CIA checks on each applicant from certain countries before issuing a visa. Additional screening for visa applicants from twenty-six predominantly Muslim countries was initiated immediately.

Patriot Act, I and II

With the passage of the USA Patriot Act on October 25, 2001, just forty-five days after the terrorist attacks, Congress gave law enforcement sweeping new powers to obtain sensitive private information about people, eavesdrop on conversations, monitor computer use, and detain suspects without probable cause. By circumventing judicial review and the First and Fourth Amendments limiting the government's ability to conduct searches, the Patriot Act bypassed the system of checks and balances that traditionally safeguard civil liberties. The balance of proof shifted from presumption of innocence to presumption of guilt. Before the legislation, the government was required to first demonstrate to a court that it had probable cause to believe evidence relevant to a crime might be found. Arrests and detentions required court supervision and involved protecting individual rights. Much of this was reversed under the Patriot Act.

However, the act was seen as an important and necessary tool to enhance the government's ability to provide for the safety and security of

American citizens, under the argument that the terrorists used America's openness to attack, and presumably were using America's respect for individual liberty to elude capture. On signing the legislation into law, President Bush commented that the Patriot Act

> will help counter a threat like no other our nation has ever faced. We've seen the enemy, and the murder of thousands of innocent, unsuspecting people. They recognize no barrier of morality. They have no conscience. The terrorists cannot be reasoned with. . . . We're dealing with terrorists who operate by highly sophisticated methods and technologies, some of which were not even available when our existing laws were written. The bill before me takes account of the new realities and dangers posed by modern terrorists. It will help law enforcement to identify, to dismantle, to disrupt, and to punish terrorists before they strike. (Office of the Press Secretary 2001b)

Under the legislation, the attorney general could certify who would be considered a terrorist. Without any hearings or legal justifications, a person could be labeled as such if the government had reasonable "suspicions" that he or she was a terrorist or would be engaged in activity that endangered national security. After effectively identifying a person as a terrorist, the Patriot Act further increased the authority of the attorney general to detain and deport noncitizens on "reasonable grounds to believe" involvement in terrorism or activity that poses a danger to national security, with little or no judicial review. Individuals who are not deportable for terrorism, but who have in some way violated their immigration status, such as overstaying a visa, could face indefinite detention.

Putting individuals on the defensive, the Patriot Act permitted detaining and deporting noncitizens who assisted in the lawful activities of groups the government identified as terrorist organizations even if the group had never been designated as such before, and regardless of whether the noncitizens knew of the designation or whether their assistance had anything to do with the group's alleged terrorist activity. This section of the legislation essentially established a person's guilt by association.

"Sneak and peek" authority was also expanded under the Patriot Act. Under this provision, law enforcement agencies could delay giving notice when conducting a search. This meant that the government could—without notifying the occupant until after the fact—enter a house, apartment, or office with a search warrant when the occupant was away, search property, take photographs, and in some cases seize physical property and electronic communications. This provision challenged the Fourth Amendment protection against unreasonable searches and seizures, which requires the government to both obtain a warrant and give notice to the person whose property will be searched before conducting the search. Expanding roving wiretap authority, the Patriot Act authorized wiretaps and other surveillance based only on probable cause. Once a telephone that a suspect used was monitored, others who used that telephone might also be subject to continuing surveillance. Internet and telephone companies were required to turn over customer information if the FBI claimed the records were relevant to a terrorism investigation. Financial institutions would monitor daily financial transactions even more closely, and be required to share information with other federal agencies, including intelligence agencies such as the CIA. Credit card firms had to disclose, without benefit of a court order, any information FBI agents requested in connection with a terrorist attack.

The proposed Patriot Act II was intended to go further than the first, and to make permanent many of its sunset provisions originally set to expire December 31, 2005. Following congressional authorization to use force, law enforcement would be allowed to conduct domestic wiretapping without a court order and access financial records without subpoena. Legal residents could be deported without a criminal charge or even evidence, based only on the suspicions of the attorney general. The government would not be required to release any information about detainees held on suspicion of terrorist activities until they were charged with a crime. Without a court order, DNA samples could be collected from suspected terrorists and anyone who might assist terror investigations.

Unlike the initial legislation, which the president had signed within two weeks of its writing, the renewal of the Patriot Act was not straightforward. The political climate in 2005 was certainly less compliant than the six weeks following the 2001 attacks, which led to more discussion and assurances regarding the reauthorization of the act. Most of the provisions of the act were renewed and other provisions were added to enhance the ability of law enforcement to detect potential threats. At the same time, another perspective saw the reauthorization as further encroachment on individual rights.

The renewal process began in February 2003 when draft antiterrorism legislation was leaked to the public. The House and Senate passed different versions of a bill that would renew the law on which they were able (in November 2005) to reach a tentative compromise on revisions that would limit some of the government's powers. A bipartisan group of senators unsatisfied with the final version, however, threatened to filibuster the legislation. A temporary extension permitted members of Congress more time to consider the measure. On March 7, 2006, Congress voted to renew the Patriot Act. The president signed the bill two days later.

The major civil liberties protection exempted libraries that provide only traditional services, such as book lending and Internet access, from receiving subpoenas without warrants. The reauthorized legislation removed the requirement that subpoenaed individuals through national security letters revealing the name of their attorney. Those who received secret national security letters, which allow examination of business records, were also permitted to appeal gag orders. A new four-year sunset was also set on certain provisions on roving wiretaps and secret warrants for books, personal records, and other items from businesses and hospitals. Public sentiment was almost evenly divided on the renewal of the Patriot Act. In a Pew Research Center survey in 2006, 39 percent indicated that the Patriot Act was a necessary tool that helps the government fight terrorism, 38 percent said it went too far and posed a threat to civil liberties, while 22 percent said they were unsure. Unfortunately, this question did not ask about specific provisions.

The Afghanistan War

After the Taliban government refused to hand over Osama bin Laden, leader of the al Qaeda terrorist network responsible for the attacks of September 11, the United States invaded Afghanistan on October 7, 2001. Because the Taliban was alleged to be training for terrorists and a co-conspirator in the attacks, American citizens overwhelmingly supported the invasion. A Gallup Poll conducted two days after the invasion showed that 90 percent of Americans supported the military response, and that another 72 percent believed that the Bush administration had waited the right amount of time to begin. The U.S. military quickly decimated the Taliban regime and much of the al Qaeda terrorist network, though Osama bin Laden eluded capture. Captured Taliban and al Qaeda fighters, incarcerated at Guantánamo Bay, Cuba, were detained under the hope they would reveal information that would aid in the fight against terrorism. Although it was later revealed that most of the detainees were not terrorists, interrogations and alleged torture of those held at Guantánamo prompted criticisms from legal and human rights organizations. In addition to charges of cruel and degrading treatment of detainees, the denial of access to legal counsel and courts and the failure to fully disclose information concerning their internment were also considered violations of international law.

To facilitate the investigation of the detainees, President Bush signed an executive order authorizing the creation of military tribunals to detain and try noncitizens involved in assisting terrorists and combatants. It was argued that if individuals supporting terrorists or enemy combatants were not entitled to the same rights as civilians, they could be prosecuted by military tribunals. Because military tribunals would not be held in public and followed weaker evidentiary rules, they were also seen as protecting sensitive information that the government deemed necessary to prevent future terrorist attacks. Critics charged that noncitizens suspected of terrorism were constitutionally entitled to the full protection of the civilian legal system. Military tribunals did not usually involve independent or impartial judges. Again, the presumption was guilt rather than innocence. Trials were not necessarily public, and there was no right to appeal.

The Iraq War

The threat of terrorism was defined more broadly than the actions of individual terrorists and extended to possible supporters of terrorism. After the fall of Afghanistan, a successful case was made for Iraq's being involved in terrorism and producing weapons of mass destruction. According to President Bush at the time,

> Saddam Hussein has a long history of reckless aggression and terrible crimes. He possesses weapons of terror. He provides funding and training and safe haven to terrorists—terrorists who would willingly use weapons of mass destruction against America and other peace-loving countries. Saddam Hussein and his weapons are a direct threat to this country, to our people, and to all free people. (Office of the Press Secretary 2003)

Although the invasion of Iraq led to Saddam Hussein's defeat and eventual capture, Americans' sense of vulnerability did not seem to diminish. According to a CNN/Gallup poll, perceptions of threat of another terrorist attack remained almost constant at just over 40 percent in the months that followed. In addition to raising concerns among individual citizens, the unilateral invasion of Iraq also alienated many of America's allies and initial supporters in the fight against terrorism. Except for Great Britain, most members of the United Nations Security Council—Germany, France, Russia, China, and later Spain—did not support the invasion of Iraq (though all eleven members have veto power). It was argued that the evidence for invading Iraq—the production of weapons of mass destruction and the connection to al Qaeda—was not compelling and that diplomatic solutions should be exhausted first. The successful military operation in Iraq changed into urban warfare, in which many American soldiers were killed, and American citizens lacked the comfort of the external validation of its major allies that the United States was doing the right thing there. No weapons of mass destruction were found in Iraq. Furthermore, in 2004, a commission investigating the 9/11 attacks found no link between Iraq and Osama bin Laden. The revelation that the Bush administration had mischaracterized the threat Iraq posed fueled further cynicism abroad toward the United States.

26   Negative Liberty

It is clear that the government faced a daunting task in balancing the rights of individual liberty and security, and that American citizens faced an equal challenge of tolerating certain restrictions on civil liberties given the degree of threat they perceived. The effectiveness and return on sacrifices to civil liberties was not immediately evident, but no further attacks occurred, despite expectations. From this point of view, the willingness to trade civil liberties for security could have topped off as the level of vulnerability to attack diminished. However, this was clearly not the case, because the level of threat did not diminish over time. Another important feature of the context of the attacks is that many of the mechanisms intended to provide safety and security in the long term made American citizens more fearful in the short term. At the time, government behavior appeared reasonable and justifiable, given the threat of terrorism and the extent to which terrorists infiltrated American society, but Bush administration's unilaterialist approach in Afghanistan and Iraq heightened feelings of threat and vulnerability. American citizens believed that it was better to have cooperation and support of its allies. Meanwhile, invading Iraq was thought to have increased the level of hatred toward the United States in the Middle East, and thereby increased the risk of future terrorist attacks.

A series of *Washington Post* and ABC News polling questions touched on this point: "Do you think the war with Iraq has or has not contributed to the long-term security of the Unites States?" Responses to this question, reported in figure 2.1, suggests that though Americans thought that the war in Iraq would make the United States safer, perceptions that the war in Iraq would make the United States more secure declined over time. When this question was asked after the invasion of Iraq, only 62 percent saw the invasion as enhancing U.S. security. This is far from the high level of support one would have expected in going to war in the first place. Although there were a series of positive milestones in the war in Iraq, the support continued to decline. The lowest level of support came a year later, when only 51 percent thought that the war had made the United States safer.

The Big Picture

In proper perspective, the initial and subsequent environments surrounding September 11 did not resemble a police or military state, though many citizens experienced aspects of one. For the most part, American citizens continued to enjoy their freedom, albeit with a little more caution than they had done before the attacks. Political tolerance was part of the administration's message. The sense of caution arose from the changing world in which Americans found themselves. The social and political climate is best described in terms of fear of both the

Figure 2.1 Has War in Iraq Contributed to U.S. Security? (Washington Post–ABC News Poll)

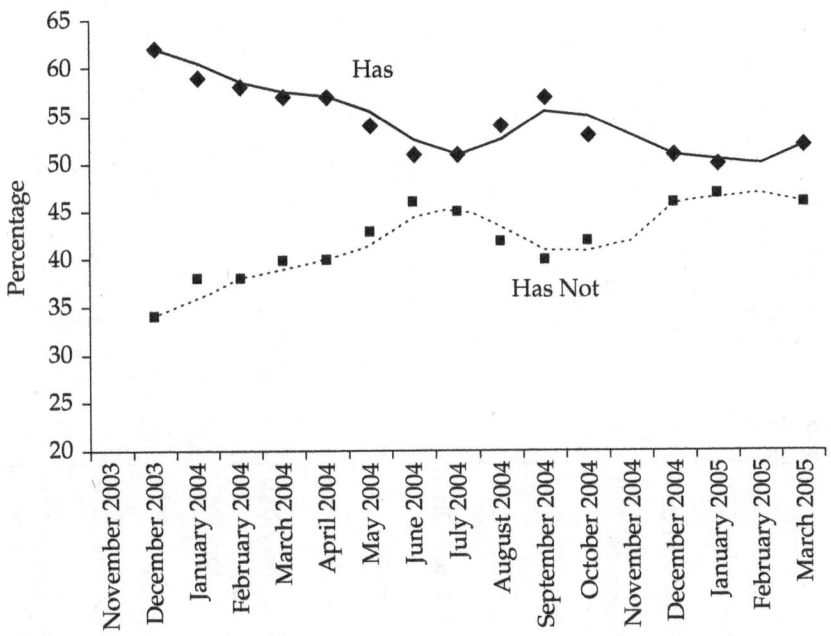

"Do You Think the War with Iraq Has or Has Not Contributed to the Long-Term Security of the United States?"

Source: Author's compilation of data from Washington Post–ABC News Poll.

possibility that other attacks were imminent and a sense of vulnerability that the government response at times exacerbated. I am not seeking to blame the government and political authorities or to suggest they manipulated or took advantage of such emotions. The point I hope to make clear is that the government was in a tenuous situation because it is almost impossible not to enhance a sense of vulnerability when attempting to warn people to be more vigilant. The automatic response, of course, is that there must be a creditable threat if the government is warning people about a possible threat, because people would not automatically assume that the government would manipulate the situation. This act alone, without any other form of government activity, is probably enough to exacerbate perceptions of threat. But, there were lapses in intelligence, the government did make false and inflammatory statements and did entertain both domestic and international activities that increased perceptions of vulnerability. This is also part of

Figure 2.2 Confidence in the Government to Prevent Attacks (Washington Post–ABC News)

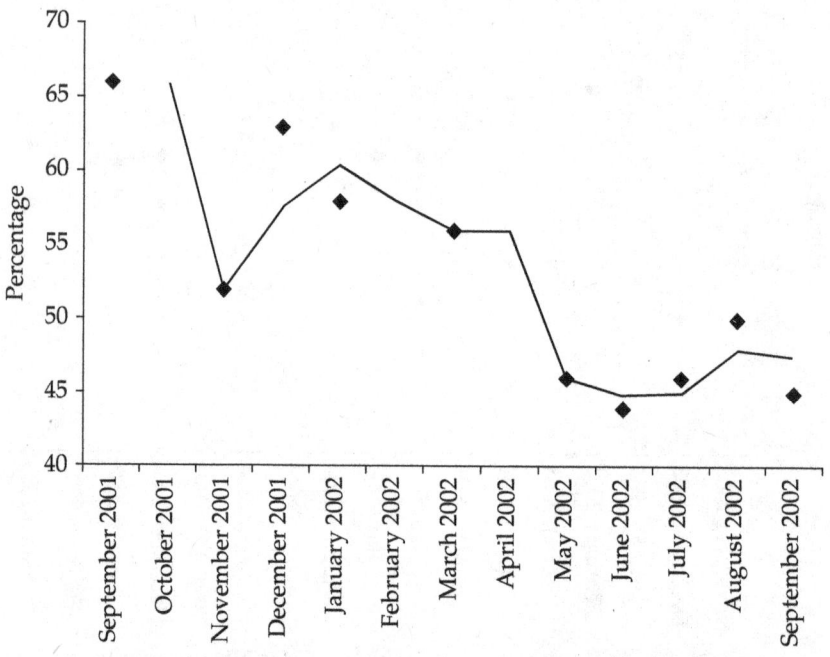

"How Much Confidence Do You Have in the Ability of the U.S. Government to Prevent Further Terrorist Attacks Against Americans in this Country?" ("A Great Deal" and "A Good Deal" Combined)

Source: Author's compilation of data from Washington Post–ABC News Polls.

the evolving context and political environment surrounding the war on terrorism.

Over time, many individuals perceived government policies as less and less effective in ensuring security from terrorism. Again, a series of ABC News polls is instructive. Figure 2.2 shows the responses to the following question concerning the effectiveness of U.S. policies: "How much confidence do you have in the ability of the U.S. government to prevent further terrorist attacks against Americans in this country?" Beginning in September 2001, 66 percent of American citizens indicated confidence. This is not as an incredibly high level of support as one might expect, but is nonetheless strong. It declines sharply, however. Almost immediately, it drops by 14 percent but nearly rebounds to its previous level just as quickly. However, after January 2002, it drops again by more than 20 percent and never recovers to the September 2001 level. I take this as prima facie evidence that government activities that were intended to bolster the confidence in the ability to combat terrorism were perceived differently and added to perceptions of vulnerability.

Implications for Subsequent Analyses of Civil Liberties Trade-offs

There are several important implications of this context on the support for civil liberties.

- We can expect that citizens, in response to the events of September 11, will concede some civil liberties for security. However, I do not think that this will be a permanent concession, especially as people began to question the activities of political authorities.
- As the context changes, the factors that determine the trade-off between civil liberties and security will likely diminish as other factors become more important.
- We can expect that perceptions of threat, which capture the most significant aspects of the context of terrorism, will be very important.
- Concern that the country as a whole is susceptible to attack will likely remain high, but not necessarily all due to terrorism. The role of government should figure into aspects of sustained threat.
- Because of government activities that exacerbated feelings of vulnerability, political trust could become an extremely important determinant of the support for civil liberties over time.

Despite the reality that being involved in another terrorist attack was probably remote, American citizens at the end of the day had a great deal to be concerned about. Initially, the concern centered on the threat of another attack, certainly understandable given that American citizens had not been attacked before, let alone by foreign terrorists from halfway around the world. The magnitude of the event and the planning were enough to heighten concern about a repeat, but political authorities and the media were telling them to be both vigilant and cautious. It is difficult to warn people about a threat of terrorism without adding to the sense of vulnerability. I will show later that there are different ways of thinking about perceptions of threat and vulnerability. For instance, though people might not think that they or their family members are likely targets, they are likely to see the country as a whole as susceptible when the government's activities are seen as threatening. This argument is a setup for a much larger discussion on the relative importance of personal threat and country level (or sociotropic) threat.

Treatment of context is also important because the role of government will figure prominently in the changing climate of threat and fluctuating support for civil liberties. It is clear that citizens will eventually shift their views of political authorities and the government. The implication is that initially Americans were willing to allow political authorities a great deal of flexibility in combating terrorism, but that this latitude will continue to diminish because of the contextual issues discussed in these chapters.

Chapter 3

Value Conflict: Civil Liberties Versus National Security

IN SITUATIONS where liberty and security collide, and enjoying one means sacrificing the other, political and social life are likely to be unpleasant. Individuals face the dilemma of tolerating a sense of threat and vulnerability to both an external enemy and the government. Both types of threat, I will argue later, can be equally menacing and indistinguishable to many citizens. Short of dissolving the social contract and starting over, individuals might be expected to tolerate restrictions on freedom and live with a certain sense of vulnerability that civil society by definition is intended to resolve. This tolerance runs counter to the belief, at least in liberal democratic theory, that empowering political authorities by surrendering some measure of civil liberties is presumed to make people safer, and therefore increase their liberty and freedom. Individual liberty and security are not supposed to clash, let alone be perceived as mutually exclusive.

However, the reality of American democratic society is that important political values frequently collide with other values and others' rights.[1] When this happens, individual citizens are expected to apply what they have learned about democracy to resolve such conflicts, which usually means that democracy suffers. Nevertheless, if security is more fundamental than self-actualization and freedom, as Abraham Maslow (1954) suggests, American citizens accustomed to freedom, broad civil liberties, and a secure society should be willing to sacrifice a great deal—even personal freedoms—to maintain a comfortable way of life. But, as I will argue, the trade-off is more complex than it seems, especially when the values being exchanged take on additional meaning within an emotionally charged context, such as the terrorist attacks of September 11, 2001. That is, asking people to compromise certain values in the abstract is one thing, but asking them to do so in real life is an entirely different one. In this chapter, I connect the trade-off between democratic values and security following those attacks to a larger literature on political tolerance.

This literature is particularly informative because it treats support for civil liberties as situational and as a compromise between perceptions of threat and democratic values. I then develop a measure of trade-offs that will be used throughout my analysis. With such a measure, I also take a first stab at describing citizen support for civil liberties following the terrorist attacks. The basic question I address is the extent to which citizens saw a balance between civil liberties and security, or whether they were willing to make wholesale concessions to the government in a time of national crisis. Where do individual citizens draw the line in their willingness to acquiesce to restrictions on civil liberties?

Studying Democratic Principles in Context

In his classic study, *Communism, Conformity, and Civil Liberties* (1955), Samuel Stouffer appraised the conflict between the support for civil liberties and the perceived threat of suspected communists, socialists, and atheists at the height of the Cold War and the Red Scare. In the 1950s, American citizens' sense of vulnerability was connected to communism as an ideology, possible invasion, and the loss of personal liberty. The emergence of the USSR and the United States as world powers following World War II led to a concern that communists would infiltrate the government and force citizens to give up their personal rights. The government's attempt to expose suspected communists led to aggressive investigations, in which American citizens suspected of being communists—or those appearing strange, different, or nonconformist—were blacklisted, administered loyalty oaths, and stripped of civil liberties. In examining the acceptance of the "two dangers" of the communist conspiracy both outside and inside the country, and support for "those who in thwarting the conspiracy would sacrifice some of the very liberties which the enemy would destroy," Stouffer revealed a great deal of intolerance among American citizens (13). Substantial majorities indicated that an admitted communist should not be permitted to speak publicly, or teach in high schools or colleges, or work as a clerk in a store. There was also a virtual consensus that communists should have their citizenship revoked, that books written by communists should be taken out of public libraries, and that the government should have the authority to tap personal telephone conversations. American citizens moderated their attitudes toward other nonconformists, such as atheists and socialists, but for the most part, they were not tolerated either. Stouffer showed, for the first time, that American citizens were not committed to a free and open exchange of ideas. This was tempered somewhat, however, by political authorities and civic leaders, who were presumed better prepared to apply democratic norms.[2]

Subsequent efforts to build on Stouffer's findings, such as the research by John Sullivan and his colleagues (1979, 1981, 1982), equalized the threat by decontextualizng the value conflict. Instead of focusing on predetermined and nonequivalent sources of threat, such as communists or atheists, Sullivan and his colleagues (1982) permitted survey respondents to identify groups they least liked; then, based on this functionally equivalent threat, they sought to determine degrees of tolerance for those groups. By leveling the playing field across respondents—whether the least-liked groups were on the political right or left, or belonged to certain racial or ethnic categories—the value conflict between tolerance and threat was grounded in equivalent contexts. This approach profoundly improved Stouffer's approach, though Sullivan, Piereson, and Marcus reported greater intolerance in 1982 than Stouffer had done in 1955. Under a content-controlled measure, American citizens were found pluralistically intolerant. That is, though in 1978 communists were still the least-liked group (29 percent), people could now identify more groups to dislike, such as the Ku Klux Klan (24 percent), to take one example. Later on in this volume, using a measure of social group affect, I will explore aspects of pluralistic intolerance that arose after the 9/11 attacks (see chapter 9).

To return to a contextualized approach, however, we see more recent research attesting to the real-life consequences of adhering to democratic beliefs. People's political and social environments shape their responses when their democratic values conflict with other values. For Jews in Skokie, Illinois, fear and threat competed with the trade-offs between freedom of expression and the rights of Nazis (Gibson and Bingham 1985). In 1977, the National Socialist Party of America attempted to march through Skokie, a community initially founded by Germans, but home after World War II to the most Holocaust survivors in the United States outside of New York City. The conflict over rights involved various measures to prevent the Nazis from demonstrating and the threat to the community that such demonstrating posed. Skokie's Jews were both terrified and infuriated at the prospect of Nazis marching in their midst. In addition to passing legal injunctions blocking the demonstration, the village board enacted ordinances designed to hinder the group from protesting, such as requiring insurance. As James Gibson and Richard Bingham (1985, 41) relate, "demonstrations creating an imminent danger of a substantial breach of the peace, riot, or similar disorder were prohibited, as were demonstrations portraying criminality, depravity or lack of virtue in, or inciting violence, hatred, abuse or hostility toward a person or group of persons by reason of reference to religious, racial, ethnic, national or regional affiliation." Although the restrictions were overturned, the case presented an ideal situation in which to study extending civil liberties for an unpopular group.

This research suggests that though local political elites tended to share the civil libertarian preferences of the community, national political leaders tended to support civil liberties. However, a national elite does not always reliably protect civil liberties, as there are many cases, such as the Red Scare, in which national political leaders have advocated repressive policies. James Gibson (1988) finds that repressive policies during this period originated with political elites, and not the general public. Similarly, following the September 11 attacks, the Justice Department ordered the FBI and law enforcement to question 5,000 Middle Eastern immigrants. Many local political leaders and law enforcement agencies resisted the FBI's requests to cooperate.

The restrictiveness of civil liberties at the state level during Vietnam War–era protests supports the contention that individual-level support for civil liberties is unrelated to repressive public policies (Gibson 1989). To give university administrators a tool to control widespread campus dissent and protest activity, criminal and civil statutes were enacted to regulate access to campuses, putting policy at odds with rights. The right to protest also conflicted with support for governmental war efforts. By contrast, the war in Afghanistan and subsequent war in Iraq, begun following the terrorist attacks of 2001 under the premise that those regimes harbored terrorists, did not result in widespread dissent.

The conflict between security and extending rights to unpopular groups may occur within communities, where the willingness to support civil liberties can be more complex and acute because a greater opportunity for threat is personalized. Gibson (1987a), for example, in examining the conflict between freedom of speech and the right to protest for the Ku Klux Klan versus the threat and fear perceived by the gay community, shows how important context can be. In 1984, members of the Ku Klux Klan planned a march criticizing the morality of homosexuality through a well-known gay community in Houston. The conflict involved the extent to which the civil liberties of Klan members should be protected over community concerns about possible violence that might result from the march. Gibson shows that, despite tolerance of the Klan reflecting a general opinion about whether unpopular groups should be allowed to demonstrate, the expectation of violence that members of the gay community associated with the Klan led to intolerance and a greater desire to restrict Klan behavior. The threat associated with the Klan was real and direct, and thus the consequences were obvious and immediate for the gay community. Whereas people would have been willing to allow the Klan to express its views about homosexuality, its wanting to take to the streets with that message was a different matter.

Using a different approach, the importance of context in civil liberties trade-off decisions can also be seen in how individuals respond when they are exposed to objective measures of aspects of their communities.

Taking the view that context can either constrain or amplify individual support for civil liberties, Gibson (1995) examines the compromise between perceptions of political freedom and conformity to racist community norms among African Americans. In communities that tolerate racists, blacks presumably would be expected to sacrifice their personal freedom to avoid the consequences of violating community norms. Gibson found the opposite, however. In local contexts tolerant of racists, African Americans had greater political freedom, and were unwilling to compromise their rights. Put another way, community tolerance of racists makes it possible for individuals to reject the need to compromise their values (see also Gibson 1992).

Against a quiescent domestic environment throughout the 1990s, scholars turned to comparative contexts to explore the individual costs of adhering to democratic beliefs when they conflicted with other values, such as when concerns about uncertainty, economic discontent, and weak support for democratic institutions competed with political tolerance among Russian citizens (Gibson 1993, 1996, 1998a; Gibson, Duch, and Tedin 1992), or when support for authoritarian beliefs and cultural norms, violence, and strong ethnic attachments competed with extending rights to political enemies in South Africa (Gibson and Gouws 2000). Political tolerance in Russia was seen as particularly problematic in light of the country's Marxist-Leninist culture that had not emphasized tolerance or liberal democratic principles. But as Russian society began to democratize, individual citizens needed to understand what was required in a democracy and to be prepared to operate accordingly. Gibson revealed that a sense of threat and vulnerability among Russian citizens was so ingrained that it interfered with political development. In South Africa, another democratizing society, individuals were also threatened by the previous apartheid system, social antagonisms interfered with the prospects for democracy. In both contexts, cultures of conflict and anxiety competed with democratic beliefs.

Explicitly contesting democratic values and taking a pluralistic value approach involving perceptions of the Canadian Charter of Rights, Sniderman and his colleagues (1996) show that conflicts over rights are inescapable, whether freedom of expression conflicts with others' rights or government surveillance of suspected terrorists competes with the fear and threat of individual citizens. The Canadian Charter of Rights protects citizens' rights and freedoms in that country by limiting government ability to pass laws or take actions that discriminate or infringe on human rights. Unlike the American Bill of Rights, it recognizes fundamental freedoms (such as those of expression and of association), democratic rights (for example, to vote), mobility rights (such as the right to live anywhere in Canada), legal rights (to life, liberty, and security of person, for example), and rights of equality. It also recognizes the multicultural heritage of Canadians, and protects official language and minority language education rights. But trade-off decisions arise with such rights as they conflict with other values. In an issue directly relevant to the present analysis involving the trade-off between wiretapping suspected terrorists and civil liberties, Sniderman and his colleagues find that individuals supported wiretapping, and political leaders supported it more than ordinary citizens did. However, the willingness to curtail civil liberties diminished as other groups were considered, such as people with antidemocratic ideas or agents of a foreign government. Canadian citizens were particularly intolerant of terriorists.

The literature suggests that, for ordinary citizens in ordinary times, civil liberties issues are likely to be remote from everyday experiences but that, in certain contexts, they assume an immediacy with direct implications for people's sense of freedom and well being. Following Gibson's 1987 assessment, we can see at least three major advantages to examining support for democratic norms within an actual context such as the September 11 attacks. First, responses to civil liberties question may be susceptible to "nonattitudes," as such issues typically are not on citizens' minds. Without immediate circumstances to orient political and social attitudes, there is often a risk that, when asked questions about civil liberties, survey respondents may either respond randomly or use another mechanism, such as social desirability or political correctness, to answer questions. Respondents may also use preceding survey questions or their perception of the interviewer to frame their answers. Dennis Chong (1993) suggests that responses to civil liberties questions are usually off-the-cuff responses. I am not suggesting that questions conducted in context are immune to survey biases, but it is quite reasonable for real experiences to anchor individuals' responses. As Chong argues, "a person gradually learns, through exposure to public discussion on the issue, to base his or her opinion on certain pertinent aspects of the issue and, at the same time, learns not to pay attention to other features of the issue deemed to be irrelevant" (890). Outside the debate over civil liberties and security, individual citizens are not likely to be aware of the consequences of their attitudes.

Second, there is a large gap between asking abstract questions with no point of reference—or, equally confusing, with different points of reference—and asking questions about specific issues they confront in their day-to-day interactions. This is the so-called abstract-applied problem. Context provides a point of reference for political and social attitudes. Information becomes more meaningful and accessible. Even in a specific context, individuals may not necessarily have more crystallized opinions unless the context raises important value conflicts. Attaching political attitudes to specific contexts, however, should allow people to form opinions more easily.

A final advantage is the opportunity to investigate the connections between attitudes and behavior. Attitudes are only approximations of probable behavior, and social scientists very rarely observe behavior directly. Although I employ rigorous, scientific methods, there is always some uncertainty in knowing whether individuals act on their political and social views. By examining the context in which political and social attitudes are formed, we have a better chance of linking it to behavior.

Conflicting Political Values

America's response to the terrorist attack reveals a "contestability of rights," in which the commitment to civil liberties collides with other cherished values (Sniderman et al. 1996). This value conflict not only parallels how individuals make normal judgments about civil liberties, but such conflict may account for why the adherence to abstract democratic norms is difficult to apply in practice. A person may sincerely believe in freedom of speech and association, but also believe in protecting society from those who use freedoms to plan or carry out criminal acts. Because ensuring liberty for some may infringe on the rights of others, support for civil liberties cannot be conceptualized in isolation from other values or goals. A decision about civil liberties inherently involves a decision about other values (Hadari 1988). As James Gibson and Richard Bingham (1985) note, support for civil liberties should not be regarded as an abstract attitude, but instead should be treated as a construct of priorities assigned in cases of value conflict. That is,

> the exercise of rights generates costs, and these costs are sometimes so substantial that conflict ensues. Previous measures of political tolerance and the support for civil liberties become inadequate because they fail to provide the subjects with information about the type of value conflict created within the particular context. (108–09)

Similarly, Herbert McClosky and Alida Brill (1983) suggest that the choice of liberty is bedeviled by the need to strike a proper balance between freedom and control. To the extent that support for civil liberties is most reasonably understood as contingent on other important values, approaches to measurement need to consider the continual play of competing forces that impinge on judgments about civil liberties. Sniderman and his colleagues (1996, 244) argue that the exercise of liberty "unavoidably collides with other values," and maintain that no right can be exercised without limitations before it clashes with the rights of others and the maintenance of order. When they collide in context, one cannot honestly support liberty and order at the same time. In the abstract, however, it is much easier to consider how values might conflict. As a result, many values, even those that are mutually exclusive, can be supported simultaneously.

Value conflict, even outside the contextual argument, is also important to civil liberty judgments because the tension it creates has been said to lead to greater tolerance. Research by Mark Peffley, Pia Knigge, and Jon Hurwitz (2001) suggests that those who experience greater value conflict, or who simultaneously rank competing values highly, engage in more complex political reasoning, which leads to greater support for civil liberties.[3]

For Saguiv Hadari (1988), a values trade-off approach presents an interesting dilemma. Value trade-off is argued to reflect a certain level of incommensurability whereby it becomes almost impossible to weigh competing values. Although the value trade-off decision inherently involves a normative decision, Hadari suggests that that approach is extremely important. It connects theoretical discussions to practical problems, which is an implicit criticism of a preoccupation with searching for utopias where values do not clash.

It is worth remarking that the value trade-off approach assumes values that are mutually exclusive or that people would have to tolerate restrictions on their individual rights if terrorism is to be successfully warded off. Because of how intensely people reacted to the attacks and how political authorities and the media framed the discourse, I assume that the context of the attacks made the choice between competing values more obvious and understandable than most other types of value considerations. After all, President Bush did declare "Freedom and fear [were] at war" (Office of the Press Secretary 2001a). With this type of framing, survey questions crafted to measure the value trade-off force an explicit choice between liberty and security. However, individuals may not necessarily perceive such value conflict, even when the tension between values is evident. Because they either cannot or do not have enough information to make the connection between conflicting values, individuals may not perceive a conflict between values. This is not unusual in the extant literature. For instance, Jennifer Hochschild (1981) in a series of in-depth interviews revealed a sense of ambivalence: many respondents appeared unaware of the underlying conflict between social welfare and traditional economic norms. Individuals seemed to find it easier living with, ignoring, and distressing normative tensions than undertaking an effort to resolve such conflicts (Hochschild 1981, 258). For Stanley Feldman and John Zaller (1992), ambivalence indicates a lack of ideological constraint. That is, American political culture is filled with inherent tensions and value conflicts that some individuals are better able to resolve more than others. Conservatives, for instance, may be better able than political liberals at reconciling anti–social welfare attitudes by appealing to the values of individualism. Michael Alvarez and John Brehm (2002), further clarifying the idea of ambivalence, argue that the relevance of multiple values need not lead to internalized conflict or irreconcilable beliefs. Instead, individuals may find the contested values acceptable (that is, not see a conflict), believe that one predisposition is more important than another, or settle on one set of values. Alvarez and Brehm (2002) also suggest that real value ambivalence is quite rare, but political conflicts involving individual rights are more likely to lead to ambivalent attitudes (2002, 69).

Trade-off Reasoning and Value Pluralism

People vary considerably in the values they hold important. When values clash, a complex cognitive process is said to govern trade-off reasoning. Philip Tetlock (1986) suggests that value trade-offs are not only unpleasant and cognitively challenging for individual citizens, but also that "people find it dissonant and threatening to their self-esteem to acknowledge that they are capable of cold-blooded trade-off decisions that require compromising basic values" (819). Although some individuals are more likely than others to think in complex trade-off terms (Tetlock 1981, 1983; Tetlock, Hannum, and Micheletti 1984), value trade-off reasoning is not such an onerous task that people cannot perform it. At the same time, people are unlikely to make sophisticated calculations of the consequences of certain trade-offs. "Trade-off reasoning should be so pervasive and so well rehearsed as to be virtually automatic for the vast majority of the population" (Tetlock 2000, 239).[4]

Trade-off reasoning is grounded in a value pluralism model. In this model, Tetlock argues that people can reason out trade-offs under certain conditions. They weigh values in specific situations, and when values are unequal, core values—such as freedom, equality, national security, perceptions of threat, or trust—govern the decision. But if core values weigh equally and values collide, simple solutions are no longer plausible, and people turn to more demanding cognitive strategies. As a result, people may differentiate values in an attempt to distinguish the impact of politics on conflicting values, or employ a form of integration to cope with trade-offs. Trade-offs also occur when the values in conflict are both important, citizens believe that it is acceptable to consider the trade-offs in question, and they see no socially acceptable way to avoid taking a stand on the issues (Tetlock 2000). Tetlock's analysis suggests that the more highly individuals ranked core values, such as freedom, over national security, the more they opposed government surveillance. Politically liberal individuals, who value civil liberties more highly than conservatives, face the greatest pressure to account for the effects of policy proposals on both values. They must also develop criteria against which to determine appropriate compromises between the two values.

The value pluralism model is useful because it emphasizes context and framing and provides a psychological explanation for selecting values. When the Bush administration framed the nature of terrorism as a war between freedom and fear in the State of the Union address a week after the attacks (Office of the Press Secretary 2001a), and the media and political experts used this frame, American citizens were likely to be aware of the value conflict between security and liberty, and thus, capable of making valid trade-off decisions. Another reason making the trade-off decision between freedom and security an easy one is that individuals did not actually have to make a formal choice between them. Though individuals had to make many choices involving security, such as how they wanted to travel or whether they should be in crowded stadiums, most individuals probably never experienced situations where they had to make an actual choice or decision about civil liberties and security. There was no national referendum asking individuals to approve government activities to combat terrorism. Government does not function like this, and it will do whatever it deems necessary to protect itself and its citizens, even if it means displeasing a large proportion of them. Individuals basically were in a situation where they had to tolerate government activities that encroached on civil liberties, but their tolerance of the trade-offs between security and civil liberties involved real consequences.

Because trade-off reasoning between civil liberties and security can be influenced by ideological predispositions, and can be interrupted by context—especially the mix of vulnerability, anxiety, patriotism, and other emotions following the terrorist attacks—chapter 4 explores the factors in value trade-offs in more detail. For now, I suggest that a cognitive process is likely to underlie how people view issues in context and respond to survey questions. Although the framing of the civil liberties and security was tied to a real context, violation of civil liberties were largely unnoticeable and in the background.

The Trade-off Measure

Based on how the trade-off between civil liberties and security was framed after 9/11, and on citizens' ability to make trade-off decisions, I adopt a value conflict conceptualization to model trade-offs between the support for civil liberties and perceptions of threat. I am ever mindful, however, of James Kuklinski and his colleagues (1991), who suggest, somewhat counterintuitively, that requiring respondents to consider competing values and the implications of democratic values does not automatically lead to endorsement of civil liberties. My value-conflict approach positions the individual's support for civil liberties against government efforts to keep citizens safe from terrorism. Both liberty and security have long been cherished American values, and though they are not necessarily at odds or zero-sum, the bases of conflict that I identify rest on the efforts of political authorities and law enforcement agencies to maintain order or provide security in the post–September 11 era. It is not terrorism per se that clashes with individual rights, but rather the government's methods of maintaining security in response.

In much of the research using a value-conflict approach to study civil liberties and tolerance, the struggle is usually between preserving individual security and tolerating the civil liberties of disliked or threatening groups. In the post–September 11 period, however, the trade-off has mainly been framed as protecting individual rights or civil liberties against the government as the government tries to defend the country against a largely external enemy, albeit one that has infiltrated American society and poses a domestic risk to public safety and security. The compromise is thus fundamental to the very idea of liberal democracy, reflected in the Bill of Rights, that citizens' rights should be protected from the government. Because the government's actions may conflict with individual rights, I expect popular perceptions of government—trust in government, political ideology, partisanship (chapter 7), and patriotism—to be important determinants of people's willingness to trade civil liberties for security.

I identified several policy dimensions along which liberty and security were contested in the immediate aftermath of the attacks. Each of these dimensions became an important public issue, and each reflects different level of difficulty:

- habeas corpus: indefinite detention of noncitizens suspected of terrorism
- racial discrimination: racial profiling
- electronic surveillance: increased wiretapping and email surveillance
- freedom of speech: schoolteachers criticizing antiterrorism policy
- right to privacy: national identity cards
- freedom of association: belonging to or supporting alleged terrorist organizations
- protection from search and seizure: search on suspicion without court order
- freedom of assembly and speech: investigate nonviolent protestors

These dimensions also cut across several policy areas, in which the trade-off is not always obvious or easy. As mentioned, individuals do not consider all rights equal and, in context, certain rights become more important than others. Because there are no absolutes in the sense that few people would agree with all or none of the civil liberties items, I expect American citizens to draw the line somewhere, and for these policy dimensions, to tell us where it is. Below is a description of the context surrounding each issue.

Habeas Corpus

I chose habeas corpus—the requirement that arrested individuals be brought before a judge and have the charges against them heard—as a civil liberties dimension because it is a fundamental right with broad support, and because it became an issue almost immediately. Many citizens were denied legal representation and detained for months without being reviewed by the courts. In public discourse after September 11, discussions of access to legal counsel and government surveillance of communication between detainees and their lawyers, uncertainty and dispute over the rights of those being held, and even over whether the names of those persons would be publicly disclosed, were considerable. Habeas corpus was also a major issue in classifying enemy combatants captured in Afghanistan, using military tribunals, and implementing the Patriot Act. I framed the survey question to refer to people suspected of belonging to terrorist organizations, rather than trying to specify the precise legal status of those who are actually detained or the rationale for their being held. The basic issue of whether people should be held indefinitely based on suspicion of belonging to a terrorist organization, without specific charges being filed against them, is something to which the average American can respond in a survey. The specific question is this:

> Some people say the government should be able to arrest and detain a noncitizen indefinitely if that person is suspected of belonging to a terrorist organization. Others say no one should be held for a long period without being formally charged with a crime. Which of these opinions do you agree with most?

Racial Discrimination

Following the September 11 attacks, individuals of Middle Eastern descent, Muslims, and people who happened to look Middle Eastern were frequently suspected of being al Qaeda sympathizers and were targets of violence and discrimination. Sporadic killings of Muslims, beatings, intimidation, fire-bombings, burning of Islamic centers, hate mail, and racial slurs were all reported, but harassment of individuals perceived as Middle Eastern took on subtler forms over time. Many were fired from their jobs and denied access to public facilities, and many of their businesses were burned and damaged. Middle Easterners also became susceptible to housing discrimination, out of the belief that they would seek to destroy high-rise buildings. Because of heightened security concerns, the Department of Defense began banning noncitizens from high-tech computer jobs and sensitive projects. As a result, many citizens with Middle Eastern backgrounds changed their names, shaved their beards, and avoided wearing traditional clothing. Support for racial profiling of blacks had been on the wane before the terrorist attacks, as I mentioned earlier, but I selected it as a dimension because it was a relatively basic issue that would perhaps take on a different level of significance in context. Racial profiling is also interesting because the role of government is less explicit. To capture this aspect of the conflict over rights and security, the following question was used to measure the support for racial profiling:

> Some people say that law enforcement should be able to stop or detain people of certain racial or ethnic backgrounds if these groups are thought to be more likely to commit crimes. This is called racial profiling. Others think racial profiling should not be done because it harasses many innocent people just because of their race or ethnicity. Which of these opinions do you agree with most?

Electronic Surveillance

For surveillance as a civil liberties issue, the role of government and the right being violated are clear. The conflict between protecting civil liberties and personal security took shape within hours of the attacks, when the FBI served many Internet service providers with search warrants for information about email addresses connected to the attacks. Through Carnivore, a search program, the FBI sifted through communications and information on web browsing habits. Unlike traditional wiretaps, in which the government is required to minimize its interception of nonincriminating or innocent communications, Carnivore scanned all email communications, from innocent Internet users as well as targeted suspects. In a voice vote on September 13, the Senate approved an amendment by Senators Orrin Hatch and Dianne Feinstein allowing the FBI greater flexibility to obtain court orders to track individual Internet users online. Calls for national identification cards, email monitoring, limits on the rights of immigrants, and cumbersome metal detectors at public gatherings gained greater support since the morning of September 11. As an example of how such authority can get out of hand, President Bush acknowledged in 2005 that he had ordered a secret program through the National Security Agency to electronically eavesdrop on American citizens without first obtaining warrants.

The following question was created to measure the conflict between the concern for electronic surveillance and security:

> Some people say that government should be allowed to record telephone calls and monitor e-mail in order to prevent people from planning terrorist or criminal acts. Others say that people's conversations and e-mail are private and should be protected by the constitution. Which of these opinions do you agree with most?

Right to Privacy

Following the need for greater surveillance and monitoring, privacy concerns were contested in the debate over national identification cards (NIDs). Because the terrorists were foreigners who had lived in the United States, using false identities but obtaining their credentials legally, the debate over NIDs revolved around the need to track foreign visitors. State motor vehicle officials and regulatory agencies asked Congress to create a national identification system, including a high-tech driver's license and a database network of driver information. Such NIDs would contain a large amount of personal information, such as current and previous addresses, family history, religion, education, fingerprint, and biometric markers. The consequences for innocent citizens raised immediate concerns. For NIDs to effectively deter terrorism, people would be subject to random checkpoints, and possibly detained for not having identification. In a less invasive requirement for driver's licenses, antiterrorism legislation, passed by Congress and signed by President Bush, empowered the departments of Homeland Security and Transportation to develop security standards for driver's licenses. Such measures could include difficult-to-duplicate holograms, encrypted magnetic strips, and other security features. I included such a measure in the analysis because it raises a more complex trade-off issue. To understand the challenge to civil liberties, individuals would have to look beyond the surface of a seemingly innocuous policy and evaluate its operational consequences in a more sophisticated way. Here is the question used to measure the trade-off between privacy and security:

> Everyone should be required to carry a national identity card at all times to show to a police officer on request. Or being required to carry an identity card would violate people's freedom of association and right to privacy. Which statement do you agree with most?

Freedom of Speech

As another basic and fundamental right, freedom of speech goes to the heart of democracy. Generally, individuals would not concede it easily, even in context. Intending to treat threats seriously, investigation into individuals expressing dissenting views appeared to challenge their ability to criticize the government and raised important questions about how much the government and individual citizens could regulate free speech.

What were once considered innocuous statements became more menacing after September 11. Antipatriotic and un-American sentiments, criticisms of government, the president, or foreign policy, or any indication of support for the terrorist attacks, triggered immediate inquires. Most notable were disciplinary actions against university faculty who were investigated and fired for criticizing U.S. foreign policy or suggesting that the United States was responsible for the terrorist attacks. The *New York Times* (Diana Jean Schemo, "The Campuses; New Battles in Old War Over Freedom of Speech," November 25, 2001, B6) reported several instances in which dissent led to disciplinary action, including one against a professor for asserting that "anybody who can blow up the Pentagon gets my vote." A university librarian was suspended for sending an email message that said American taxpayers "fund and arm an apartheid state called Israel, which is responsible for untold thousands upon thousands of deaths of Muslim Palestinian children and civilians." The following question was used to capture the choice between freedom of speech and security:

> Some people say high school teachers have the right to criticize America's policies toward terrorism. Others say that all high school teachers should defend America's policies in order to promote loyalty to our country. Which of these opinions do you agree with most?

Freedom of Association

Another component of civil liberties raised in the context of the terrorist attacks involved the extent to which American citizens aided and materially supported foreign terrorist organizations. By executive order, the Treasury Department initially authorized to impound the U.S. assets of anyone at home or abroad suspected of aiding or financing State Department-designated terrorist organizations. Foreign banks that declined to cooperate with Treasury's order were subject to having their assets in the United States seized. It was thought that sharing financial information between agencies, freezing assets, and employing other economic sanctions would incapacitate terrorists' ability to carry out future attacks. This order, as a tool to combat terrorism, was deemed largely benign and successful, but civil liberties concerns were raised because individual citizens seemed to get caught up in its web. Under the Patriot Act, belonging to an organization suspected of terrorist activities, financially aiding such organizations, or attending meetings at which a representative of those organizations spoke, became illegal. Many individuals came under suspicion for associating with organizations alleged to have terrorist ties. Many citizens were charged with belonging to sleeper cells and providing material support. This dimension of the conflict over civil liberty and security is important because it captures a major component of the Patriot Act that individuals may find relatively easy to concede. The civil rights issue being challenged in this trade-off is not obvious and seemingly harmless. The question used to measure such a value trade-off is:

> Some people say it should be a crime for anyone to belong to or contribute money to any organization that supports international terrorism. Others say that a person's guilt or innocence should not be determined only by who they associate with or the organizations to which they belong. Which of these opinions do you agree with most?

Protection from Search and Seizure

Restraints on "sneak and peek" search warrants were dramatically altered in the Patriot Act. Whereas conventional search warrants required notice of a search and demanded that the locations to be searched be specified, the Patriot Act enhanced surveillance powers by allowing search and seizure based only on suspicion. Eliminating the need for probable cause, thus circumventing the Fourth Amendment, law enforcement agencies could be granted access to all personal information, such as personal records from libraries, doctors, and financial and educational institutions. Secret evidence such as rumors, stereotyping, and faulty translations has been used to prosecute and deport citizens. Search and seizure issues are also ingrained in the psyche of Americans. It reflects a direct issue on which the choice between civil liberties and governmental authority should be very clear. The following question was used to reflect an aspect of the search and seizure issue:

> Some people say that law enforcement should be free to search a property without a warrant solely on the suspicion that a crime or a terrorist act is being planned there. Others say that protection against searches without a warrant is a basic right that should not be given up for any reason. Which of these opinions do you agree with most?

Freedom of Assembly and Protest

Despite challenges to civil liberties, virtually no protests or demonstrations followed the attacks of September 11. Although the decision to invade Afghanistan did lead to protests and questions about the government's response to terrorism, the administration and the government received broad support. Attempting to minimize the level of dissent on the war and criticism of President Bush, the government's response to protestors and demonstrations became more punitive and restrictive. Not only were the types of demonstrations that could be held limited, but protestors could be intensively surveilled. Penalties for protesting became more punitive as arrests without cause and bail became excessive and civil disobedience—disrupting traffic, or blocking street or sidewalks—was no longer tolerated. Although these steps were viewed as preemptive and necessary, citizens were intimidated from expressing dissenting views. Different from the other dimensions, this issue was relatively subtle following the attacks of September 11. Thus, when individuals were presented with questions about protest activity, they may have answered more generally. The question to measure the tension between freedom of assembly and security follows:

> Some say that people who participate in nonviolent protests against the United States government should be investigated. Others say that people have the right to meet in public and express unpopular views as long as they are not violating the law. Which of these opinions do you agree with most?

Distribution of Responses to Civil Liberties Items

Based on the framing of the compromise between civil liberties and security, the series of survey questions reflect the specific rights contested in the wake of the September 11 terrorist attacks. Although these items represent the most highly contested civil liberties issues from the time of the attacks to the field date of the survey, they do not capture several important challenges that arose later, such as the use of military tribunals, material witness statutes and deportations, neighborhood watch programs, fingerprinting of immigrants, and restrictions on weapons permits. One of the most notorious policies challenging civil liberties, outside of the immediate context of the attacks, involved the National Security Agency (NSA) secret spy program that involved listening on telephone calls and email between people in the United States and other countries. Given the reactions to other alleged policies of the administration (like torture and secret prisons) and its diminished support, a surprisingly large percentage (56 percent in an ABC News and Washington Post Poll) viewed such an activity acceptable. Because the threat of terrorism continues, and because many co-conspirators and illegal combatants captured during the invasion of Afghanistan have not gone to trial—which will inevitably lead to further debates on civil liberties—many of these issues have yet to be resolved legally. However, I hope to make clear where American citizens stood after the attacks of September 11.

The survey items presented in figure 3.1 are a snapshot of the support for civil liberties following the terrorist attacks. As expected from the political tolerance literature, American citizens were committed in the abstract to protecting civil liberties. Since the beginning of research on the support for democratic values, American citizens have generally expressed greater support for democratic principles expressed as abstractions (McClosky 1964; Prothro and Grigg 1960; Sullivan, Piereson, and Marcus 1982). When democratic principles were tied to specific situations and contexts, however, public support for democratic norms and civil liberties almost invariably weakened.

This abstract versus specific distinction in the support for civil liberties is true in the first wave of National Civil Liberties Survey (November 15, 2001, to January 15, 2002) as well.[5] In response to an abstract trade-off question about giving up some civil liberties to curb terrorism in this country, 55 percent favored protecting civil liberties. Although this is a slight majority, such a level of support raises serious questions about the degree to which individuals are committed to democratic ideals in a national crisis. It is quite possible that respondents were thinking about specific civil liberties, even though the question was phrased generally and appeared before the battery of specific civil liberties questions in the questionnaire. But this percentage of abstract support for civil liberties is lower than other polls following the September 11 attacks. In a collection of public opinion polls conducted in the aftermath of the terrorist attacks, Leonie Huddy, Nadia Khatib, and Theresa Capelos (2002) report a series of questions similar to our abstract civil liberties question. A CBS News/New York Times poll, taken two days later, reported that 74 percent of Americans were willing to concede their civil liberties. This percentage increased to 79 percent a month later. A Los Angeles Times poll also conducted on September 14 showed that 61 percent were willing to give up civil liberties to curb terrorism. More in line with my result, on September 17, a Princeton Research Associates and Pew Charitable Trust poll showed that 55 percent were willing to give up civil liberties, but this proportion increased to 63 percent three days later. It would probably be more comforting for civil libertarians if support for democracy in the present study were higher.

Several polling organizations asked general survey questions about the trade-off between civil liberties and security following the Oklahoma City bombing. Results from these polls are reported in table 3.1. In 1995, 62 percent of American citizens thought increasing government surveillance went too far. A year later, this number decreased to 53 percent. In a 1995 Los Angeles Times Poll, 70 percent were generally concerned that new measures enacted to fight terrorism would end up restricting

Table 3.1 Early Polling Questions on Civil Liberties Trade-Offs (Percentages)

Gallup	For each of the following measures – please tell me whether you would support it as a way to reduce terrorist attacks, or whether you think it is going too far... Increasing surveillance of U.S. citizens by the government		
		April 1995 (n = 601)	July 1996 (n = 649)
	Support	38	47
	Going too far	62	53
Los Angeles Times	In order to curb terrorism in this country, do you think it will be necessary for the average person to give up some civil liberties, or not?		
		April 1995 (n = 1,032)	
	Necessary	53	
	Not necessary	47	
	Would you be willing to give up some civil liberties if that were necessary to curb terrorism in this country, or not?		
		April 1995 (n = 1,032)	August 1996 (n = 1,572)
	Willing	57	58
	Not willing	43	42
	How concerned are you that new measures enacted to fight terrorism in this country may end up restricting some of our civil liberties?		
		April 1995 (n = 1,032)	August 1996[a] (n = 1,572)
	Concerned	70	65
	Not concerned	30	35
Princeton Research Associates	In order to curb terrorism in this country, do you think it will be necessary for the average to give up some civil liberties, or not?		
		March 1996 (n = 1,500)	April 1997 (n = 1,206)
	Necessary	32	32
	Not necessary	68	68

Source: Author's compilations.
Note: All percentages were recalculated excluding the "don't knows" and "refusals."
[a]To maintain consistency with the previous year, the four response categories (that is, "very concerned," "somewhat concerned," "not too concerned," and "not concerned") were collapsed to two categories.

Figure 3.1 Civil Liberties Versus Security Responses, 2001

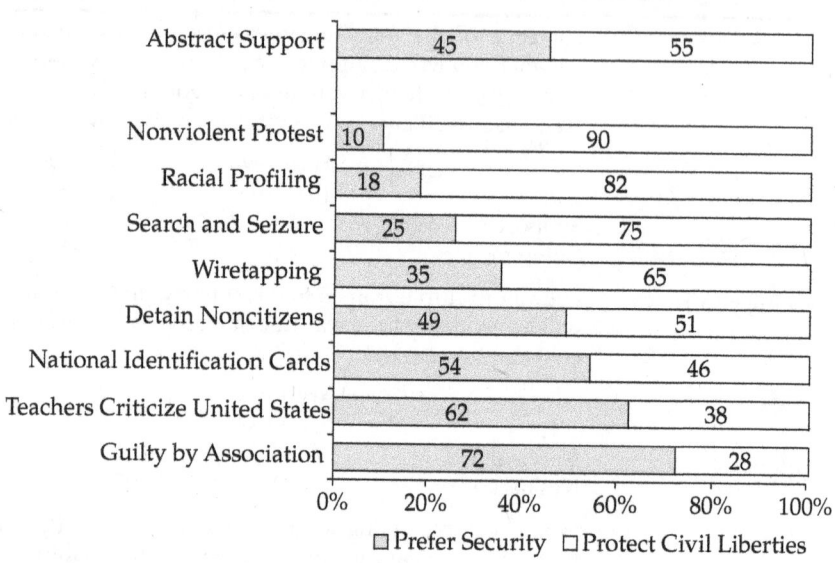

Source: National Civil Liberties Survey (2001).

civil liberties, though this percentage decreased by 5 percent a year later. Seemingly inconsistent with this level of concern, though 53 percent of respondents considered it necessary for the average person to give up some civil liberties, 57 percent were personally willing to do so. Over time, there was virtually no change. In a 1996 Princeton Research Associates poll, 32 percent thought it would be necessary for the average person to give up civil liberties. To the extent that the term *civil liberties* elicits the same reaction as more specific values, about which I am extremely doubtful, this could not account for the lukewarm support abstract civil liberties received following the terrorist attacks. Rather, it attests to the influence of the threat of terrorism, and perhaps evidence of the beginning a "new normal."

Figure 3.1 also shows responses to specific civil liberties contested after the 9/11 attacks. It is clear that though many responses to some specific civil liberties break down relative to the abstract question, others elicit greater protection from government encroachment. In moving from the abstract trade-off to specific trade-off questions, support depended on the particular civil right being contested. When the value trade-off decision was framed as a question about the need to be safe and secure versus judging people guilty by association, 72 percent supported treating people as guilty based on their associations. Although people's willingness to judge others guilty by association is extreme, other applications of the value trade-offs reveal a similar but lesser willingness to concede civil liberties for personal security. In a decision involving support for freedom of speech, 62 percent thought that schoolteachers should not be allowed to criticize U.S. antiterrorism policy. Regarding the right to privacy, 54 percent supported requiring NIDs.

At the same time that a majority of Americans were willing to concede some civil liberties and freedoms, majorities favored safeguarding certain liberties. In the habeas corpus question framed as the ability to detain noncitizens suspected of belonging to a terrorist organization, 51 percent supported the civil libertarian position. In a trade-off of the right to privacy by allowing telephone conversations and email communications to be monitored, 65 percent took the civil liberties position. On the issue of circumventing Fourth Amendment rights by allowing law enforcement to conduct a search of a residence without a warrant if it is suspected that terrorist acts are being planned there, 75 percent gave a civil liberties response. When the right to privacy issue was framed as racial profiling—the ability to stop and detain people of certain racial or ethnic backgrounds because they are thought to be more likely to commit crimes—only 18 percent preferred security to civil liberties. The least support for security at the expense of civil liberties—10 percent—was given when the trade-off involves freedom of speech and assembly, framed as whether nonviolent protesters against the U.S. government should be investigated. In short, rights that directly affect American citizens seemed to elicit greater desire for protection than those intended for suspected terrorists. There was no wholesale concession of civil liberties. A majority preferred security over civil liberties in only three instances. From this perspective, where American citizens were willing to draw the line is clear, at least at this one moment in time which happens to be one of the most frightful positions Americans have faced. Despite the fact that most of the civil liberties restrictions were unnoticeable by the average citizen, the idea itself of restricting civil liberties was seen as problematic.

The previous discussion simplified the survey results in terms of the support for civil liberties, rather than of the concern for security. It is important to not lose sight of the conflict posed in each of the civil liberties questions. As an example, a respondent exposed to the search and seizure question is faced with a balanced question in the choice between the willingness to allow law enforcement to search one's property without a warrant and the idea that privacy is a basic right that should not be given up for any reason. When the choice between them comes down to which is most cherished, respondents are expected to weigh the relative importance of both and then decide which is most important to them.

Figure 3.2 shows the percentage of respondents who gave consistently security (0) or civil liberties (8) responses across all of the items in all three waves (see appendix B for the details of all three waves of the survey). It is clear from this graph that, in all three waves, respondents

Figure 3.2 Distribution of Civil Liberties Responses

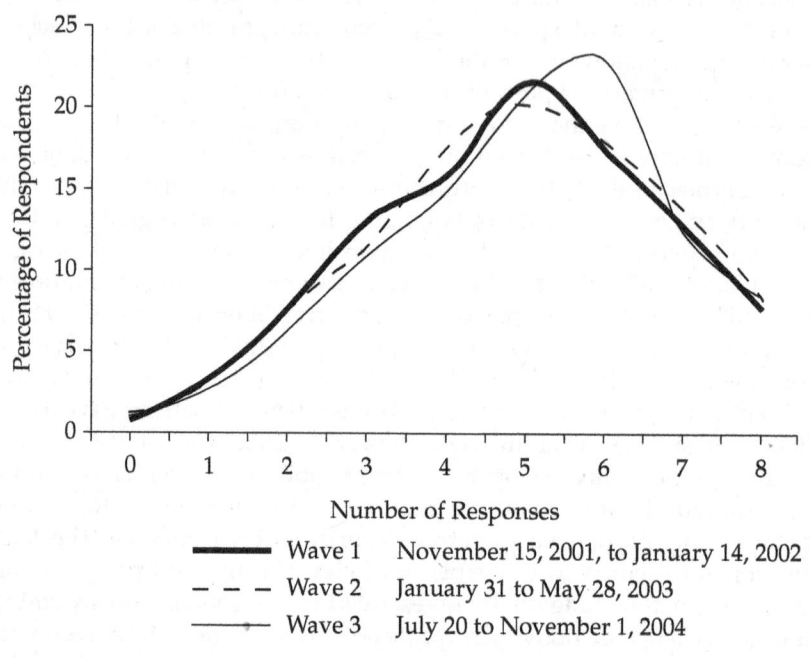

Source: National Civil Liberties Survey (2001, 2003, 2004).

are no way near an absolute or unequivocal support for civil liberties or security. Preference for civil liberties over personal security is not a matter of people agreeing on a few items, but of consistently supporting the same position over a wide range of issues. In the first wave, less than 1 percent endorsed a security position across all of the items, and only 8 percent consistently preferred a civil liberties position. Sixty-one percent of first wave respondents answered at least 5 (a majority of the items) in favor of protecting civil liberties. This did not change much later in the second wave. In the third wave in 2004, there was a noticeable increase in support for civil liberties. Less than 1 percent continued to stake a strictly security claim, and 8 percent held a strictly civil liberties position. Sixty-five percent in the third wave answered a majority of the items in favor of civil liberties.

The intercorrelations (tau b values) between the trade-off items in table 3.2 reveal a series of moderate relationships. Falling well short of perfect colinearity, each item reflects a unique component of the conflict over rights. Knowing how individuals responded to the abstract support for civil liberties is a good predictor of support for NID, the detention of noncitizens, search and seizure, and electronic surveillance. Racial profil-

Table 3.2 Correlation Matrix of Civil Liberties Items, 2001

	1	2	3	4	5	6	7	8
1. Abstract support	1.0							
2. Identification card	.22**	1.0						
3. Guilt by association	.14**	.12**	1.0					
4. Detain noncitizens	.17**	.18**	.18**	1.0				
5. Racial profiling	.09*	.10**	.04	.19**	1.0			
6. Teachers criticize	.06	.18**	.15**	.19**	.07*	1.0		
7. Search and seizure	.16**	.20**	.13**	.25**	.15**	.18**	1.0	
8. Wiretapping	.26**	.22**	.13**	.25**	.23**	.10*	.31**	1.0
9. Nonviolent protest	.05	.14**	.08	.14**	.06	.16**	.13**	.12*

Source: National Civil Liberties Survey (2001).
Note: Entries are tau-b's, listwise N = 1,095.
*p < .05; **p < .01.

ing, teachers criticizing U.S. policies, and nonviolent protest are generally unrelated to each other and to other civil liberties items.

An index derived from the combination of these questions about the trade-off between civil rights and security is the principal dependent variable in this book. I do not consider the determinants of the individual items unimportant, but the focus of this analysis is on the general sense of the compromise. As a result, the extent to which these items can be combined to form a single reliable scale is paramount. Assessing whether the civil liberties and security items reflect an underlying or latent value dimension is probably asking a great deal. Whereas many of the reliable indices in the social sciences (such as self-esteem, conservatism, dogmatism, and authoritarianism) were structured by independent conceptualizations, each item was written to reflect an important contested civil right in the context of the terrorist attacks. In planning the survey it was not clear whether citizens structured their civil libertarian beliefs along the lines indicated by these items. Additionally, though the specific tradeoff aspect may appear straightforward, the trade-off and value conflict approach may also make answering the questions difficult for some respondents. Because there is no middle position for respondents who might be able to understand both sides of the issue, the trade-off approach may compel some to take positions they may not totally support. These combined factors may diminish with the coherence of the items.

In spite of such drawbacks, a factor analysis using principled components factor extraction of the civil liberties and security items reported in table 3.3 suggests that the individual items form a reliable scale, though it goes without saying that it could be higher. Although the items produced three latent dimensions with eigenvalues of greater than 1.0, the factor loadings indicate that the first factor most likely represents the

Table 3.3 Factor Analysis of Civil Liberties and Security Items, 2001

	First Factor	Second Factor	Third Factor
Wiretapping	.53	−.33	−.15
Search and seizure	.60	−.02	−.55
Detain noncitizens	.55	−.37	−.32
Identification cards	.41	−.50	.43
Teachers criticize	.52	.46	−.16
Guilt by association	.59	−.16	.30
Racial profiling	.62	−.13	.10
Nonviolent protest	.34	.54	.51
Eigenvalue	2.08	1.04	1.02
Variance explained	.26	.13	.13
Cronbach's alpha	.66		

Source: National Civil Liberties Survey (2001).
Note: Principle Components Factor extraction, with no rotation.
N = 1,104

civil liberties trade-off. With the exception of nonviolent protest, which was not a major concern for many people in the immediate aftermath of the attacks, the civil liberties items load moderately high on the first factor, which explains 26 percent of the variance—twice as much as the remaining two factors.[6] Wiretapping, search and seizure, detaining noncitizens, freedom of speech, guilt by association, and racial profiling are all clearly associated with the first factor. Although using factor scores would be appropriate in constructing a scale for the value of the civil liberties trade-off, for ease of interpretation and to recapture missing cases, I chose to rely on an index based on the percentage of civil liberty responses out of the eight trade-off items.[7] Correlated at .98, a factor score and my summary measure capture an essentially identical underlying civil liberties dimension. The reliability coefficient (Cronbach's alpha = .66) suggests that these items can be combined in a single index.

Bivariate Analysis of Civil Liberties Trade-offs

Examining the convergent validity of the civil liberties trade-off index with social demographic and attitudinal factors is my first stab at understanding what is involved in the value compromise. This is very much a kitchen sink approach to analysis, trying out relevant factors related to the trade-off decision without first laying out theoretical expectations for each. My intent is to explore the convergent validity of the trade-off measure. Table 3.4 shows the univariate statistics for the civil liberties trade-

Table 3.4 Mean Civil Liberties Responses by Social Demographics, 2001

		Mean	SD	r/Significance Level	N
Race-ethnicity	African Americans	67.4	20.7	.18/.00**	322
	Latinos	54.0	22.9	−.10/.00**	152
	Whites	57.6	22.8	−.10/.00**	878
Gender	Female	57.9	21.8	−.06/.04*	783
	Male	60.4	23.9		602
Education	0 to 11 years	61.0	21.7	.10/.00**	108
	High school graduate	55.6	21.7		381
	Some college	59.7	23.6		382
	College graduate	64.8	22.3		347
	Advanced degree	61.9	26.6		147
Age	18 to 24	68.6	21.0	−.16/.00**	123
	25 to 29	59.9	22.1		107
	30 to 39	59.7	21.3		255
	40 to 49	60.9	23.3		295
	50 to 59	57.6	22.8		234
	60 and older	51.0	23.9		87
Community size	Urban	62.5	24.2	.04/.14	359
	Suburban	57.2	22.7		254
	Small city, town	60.7	21.8		446
	Rural	57.7	23.5		264
Region	Northeast	58.8	22.0	−.01/.78	236
	Midwest	59.3	23.6		328
	South	59.4	23.5		509
	West	58.6	22.0		219

Source: National Civil Liberties Survey (2001).
*p < .05; **p < .01.

off index by various demographic variables, and table 3.5 shows the same by attitudinal variables. The next chapter develops the underlying theoretical connection of the various factors. For now, I consider social demographic explanations to reflect broader historical and cultural contexts, and the attitudinal measures to reflect different reactions to the terrorist attacks. However, this cursory view of the univariate statistics is a good start in anticipation of developing a theoretical model.

Clearly, race and ethnicity will be an important part of the story behind the willingness to compromise civil liberties for security.[8] African Americans appear more committed to civil liberties: 10 percentage points higher than whites, and 14 percentage points higher than Latinos.

Table 3.5 Mean Civil Liberties Responses by Attitudinal Measures, 2001

		Mean	SD	r/Significance Level	N
Ideology	Very liberal	62.7	24.1	−.21/.00**	79
	Somewhat liberal	64.4	22.0		327
	Moderate	56.2	21.6		107
	Somewhat Conservative	56.3	22.1		586
	Very Conservative	53.7	23.2		116
Partisanship	Strong Democrat	62.9	21.3	.10/.00**	274
	Democrat	55.0	23.3		259
	Independent	63.1	21.9		318
	Republican	59.4	21.6		178
	Strong Republican	51.5	21.7		188
Political trust	Very trusting	49.7	24.5	−.15/.00**	95
	Trusting	55.8	21.0		355
	Low trusting	58.6	23.2		164
	Moderate	65.2	25.4		19
	Low nontrusting	61.9	21.4		165
	Nontrusting	63.0	22.9		384
	Very low nontrusting	63.9	28.1		62
Political interest	Very interested	57.8	24.3	−.07/.07	344
	Somewhat interested	58.4	22.4		710
	Not very interested	61.9	23.3		200
	Not at all interested	62.5	21.4		94
Patriotism	Very proud	57.1	22.0	−.25/.00**	1057
	Proud	69.7	22.7		193
	Somewhat proud	74.3	23.1		79
	Not very proud	90.2	9.5		19
	Not at all proud	78.8	43.5		10
Sociotropic threat	Very concerned	52.7	22.0	−.22/.00**	514
	Somewhat concerned	61.0	22.0		653
	Not very concerned	68.5	24.2		164
	Not at all concerned	64.4	22.6		48

Source: National Civil Liberties Survey (2001).
Note: See appendix C for specific question wording. Political trust is an additive index based on two questions.

Such racial and ethnic distinctions raise important questions about how aggrieved groups in American society respond when an external enemy attacks the country. Because these differences remain robust in the following chapters, additional analyses are required to determine whether there is something unique about the experiences of blacks, or if the significance of race captures indirect differences in psychology or political orientations. Chapter 8 is devoted to race and ethnicity.

Another important distinction relates to the effects of age. As age increases, so does the concern for security. Whereas eighteen- to twenty-four-year-olds supported protecting civil liberties (69 percent), older individuals (forty- to forty-nine-year-olds at 61 percent, fifty- to fifty-nine-year-olds at 58 percent, and sixty and older at 51 percent) were more willing to trade them for increased security (Abramson and Inglehart 1995; Inglehart and Welzel 2005). The conservative effects of aging are well documented in the sociological and psychological literature, but here too it is important to question whether age distinctions reflect other tendencies, such as greater awareness and susceptibility to threat. I do not anticipate the effects of age to be as dominant as race in explaining the trade-off between civil liberties and security. Gender differences also appear entirely negligible, though men were more protective of civil liberties. Education washes out as well: both those with advanced degrees and those with only a high school education or no diploma were less committed to civil liberties than those with some college or with an undergraduate degree. Size of community and region of the country hardly differ from one another in the average level of support for civil liberties, though it might have been reasonable to expect those in urban areas or in the Northeast to be more sensitive to the threat of terrorism and to have heightened security concerns. This finding departs dramatically from Stouffer's, which indicated significant urban support for political tolerance and civil liberties. In a different paper (Davis, Haspel, and Silver 2005), we have argued that a big difference since Stouffer's 1955 study is that with growth of cities and urbanized areas subjective definitions of place are less relevant. That is, people's subjective and objective definitions of place are notably different. But, despite this discrepancy, objective measures of place predicted neither support for civil liberties nor perceptions of threat.

Attitudinal measures reflect a different component of the trade-offs individuals are willing to make in context. Political ideology is an important explanation for the trade-off decisions between security and civil liberties. As one might expect from the traditional distinctions between liberals and conservatives, political liberals were significantly more protective of civil liberties than both moderates and conservatives were. Individuals at the ideological extremes are 10 percentage points different on the civil liberties scale. Partisanship reflects a similar response to civil liberties whereby strong partisans are 11 percentage points different. This interesting dynamic is explored further in chapter 7. The extent to which people trust the federal government is another important attitudinal component in the trade-off decision. People who trust government less cannot be expected to concede their civil liberties to it, even during a national crisis. To the contrary, those who trust the least might take the position that it is during national crises that people should be most wary of the government. Individuals who trust the government most support civil liberties 14 percentage points less than those who never trust the government. Political interest is not strongly related to the trade-off decision and was generally high following the attacks anyway. But the expectation was that individuals who followed politics more closely would be better informed about the issues surrounding trade-off decisions, and thus lean more to one side than another. These findings do not strongly support this expectation.

The more patriotic were more likely to support the war on terrorism by giving the government broader latitude on civil liberties. This actually makes perfect sense: those who are more attached to the political system are more willing to give political authorities more discretion than those less attached.

Conclusion

Following the attacks of September 11, then, Americans came to understand the sacrifices and compromises they would have to make to manage their heightened sense of vulnerability. This conflict between democratic norms and security, but not necessarily the related decision-making process, was new terrain for most Americans.

The political tolerance literature has been extremely useful to structure my approach to this analysis. Individual citizens were asked to tolerate government's encroachment on civil liberties in the same way that many unpopular groups in American society challenge the democratic resolve of many of its citizens. The specific trade-offs American citizens were asked to accommodate also presented a different challenge to the traditional political tolerance approach. Individuals vary considerably in how willing they are to exchange civil liberties for security. The extent to which the glass is half full or half empty will become clearer as I proceed. But, based only on the raw distributions and bivariate relations, support for civil liberties varied considerably following the attacks of September 11. Most Americans were not willing to make a wholesale concession to the government, though such a concession ultimately depends on precisely which civil liberties are in question.

Chapter 4

Explaining the Support for Civil Liberties

AMERICAN CITIZENS drew on a variety of values, beliefs, and emotions to make sense of the unfamiliar compromise between protecting civil liberties and enjoying greater security after September 11. Individual decisions were likely made through a variety of perceptual screens, such as sense of threat and vulnerability, trust in government, liberal or conservative ideology, patriotism, and racial experiences. Although there are probably as many reactions to the terrorist attacks as there are citizens, my interest here is not in taking account of all possible reactions. My interest is rather to determine the extent to which there was a shared or systematic set of values that helped citizens make their civil liberties trade-off decisions. The question I explore is pivotal. Was there a common set of political beliefs or predispositions among American citizens? If so, could it explain their level of support for civil liberties following the terrorist attacks?[1]

In the last chapter, I introduced the concept and measure of the trade-off and reviewed generally some of the factors that might influence how such decisions were made. I provided, however, little theory to explain such reactions to government and its proposed policies to combat terrorism. Here I rely on the literature to better understand the decision process involved in accepting limitations on civil liberties for security, and vice versa. I argue that the attacks of September 11 created deep emotional reactions that influenced individual perceptions of the trade-off, but that many reactions to civil liberties, political authorities, and heightened sense of vulnerability were grounded in a larger belief system that existed well before the attacks. Thus, when the country faced the attacks, the event and how it was subsequently framed by political authorities conditioned individual perceptions, but individual reactions to the event were also constrained or bolstered by existing belief systems. Individuals do not acquiesce easily to values and beliefs they find objectionable, but experience and established beliefs help define how context is interpreted.

Accounting for the varied reactions to the terrorist attacks is complex, requiring some clairvoyance to include the right mix of survey questions. The theoretical framework I develop will guide both the analysis of the compromise between civil liberties and security and subsequent analyses. I hypothesize that an individual's willingness to trade civil liberties for security will be highly predictable from his or her sense of threat from terrorism and trust in government—perceptions transformed incredibly by the terrorist attacks. Both trust and a sense of vulnerability increased in unison. It is important, however, to consider a range of alternative attitudes that might also account for the willingness to make the trade-off.

A theoretical model outlining the expected determinants of support for civil liberties is presented in figure 4.1. This model assumes that the decision to support civil liberties was not made before or simultaneously with other perceptions. The direction of causality is assumed to flow in only one direction. From a temporal perspective, the decision to support civil liberties over security and vice versa did not "cause" a heightened sense of threat, patriotism, or trust in political authorities, though it is not difficult to imagine that the decision to either protect or sacrifice civil liberties in the face of real consequences and to be placed in such a position could affect some people in important ways. Because political and social attitudes, regardless of the timing of precipitating events, are measured contemporaneously, expected causal relationships may also work in the opposite direction. Based on this logic, it is quite possible for the decision concerning the support for civil liberties to exacerbate a sense of vulnerability and reduce political trust. Thus, though my main interest is in exploring the direct explanations of the support for civil liberties, I do not treat other factors—such as political trust, patriotism, and political ideology—as completely exogenous throughout the book. In later chapters I further explore the influence of those factors on the terrorist attacks.

Perceptions of Threat and Vulnerability

As one of the explicit measures of context, the level of threat should be the most important indicator of the choice between civil liberties and security in the immediate aftermath of the terrorist attacks. Although I rely on the terms *threat*, *concern*, and *vulnerability* to capture the range of emotional reactions, I recognize that threat, anxiety, fear, and vulnerability are all deeply intertwined emotional reactions that lead to similar psychological consequences. Threat, fear, and anxiety exist along a continuum. The essential difference is that fear is an emotional reaction to a consciously known and immediate threat, and anxiety is an emotional reaction to an ill-defined threat, for which individuals anticipate the worst. Many Americans experienced a deep sense of fear from the at-

Figure 4.1 Theoretical Model of the Civil Liberties and Security Trade-Off

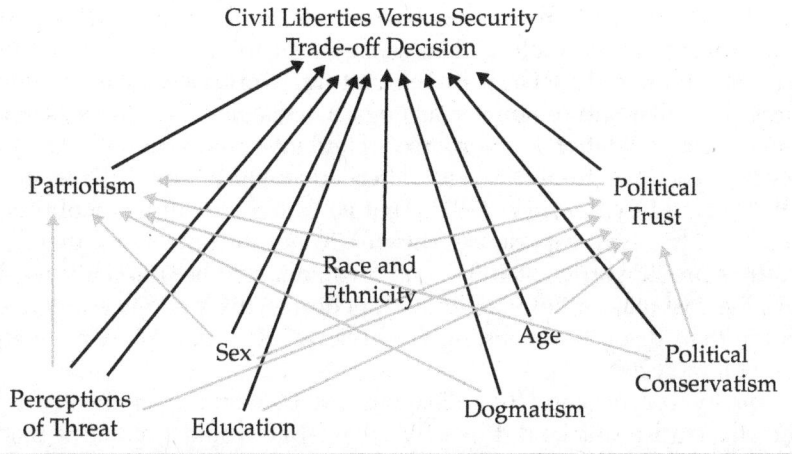

Source: Author's compilation.

tacks. As people began to anticipate an unknown risk, however, the emotional reaction is perhaps most appropriately described as anxiety, which can be just as debilitating and politically important as fear. Because the basis of both fear and anxiety is a concern that something bad is going to happen (or is happening) or a perceived threat and vulnerability, I use these terms *threat* and *vulnerability* rather than *fear* and *anxiety* to describe a range of emotions experienced after the terrorist attacks.

One of the few attempts to comprehend the consequences of threat, terror management theory (TMT) links individual reactions to a heightened sense of threat and anxiety to political and social behavior. Although it does not explain why people perceive threats or why they become vulnerable, it does explain how the emotional consequences of threat lead to support for political authorities, national identity, and the trade-off of civil liberties for security. According to TMT, the desire for survival and the awareness of the inevitability of death heightens individual perceptions of threat and potential for terror, but individuals can manage their anxiety by employing direct, rational, and threat-focused defense mechanisms (Greenberg et al. 1990; Pyszczynski, Greenberg, and Solomon 1997). The initial response to heightened awareness of death is to engage in simple, threat-focused defenses to eliminate conscious thoughts of it. Individuals also seek to bolster their self-esteem by intensifying their loyalty to their cultural worldviews. In threatening situations, people seek a connection to a larger belief system and the validation of others, such as families, ethnic or racial groups, or nations, which enables them to view themselves as valued and part of an enduring culture. A strong attachment to cultural worldviews or belief systems facilitates effective terror management because it increases self-esteem and provides individuals with a sense of meaning, permanence, and symbolic immortality. Faith in the cultural worldview is maintained through secular and religious teachings, associated cultural rituals, continual social validation in interpersonal and intergroup contexts, and defensive reactions to those with alternative worldviews (Greenberg, Solomon, and Pyszczynski 1997). That is, "different cultures mold their members' transient experiences differently, but fortunately for them, all cultures provide order, stability, and meaning. And because cultures do this, the vast majority of people can function securely, safely entrenched within their death transcending worldviews" (Pyszczynski, Greenberg, and Solomon 2003, 17).

Tom Pyszczynski and his colleagues (2003) maintain that the September 11 terrorist attacks did exactly what TMT would predict: it made thoughts of individual mortality more salient and accessible by making death a pervasive part of reality and attacking important cultural symbols. Americans attempted to mitigate their sense of vulnerability by seeking validation of their worldviews, greater self-esteem, and more interpersonal contact. I take this one step further. Under a heightened sense of threat, I expect people to gravitate toward political institutions and support policies that provide security and affection. A heightened sense of anxiety and threat should lead to greater attachment to the political system. Several studies have shown that simply reminding people about various threats and their own mortality can influence political and social behavior, such as increasing allegiance to America and nationalism (Greenberg, Solomon, and Pyszczynski 1997) and inducing greater support for President Bush and his counterterrorism policies (Landau et al. 2004).

A heightened sense of fear of terrorism is expected to compel people to concede civil liberties for greater security. If the cultural worldview were represented by allegiance to country, an increased sense of patriotism, attachment to the national community, and intolerance of dissent would create a greater acceptance of governmental policies to combat terrorism. TMT would also predict greater hostility toward others, in particular, those who threaten their cultural worldview. In chapter 9, I follow up on the relation between threat and the rejection of out-groups, but for now I consider TMT a useful explanation for why civil liberties suffer under heightened levels of threat. People who feel more vulnerable are driven to mitigate the threat.

Consistent with the effects of TMT, perceptions of threat can also exert a cognitive influence on the willingness to trade civil liberties for personal security. According to Joseph LeDoux (1996), perceptions of threat enhance attention to contemporary information and the source of anxiety, whereby cognitive functioning becomes impaired and the decision-making process deteriorates. The amygdala—the fear command center in the brain—tells the rest of the brain and body to shift efforts away from nonemergency services, such as digestion and immunity, and redirect them to the source of anxiety. Many studies show diminished cognitive processing among individuals experiencing high-threat conditions (Lerner and Keltner 2001; Mathews and MacLeod 1986).[2] Following this logic, when a heightened sense of threat constrains individual decision making, people may be more likely to rely on heuristics and norms that support government efforts to relieve their sense of anxiety, without considering the full range of options or consequences. Irving Janis and Seymour Feshbach (1953) observed that highly anxious individuals support persuasive messages they perceive as moderating their level of threat. As the media and political elites favoring governmental policies promised to do this, individuals under a heightened sense of threat would find such information more acceptable. This is consistent with experimental research after the September 11 attacks, showing that fear enhanced support for cautionary public policy measures (Lerner et al. 2003), which, I argue, involved granting greater latitude to the government to prevent terrorism.

In measuring threat, my approach is consistent with the findings of James Gibson and Amanda Gouws (2003) and of Leonie Huddy and colleagues (2002), which treat individual perceptions of threat as separate but related concepts: personal or egocentric threat and sociotropic threat. Gibson and Gouws (2003) distinguish between sociotropic threats and egocentric threats. Sociotropic threat is one to the larger society and the existing political order. Egocentric threat is threat to the individual. A sociotropic threat against society or cherished values and norms usually outweighs a sense of personal threat in leading people to act in antidemocratic or intolerant ways. Huddy and her colleagues (2002) examine the distinctions between personal threat and national threat among residents of Queens and Long Island after 9/11. Personal and national threats were found to be distinct but highly correlated concepts. That is, the more people believed there would be other terrorist attacks on the United States, the more they were concerned for themselves. Interestingly, despite the subjects' proximity to the World Trade Center, perceptions of national threat were more important than those of personal threat in determining support for national policies. As a single item measure, respondents are asked about a generalized concern that the United States might experience another attack: "All in all, how concerned are you that the United States might suffer another terrorist attack in the next three months?"

Personal threat is a more complex concept because individual citizens might perceive personal threat from terrorism or perceive a greater risk of being involved in a terrorist attack in a variety of ways. As a result, personal threat is based on a multi-item index. Asking respondents explicitly about their personal concern for a general another attack would have likely elicited many different points of reference. Instead, the range of personal threat measures cover a variety of instances in which respondents might have perceived a personal threat to them or someone in their family. The following questions were used:

- How concerned are you about flying on airplane?
- How concerned are you about opening your mail?
- How concerned are you about the safety of food and drinking water?
- How concerned are you about going into tall buildings?
- How concerned are you about being in large crowds or stadiums?

Figure 4.2 shows the distribution of responses to sociotropic and personal threat questions (see appendix C for the specific wording of the questions). The most striking feature in this graph is that American citizens were more concerned about the country coming under attack than they were about being personally attacked. Combining the top two threat categories ("somewhat concerned" and "very concerned" responses), 85 percent of respondents were concerned that the country would suffer another attack, and only 49 percent were concerned that they personally would be. Such a discrepancy is not surprising, but certain aspects of terrorism did intensify people's sense of personal threat. For instance, people were understandably concerned about airline security. With added security measures, it took more than a year for airline travel to match pre-attack levels.

People seemed only moderately threatened by going into tall buildings and being in large crowds, despite fresh images of airplanes flying into buildings. Being in large-scale venues, such as for professional sports events or concerts, were not thought of as risky. Only 37 percent of respondents considered it an important concern. The anthrax attacks were perpetrated through the mail and subsequently shut down postal facilities, but only 33 percent of respondents were seriously concerned about opening their own mail. However, the anthrax attacks highlighted the risks of bioterrorism and contamination of the water and food supply, and obviously heightened a concern for the country as a whole and not for people personally. This sociotropic threat should be more closely aligned with the willingness to concede civil liberties. For subsequent analyses, I use that single item as a measure of sociotropic threat, and a scale based on the mean of the responses to the five personal threat items

Figure 4.2 Distribution of Responses to Sociotropic and Personal Threat Items

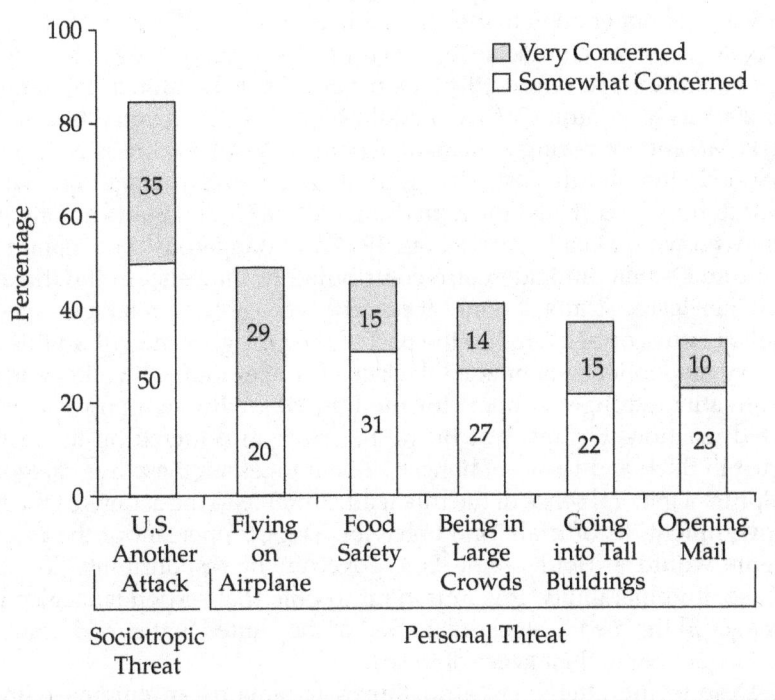

Source: National Civil Liberties Survey (2001).

as a measure of personal threat. This scale is intended to simplify analyses, but also capture a general sense of personal vulnerability.[3]

As a follow-up to the sociotropic threat question, an open-ended question probing respondents' causes of concern was included in a survey of the state of Michigan in the summer of 2005.[4] Despite the time gap and different sample, the verbatim responses are useful in understanding the force behind the sustained sense of threat and vulnerability among American citizens. Even at this late date, I suspected that many of the policies the Bush administration proposed, which were intended to make people feel secure in the long term, had the opposite effect in the short term. Following the closed sociotropic threat question, respondents who were either "very concerned" or "somewhat concerned" about the United States coming under another attack (63 percent), were asked an open-ended follow-up question: "What is causing you to be concerned about the possibility of another terrorist attack?" Respondents were able to answer in their own words. A content analysis of the verbatim responses, reported in table 4.1, suggested a classification of nine categories. Most respondents (40 percent) conveyed a sense of fatalism about national security. Many respondents thought that national security measures were not enough to prevent another and inevitable attack. Because this survey was conducted between May and July of 2005, survey respondents may have used the terrorist attacks on London in the summer of 2005 as an example of what could happen in the United States. The next category receiving a substantial percentage of responses was the situation in the Middle East. The gist of these responses suggested that the war in Iraq exacerbated the hatred toward the United States among people who were already seen as fanatical and dangerous. The inability to capture Osama bin Laden also contributed to the belief in the threat of another terrorist attack. Only 9 percent were able to reference specific policy issues or behavior on the part of the U.S. government. In this category, respondents mentioned the lack of cooperation with allies and not cultivating stronger support for the Iraq war. Although only 5 percent cited reactions to President Bush, the criticism centered on the lack of trust in Bush and issues of honesty. Taken together, these five categories capture a general sense of the threat attributable to the actions of the U.S. government, its officials, and behavior. Thus, 76 percent of the respondents would attribute some U.S. government responsibility for their sense of vulnerability. It is important to note that respondents also link images in the media, a general hatred of the United States, and domestic consequences to their sense of threat.

Despite the attentiveness to threat, it remains an enigma (Gibson 2006). Table 4.2 reports the mean levels of threat by social demographic factors. Based on this bivariate analysis, race plays a significant role in personalizing threat. Blacks expressed greater personal threat than whites and Latinos did, and Latinos registered higher than whites. It is my speculation that, given African Americans' tendency toward greater stress than other groups, this may create greater sensitivity to threatening and stressful situations. In general, gender, as revealed in psychological studies of posttraumatic stress, is also an important factor in individual reactions to the terrorist attacks, because women were more sociotropically and personally threatened by the terrorist attacks than men were. Less educational attainment is related to higher sense of threat. Although younger individuals reported lower levels of sociotropic threat, they also reported higher levels of personal threat. As expected, urban residents registered higher personal threat than their counterparts. Because the terrorist attacks and the anthrax largely unfolded in the Northeast, it would have been reasonable to expect that individuals living in this region would perceive a heightened sense of personal threat. Those in the Northwest and West, however, registered a heightened sense of sociotropic threat. I suspect that residents in the West may have thought

Table 4.1 Open-Ended Response to Sociotropic Threat Question, 2005

"What is causing you to be concerned about the possibility of another attack?"

1. National security – 40 percent
Examples: "If it happened once it can happen again."
 "Not enough security."
 "The London attack."

2. Situation in the Middle East – 22 percent
Examples: "Everything is going on in Iraq."
 "They have not caught Bin Laden."
 "In a country we should not be in."

3. World situation/American foreign policy – 9 percent
Examples: "America went to Iraq without approval from European Union."
 "Our lack of friendship toward other countries."
 "The USA takes control over other countries."

4. Immigration – 6 percent
Examples: "Letting too many people in the country without knowing who they are."
 "Everything is still going on, letting them come to this country."
 "It's so easy to come here and do whatever they want to, we let everybody in."

5. Trust in Bush and political leaders – 5 percent
Examples: "Don't like the way the Bush administration is handling all of this."
 "The way the country is being run."
 "The government is lying to the public."

6. Media – 5 percent
Examples: "Listening to the media."
 "Things you hear in the news."
 "See it on the news everyday."

7. General hatred toward the U.S. – 4 percent
Examples: "Widespread hatred of the U.S. around the world."
 "The amount of hate that George W. has created for Americans around the world."
 "Because so many countries dislike us."

8. Domestic consequences – 4 percent
Examples: "Prices of gas going up."
 "The rate of inflation and the rise of gas."
 "Jobs are leaving."

9. Personal issues – 2 percent
Examples: "I'm a firefighter."
 "Have parents and children who are living abroad."
 "Son in the military."

Source: Author's compilations of data from 2005 State of the State Survey, May 2005 to July 2005. Institute for Public Policy and Social Research. Michigan State University.
Note: These data come from a survey that is part of the quarterly State of the State Surveys series in Michigan. N = 577.

Table 4.2 Mean Threat Perceptions by Social Demographics, 2001

		Sociotropic Threat	r/Significance Level	N	Personal Threat	N	r/Significance Level
Race-ethnicity	African Americans	3.14	−.02/.36	320	2.66	320	.23/.00**
	Latinos	3.31	.04/.14	158	2.59	158	.14/.00**
	Whites	3.16	−.02/.49	885	2.13	887	
Gender	Female	3.22	.08/.00**	791	2.43	795	.21/.00**
	Male	3.23		605	2.06	606	
Education	0 to 11 years	3.29	−.08/.00**	107	2.39	109	−.16/.00**
	High school graduate	3.20		381	2.39	382	
	Some college	3.09		383	2.16	383	
	College graduate	3.10		349	2.07	349	
	Advanced degree	3.11		146	2.04	148	
Age	18 to 24	2.77	.14/.00	121	1.98	123	−.01/.68
	25 to 29	3.28		107	2.33	107	
	30 to 39	3.09		254	2.28	255	
	40 to 49	3.24		298	2.41	298	
	50 to 59	3.10		235	2.24	235	
	60 and older	3.31		340	2.17	341	
Community size	Urban	3.18	.00/.87	355	2.34	359	.04/.14
	Suburban	3.21		257	2.21	257	
	Small city, town	3.04		447	2.22	448	
	Rural	3.20		264	2.22	264	
Region	Northeast	3.20	.03/.32	234	2.22	236	.04/.16
	Midwest	3.11		331	2.25	332	
	South	3.13		610	2.30	611	
	West	3.25		221	2.19	222	

Source: National Civil Liberties Survey (2001).
*p < .05; **p < .01.

specific landmarks, such as the Golden Gate Bridge in San Francisco or the Space Needle in Seattle, were the next logical targets.[5]

Trust in Government

Next to perceptions of threat and vulnerability, political trust is expected to be an important influence on the trade-off of civil liberties and security. I argue that people are willing to concede their rights and freedoms to political authorities only to the extent that they have faith in the authorities' ability to ensure that things do not get out of hand. Concession of civil liberties is predicated on the belief that it is temporary and will be returned. Without trust in political authorities and the government, threat alone does not compel individuals to transfer their rights. But political trust can stand alone in the willingness to hand over civil liberties.

Putting it another way, trust in government may be thought of as a resource on which the government can draw when it needs latitude from its citizens to tolerate restrictions on civil liberties (Weatherford 1987). People who trust the government should not have as much trouble conceding their rights and liberties as those who do not trust it, because they expect that such rights will not be used against them and, as mentioned, that their rights will be fully restored after the threat dissipates. Less trust leads to alienation and frustration, making it difficult for the government to implement policies, even those it finds necessary in times of national crises. Although trust is directly related to the trade-off between civil liberties and personal security, I consider the possibility that threat may be either exacerbated or minimized by trust in government.

Fluctuations in the political trust measure, such as its rise and fall after the 9/11 attacks (which I will explore in chapter 6), have raised important questions and disagreement about what "trust in the government in Washington" means to survey respondents. Arthur Miller (1974) argues that the traditional trust measure, at the time, captured a growing dissatisfaction with and alienation from the political regime. Political trust was seen as a belief in the legitimacy in government. Jack Citrin (1974), taking a different view, suggests that political trust is an assessment of the effectiveness and performance of political authorities, with negative perceptions of political leaders as the main causes of distrust (for an evaluation of this controversy, see Abramson 1983). In the context of September 11, when respondents answered the trust question, they were most likely thinking about political leaders rather than the political system overall. In context, political trust and political evaluations are incredibly responsive to societal events and, as a result, become intertwined—unlike strict perceptions of the political system. Marc Hetherington and Michael Nelson (2003) show that political trust following the attacks was highly susceptible to a "rally-round-the-flag" effect, in which people, responding to an external threat, gave greater support to political authorities. Virginia Chanley (2002) also shows that a renewal in political trust after the attacks as a result of increased attention to international concerns. Such a rally in trust did not of course last very long because citizens began to rely on other criteria and events to evaluate the government, such as the invasion of Afghanistan and the war in Iraq, on which there was substantial disagreement.

I use the most frequently used political trust items to the capture of resurgence in political trust following the terrorist attacks of September 11. There is no doubt that the increase in trust was a direct result of the attacks, and diminished trust a reaction to governmental efforts to provide safety and security from terrorism, such as the Patriot Act and the challenges to civil liberties. Trust is an important component in my analysis because higher levels of political trust, and political capital more generally, make governing easier. As trust in government increases, so does acquiescence to governmental policies and support for government spending. If the willingness to trade civil liberties for security translates into a concession of greater power to government, then trust and confidence in government should become far more significant.[6]

Liberal and Conservative Political Ideology

In the first year after the September 11 attacks, it was difficult to discern so-called liberal and conservative divisions regarding the appropriate response to the terrorist attacks. Both political parties within Congress worked closely to support the president's agenda to combat terrorism, and the usual ideological antagonisms was virtually nonexistent among the mass media and the public. Reactions to the attacks muted many of the normal ideological divisions about government efforts to provide for safety and security. However, the willingness to acquiesce, or to remain silent, should not be interpreted as capitulation. Underlying the reactions to the events, individual political beliefs and ideological values should influence the willingness to concede greater power to political authorities. Several scholars, such as George Lakoff (2002) and Michael Milburn and Sheree Conrad (1996), argue that liberal and conservative worldviews stem from different social processes that result in drastically opposed social and political attitudes. Strict conservatives hold that life is difficult and dangerous, and that people have to be self-disciplined to survive. Self-discipline and obedience to authority leads to success in life. Competition is important as an indicator of morality. Rewards given to those who have not earned them through competition removes the incentive to become self-disciplined (Lakoff 2002, 68). Strict liberals, by contrast, view the world as requiring nurturing, empathy for others, and social conscience. Bonds of affection, respect, interdependence, and tolerance should govern the world. For liberals, support for authority cannot be grounded in dominance; it must stem from wisdom, reasoned judgment, and empathy (Lakoff 2002, 113).

Political conservatism has also been viewed as motivated social cognition, in which individuals adopt conservative political attitudes as a defense against various threats. High levels of threat and anxiety may increase the appeal of political conservatism for its ability to simplify, control, and bring order to the external (and internal) world (Jost et al. 2003; Wilson 1973). Because conservatives are more sensitive to negatively framed than to positively framed messages, as well as to the possibility of loss, the salience of one's mortality has been linked to behaviors associated with conservative and right-wing ideological positions (Altemeyer 1996). To avert anxiety and reduce conflict, conservative tendencies may stem directly from a desire to control uncertainty by employing a rigid, simplified, and inflexible value structure.

Such strong ideological differences have been connected to perceptions of civil liberties and reactions to threat (McClosky 1964; McClosky and Brill 1983; McCutcheon 1985; Sullivan, Pierson, and Marcus 1982). Far more than liberals, conservatives have been associated with beliefs about duty, respect for authority, and the primacy of law and order. Liberals, on the other hand, are often seen as willing to risk some social instability to promote certain changes (McClosky and Brill 1983). They also, McClosky and Brill (1983) maintain, tend to think of rights as natural and inalienable—things that government cannot take away—whereas conservatives tend to view rights as more situational and contingent.

In the context of the terrorist attacks, normal ideological predispositions are expected to be important determinants of how individuals respond to the trade-off between civil liberties and security. During national crises, people can be expected to bring their political predispositions to the event, but the nature of crisis and the framing of the event are likely to create reactions that govern individual responses. In this analysis, I rely on a three-part question on ideological self-classification that places people on a seven-point scale, from strong conservative to strong liberal.

National Pride and Patriotism

As TMT predicts, the terrorist attacks of September 11 produced remarkable expressions of patriotism and feelings of national identity among American citizens. Forced to reflect on their sense of mortality, American citizens easily gravitated to the country, its symbols, and its values. Patriotic symbols and outward expressions of pride in the United States were displayed with intense zeal, revealing a deep sense of social unity. The American flag was plastered on buildings, homes, cars, and clothing. At the same time, people acknowledged the heroism of the rescue workers by wearing and displaying the symbols of the New York City fire and police departments. Other signs of patriotism reflected disdain and anger toward Osama bin Laden. The rush to donate to relief funds and blood showed a strong sense of charity and commitment to the political community.

Intense affect toward the political community, feelings of national pride, and loyalty and love of country were seen as a positive by-product of the terrorist attacks. This type of affect toward the government can be expected to influence support for policies intended to provide for the country's safety and security, even when such policies may be inconsistent with protecting democratic norms. From an Eastonian perspective, affect toward the political community is distinct from perceptions of political authorities and the political rules (Easton 1975). Because the trade-off between civil liberties and security represents the political rules and democratic norms aspect of support for the political system, I expect that, in times of national crisis, patriotism or affect toward the political community leads to protecting that community and its authorities at the expense of systemic and democratic values.

The resurgence in American patriotism was viewed as a positive outgrowth from a terrible event, but taken to an extreme, it can undermine democratic values and processes. Patriotism can, but does not necessarily, take on chauvinistic tones, narrowly defining who and what may be considered American and rejecting out-groups that may not fit traditional American characteristics. A strong sense of patriotism and rallying people to support the common cause is associated with intolerance (Adorno et al. 1950; Gomberg 2002; O'Leary 1999) and social dominance (Sidanius et al. 1997). Research by Robert Schatz and Ervin Staub (1996) and Schatz, Staub, and Lavine (1999) shows that blind patriotism is strongly associated with political conservatism and the belief that U.S. national security is vulnerable to foreign threat. This result informs the findings of Jon Hurwitz and Mark Peffley (1987) and John Sullivan, Amy Fried, and Mary Dietz (1992) that patriotism is associated with aggressive views on national defense and security. Although patriotism can take several different forms, I adopt a simplified view, relying on a five-point national pride question that has been used as a symbolic form of patriotism.[7]

Dogmatism

Extending beyond the sense of inflexibility that arose from political conservatism, the nature of the discussion and framing of solutions and possible responses to the terrorist attacks was characterized in very rigid and dogmatic terms. There was essentially no middle ground in the battle between good and evil, or between freedom and repression. Either people supported America and its response to the attacks, or they did not, and were thus perhaps part of the problem. Dogmatism as an individual-level trait is related to a larger set of social and political attitudes. Milton Rokeach (1960) developed the concept to measure authoritarianism devoid of ideological biases and political content. He defined it as a closed cognitive organization of beliefs about reality, manifested in an inclination to be close-minded, intolerant of others, and deferential to authority. Strict dogmatists were viewed as having a pervasive outlook of fear and pessimism and a concern for power. According to Rokeach, the need for defense against threat is an important factor leading to a close-minded belief system. As the level of threat increases, the cognitive need for information weakens until existing information is used to rationalize, justify, or deny subsequent beliefs. "The closed system is nothing more than the total network of psychoanalytic defense mechanisms organized together to form a cognitive system and designed to shield a vulnerable mind" (69). Psychological insecurity and inflexibility, and the level of dogmatism in particular, are expected to influence people's willingness to trade civil liberties for personal security. A scale derived from a set of six items, drawn from the work of Gibson and others, was used to measure dogmatism.[8]

Race and Ethnicity

As American citizens reached out to each other for comfort and assurance, the possibility that other groups might respond differently to the terrorist attacks, and to government policies increasing security at the expense of civil liberties, received very little attention in the mainstream media. Although the media framing was one of unity and solidarity, it masked significant underlying racial and ethnic differences in perceptions of threat and support for civil liberties. Several indicators, however, suggested that blacks and Latinos might have different reactions to and interpretations of both the September 11 attacks and the trade-offs between civil liberties and security.

Race and ethnicity are so important to understanding the reactions to the terrorist attacks that I devote an entire chapter to their effects (see chapter 8). For now, racial and ethnic differences stem from differences in perceptions of threat and attachment to the political system. I argue that a heightened sense of black identity or consciousness, coupled with lower levels of trust in political leaders, is likely to be discordant with the reactions of members of the dominant culture. First, because blacks' long struggle for equality and civil rights and because of their sense of disaffection from the political system, they should show a stronger commitment to civil liberties than whites and Latinos are, but at the same time guarded against the government's increasing authority and invasion of individual rights, both domestically and internationally (Stanford 2002). In short, African Americans should be reluctant to concede rights they have worked very hard to achieve and loath to empower a government in which they have little confidence, even for the sake of personal security. Although politically alienated individuals may not actively undermine the government's efforts when it is faced with national crisis (Sears and McConahay 1973; Sears et al. 1978), they will find it difficult to change their mistrust of government.

Second, from a TMT perspective, after September 11, because of the salience of racial consciousness in guiding social and political behavior (Allen 2000; Allen and Bagozzi 2001; Allen, Dawson, and Brown 1989; Dawson 1994; Gurin, Hatchett, and Jackson 1989; Tate 1994), blacks should be more likely to gravitate toward others in their in-group than to the government, which appears more menacing in times of crises. African Americans share the sense of a threat from terrorism, but in them it is likely to be exacerbated by the image of an empowered government and law enforcement. The cultural worldview of African Americans as a group is likely to be a critical source of self-esteem and meaning, which they need to cope with the sense of threat, given that the support and security from the larger political community is more tenuous. Others may find the government's response to the terrorist attacks comforting and reassuring, but blacks may feel less secure.

Although Latinos often suffer degrading experiences such as those of African Americans, their political orientations and core values—particularly of native-born Latinos—tend to be more closely aligned with the dominant culture than those of African Americans (de la Garza, Falcon, and Garcia 1996). The Latino acculturation process, like that of European immigrants, is said to facilitate Latinos' accepting certain political values, such as greater political trust. However, Latinos' sense of consciousness from identifying with a larger distressed community, and from not being totally accepted as Americans, may lead to a peripheral, outsider's assessment of the political system (Fuchs 1990; Portes and Rumbaut 2001). Jamie Arndt and his colleagues (2002) suggest that a heightened sense of threat among Latinos leads to a tenuous identification with other Latinos, and a stronger one with the larger political culture.[9] "Mortality salience leads Hispanics to move away from their in-group when situational factors made identification with that group a potential threat to self-esteem" (39). In response to the attacks of September 11, threat alone can increase support for the political system.[10] Hence, I expect Latinos' perceptions and internalization of threat from the attacks to be similar to those of the dominant culture (because of acculturation), but at the same time, to reflect a peripheral and critical view of the political system (because of their ethnic consciousness). Exposure to the threat of terrorism is expected to intensify Latino attachment to the American political community.[11]

Demographic Factors

Social background explanations reflect broader historical, cultural, and economic contexts in which the trade-offs between civil liberties and further empowering the government may be evaluated. I include formal levels of education in the model because it has been instrumental in shaping political behavior and support for civil liberties. Educational attainment can reflect a variety of different processes, such as cognitive sophistication, successful sorting, indoctrination in certain types of belief systems, and exposure to different individuals and perspectives. Through the educational experience, individuals acquire the knowledge to understand what is required in a democracy (Lawrence 1976; McClosky 1964; Nunn, Crockett, and Williams 1978; Prothro and Grigg 1960; Stouffer 1955). Democratic values are considered complex ideas, requiring considerable education to comprehend the implications of support. Lawrence Bobo and Frederick Licari (1989) show that educational achievement enhances the protection of civil liberties more than cognitive sophistication or actual measures of knowledge does. Cognitive sophistication, in turn, accounts for a substantial portion of the influence of education on support for civil liberties, but it does not replace educational achievement. Ewa Golebiowska (1995) argues that education is tied to greater support for civil liberties because it influences individual value preferences and priorities. In the context of the September 11 terrorist attacks, education is expected to take on special significance: educational achievement will influence support for civil liberties directly and involve certain skepticism of government, but may also help integrate complex and emotional information. American citizens were bombarded with technical and emotional accounts of terrorism, news about world events, and information on governmental policies intended to protect the country. The less sophisticated may be more accepting of emotional appeals, and more threatened, than the more sophisticated. Understanding the implications of heightened vulnerability requires the ability to assimilate and integrate information. Educational attainment is thus more than just an indicator of social background: it becomes an integral evaluative component to the trade-off between civil liberties and personal security.

Despite an initial minimal showing, gender may become an important factor in the trade-off because of a more heightened level of anxiety that women experienced after the attacks of September 11 (Pulcino et al. 2003). But the underlying processes governing gender differences are not simple, not by any means. Following the terrorist attacks, studies of anxiety show that emotional responses were greater among women than men (Pulcino et al. 2003; Schuster et al. 2001). Previous exposure to traumatizing events, responsibilities as the primary caretaker in the household, and concern for community were found to make women more susceptible to emotional distress (Pulcino et al. 2003). From a TMT perspective, Sandra Thomas (2003) suggests that women were distinguished from men after the attacks in the degree to which they expressed a strong need to connect with and "nest" with loved ones, and in their propensity to criticize government policies.

Women have also been shown to have a weaker attachment to civil liberties than men have. Stouffer (1955) initially noted consistent gender differences in support for civil liberties, which later studies confirmed (Nunn, Crockett, and Williams 1978, for example). Gender differences were considered to stem from women's traditional responsibility for the household, which exposed them to less diversity than men, as well as fewer opportunities to develop an attachment to norms that would translate to support for civil liberties. Golebiowska (1999) suggests that, because of less psychological involvement in politics and political knowledge, women may be less prepared to support civil liberties. There seems to be a consensus expecting women to trade civil liberties for greater security, but the government's failure to satisfy women's heightened sense of threat from terrorism may more closely reflect individual motivations than other theories.

The final variable in the model is age. Younger individuals are generally more committed to democratic norms than older individuals are (Davis 1975; McClosky and Brill 1983; Nunn, Crockett and Williams 1978; Stouffer 1955). In the context of September 11, the willingness to trade civil liberties for personal security is expected to increase with age. The attacks may have created a more intense emotional reaction among older people, especially the elderly, who may have felt more vulnerable and personally threatened. Older individuals can therefore be expected to gravitate to the government, and to policies intended to provide greater security from terrorism.

In short, these demographic factors are more than statistical controls. Each reflects meaningful reactions to the attacks and to the trade-off decision.

Multivariate Analysis

Taken together, these theories and expectations form a model to explain the compromise between civil liberties and security. Table 4.3 reports the results of two ordinary least squares (OLS) regression equations testing the influence of the various determinants on the trade-off decision.

Model 1 establishes the independent and additive effects of the various explanations, and model 2 incorporates the conditional effects of sociotropic threat and political trust. Sociotropic threat is explicitly considered to exacerbate the extent to which people trust the political authorities. Such conditional relationship arguably may exist among other variables, but the relationship between sociotropic threat and trust was found to be more powerfully interdependent. Standardized regression coefficients from model 1 are also reported to establish the relative importance of the explanatory variables. The results from the equations offer important and substantive insight into the decision involved in the support for civil liberties in a national crisis. It is clear that the compromise between civil liberties and security was neither random nor capricious; rather, the decision was predicated on a mix of reactions to the context itself and preexisting values.

One of the most important predictors of civil liberties trade-offs is sociotropic threat. As TMT predicts, a heightened sense of sociotropic threat from the attacks led respondents to trade civil liberties for greater personal security. The higher the level of concern about another terrorist attack on the United States, the more people preferred security to civil liberties. Reflecting the sense that individuals were not personally concerned about the risk of terrorism, personal threat was unrelated to trade-off decisions in the context of the terrorist attacks. That Americans' response to the trade-off was not influenced by personal threat is an important and somewhat unsurprising result. Because the media and political authorities controlled the information, and as a result, how people thought about terrorism, the initial focus on terrorism emphasized the threat to the country as a whole and not to individuals, though innocent citizens were probable targets. With the exception of warnings by the Bush administration to purchase duct tape and plastic sheeting which came later, citizens were generally not forced to personalize the threat or question their personal risk. As a result, most people did not have to shift their daily routines in response to the attacks. On the other hand, people did seem to understand that an attack on the United States was likely.

Similarly, high levels of psychological insecurity or dogmatism were associated with a willingness to concede civil liberties. Consistent with theoretical expectations, the greater the psychological insecurity, the more respondents were willing to allow the government greater leeway to fight the domestic war on terrorism. Heightened levels of dogmatism—or, put simply, closed-mindedness—led to accepting personal security and order over protecting civil liberties and freedom. Whereas a dogmatic belief system is seen as a defense against threatening situations, an important consequence of such a belief system is that it goes beyond threat, ideology, and patriotism to predispose individuals to certain types of political beliefs, and that it increases the appeal of certain

Table 4.3 OLS Regression of Determinants of Civil Liberties Trade-Offs, 2001

	Model 1	Beta	Model 2
Sociotropic threat	−4.74** (1.00)	−.15	−3.57 (2.42)
Personal threat	−1.31 (.98)	−.04	−1.31 (.98)
Political trust	−1.11** (.34)	−.09	−.38 (1.44)
Patriotism	−4.40** (1.09)	−.12	−4.51** (1.11)
Conservative	−1.90** (.62)	−.10	−1.89** (.62)
Dogmatism	−4.49** (.75)	−.18	−4.49** (.75)
African American	8.38** (2.07)	.12	8.34** (2.07)
Latino	−5.19* (2.41)	−.06	−5.09* (2.41)
Education	.80 (.65)	.04	.78 (.65)
Sex (1 = female)	−.41 (1.30)	.01	−.41 (1.30)
Age	−1.61** (.36)	−.13	−1.61** (.36)
Sociotropic threat × political trust			−.24.45 (1.07)
Constant	127.91** (5.84)		124.76** (8.33)
R^2/adjusted R^2	.20/.19		.20/.19
Root MSE	20.74		20.74
N	1081		1081

Source: National Civil Liberties Survey (2001).
Note: Standard errors in parentheses.
*p < .05; **p < .01.

types of messages. After the attacks, highly dogmatic individuals were more willing to accept governmental policies intended to provide for their security at the expense of their civil liberties. The sense of vulnerability that people experienced after September 11 may have contributed to their thinking dogmatically, but dogmatism is a psychological predisposition that people also carry around with them regardless of context.

Also, individuals with greater trust and faith in political authorities were more willing to acquiesce to the government and its policies than individuals with less faith in government. As I alluded to earlier, trust in the government and political authorities matters a great deal because with trust is a belief that when people concede their rights and liberties that it will not be used against them and returned in full once the crisis subsides. People who do not trust government probably know otherwise and respond differently. In this case, civil liberties are not traded for security because of the perception that government will abuse their rights and hold their rights against them, and potentially take other liberties. As an example, people who were initially distrustful of government can turn to the President Bush's 2006 domestic surveillance program for evidence of how civil rights concession might be exploited.

Ideology and patriotism also perform as expected. Self-reported political ideology carried a great deal of weight in determining the trade-off. Even after adjusting for the effects of trust in government, a sense of threat from terrorism, and other attitudinal and demographic differences, liberals were more likely than conservatives to favor maintaining civil liberties over security. Other political beliefs are also important to how people react in the context of a terrorist threat. I expected that underlying national pride was a sense of authoritarianism, intolerance, and concern for order. However, table 4.3 shows that patriotism has an independent effect on support for civil liberties. Citizens with a strong sense of national pride were more willing to trade civil liberties for greater security. Even after adjusting for the effects of other factors, including threat and trust in government, a move of one rung up the national pride measure is associated with a decline of almost 5 percentage points in support for civil liberties. Interestingly, patriotism does not lead to defending the underlying values of the democratic political system. Rather, high levels of patriotism place democracy at greater risk because, in context, patriotism translates into support for political authorities and their policies. That political authorities can call upon such support makes patriotism extremely important. The downside is that patriotism can also be exploited and used like other forms of political capital. Such a view of patriotism does not comport well with the traditional view that it is connected to the symbols and values of the American political system.

Table 4.3 supports the expectations for blacks and Latinos and begins to provide important details about racial and ethnic reactions to the political system in times of crisis. Blacks are less willing than whites to trade civil liberties for personal security, scoring slightly more than 8 percentage points higher than whites on the scale. It is my speculation that the historical struggle to secure civil rights and liberties, and a distrust of government, may make giving up civil liberties especially difficult, even during a national crisis. Despite high levels of national pride (blacks did not differ from whites on this measure), cultural and historical experiences are powerful forces in defending individual rights. By contrast, Latinos score 5 percentage points lower than whites on the scale, everything else being equal. That is, they are more willing than whites to give up civil liberties for greater personal security. I revisit this intriguing and complex finding in chapter 8.

Finally, demographic factors make only a limited contribution to understanding the trade-off decision. I had high expectations for gender and educational attainment, but they are virtually inconsequential. Beyond the independent effects of threat and political ideology, age is a strong factor, with older individuals more likely to trade civil liberties for security. Older individuals normally show a weak attachment to civil liberties regardless of context, but after September 11 they could be expected to be sensitive to the heightened sense of vulnerability and patriotism.

Behavior under Equivalent Threat

In the face of a heightened sense of vulnerability and threat, an unequivocal defense of individual liberties has been deemed by some as tantamount to constitutional suicide. They argue that, by defending individual liberties to the hilt, we leave ourselves vulnerable to those who would exploit our open society to achieve evil ends, and ultimately destroy democracy. Others, on the other hand, have deemed a willingness to sacrifice civil liberties to preserve democracy as self-contradictory: we are to concede the very rights that we are trying to defend. Using the statistical results to simulate different responses to the terrorist attacks under different scenarios, I am able to ask the question: under equivalent threatening situations, do people maintain their civil libertarian views, or do they cave in to their sense of vulnerability by trading civil liberties for security? As I mentioned earlier, the willingness to concede civil liberties is likely to be affected jointly by the level of threat and the level of trust in government. That is, the effects of the threat will depend on how much people trust the government, and the effects of trust will depend on how threatened by terrorism people feel.

Using the coefficients from model 2, figure 4.3 illustrates the predicted trade-off response to the conditional effects of threat and political trust. One way to interpret these estimates is to view them as simulating civil liberties responses, varying the levels of both sociotropic threat and po-

Figure 4.3 Effects of Trust in Federal Government and Sociotropic Threat on Support for Civil Liberties

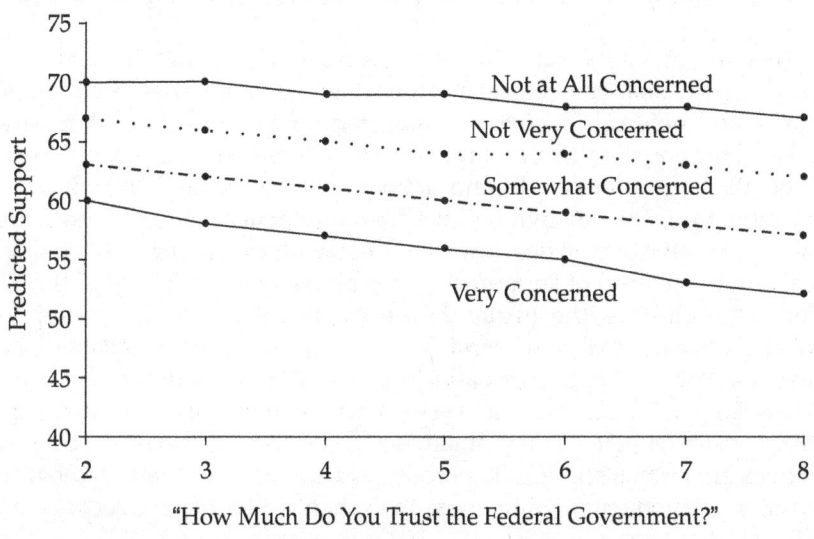

Source: National Civil Liberties Survey (2001).

litical trust. For instance, figure 4.3 shows the predicted civil liberties responses that are conditional on how much people trust the federal government and the level of sociotropic threat. Taking into account that the effect of trust on support for civil liberties depends on how threatened people feel, each line represents a different degree of sociotropic threat. At almost every level, increased political trust is associated with decreased support for civil liberties. Especially among those who claim at least some trust in the federal government, greater concern about another terrorist attack is associated with greater willingness to cede some civil liberties for greater security and safety. The two variables clearly interact with one another, however. At low levels of trust in the government, those most concerned about another attack differ little from those with little or no concern in their support for civil liberties. The predicted civil liberties line for individuals who are not concerned about another attack is essentially flat, meaning that under no level of trust are they willing to concede their civil liberties for security. However, among those who have some or significant trust in the government, greater concern about another attack is associated with markedly less support for civil liberties. In short, trust in government and threat can combine to have powerful effects on support for civil liberties. At one extreme, individuals who do not feel threatened and "never" trust the government sup-

82   Negative Liberty

port civil liberties positions between 67 and 72 percent of the time. At the other extreme, those who do feel threatened and "always" trust the government support the civil liberties positions only 46 to 50 percent of the time.

Like the previous chart, figure 4.4 is based on model 2 in table 4.3. That is, the relations between support for civil liberties, sociotropic threat, and political ideology are adjusted for the effects of other variables in the equation (for example, personal threat, trust in government, dogmatism, faith in people, and national pride). On the whole, liberals are more protective of civil liberties than moderates, and moderates are more protective of civil liberties than conservatives. But for each ideological group, the level of support depends on the perceived level of threat. For all three groups, the greater the sense of threat, the lower the support for civil liberties. Extreme liberals who are not concerned at all about the likelihood of another terrorist attack support 74 percent of the civil liberties positions. Liberals who are very concerned about another attack support register 64 percent. The analogous percentages for extreme conservatives are 66 percent and 50 percent. Thus, whatever their ideological position, respondents' willingness to exchange liberties for security in-

Figure 4.4   Effects of Liberalism-Conservatism and Sociotropic Threat on Support for Civil Liberties, 2001

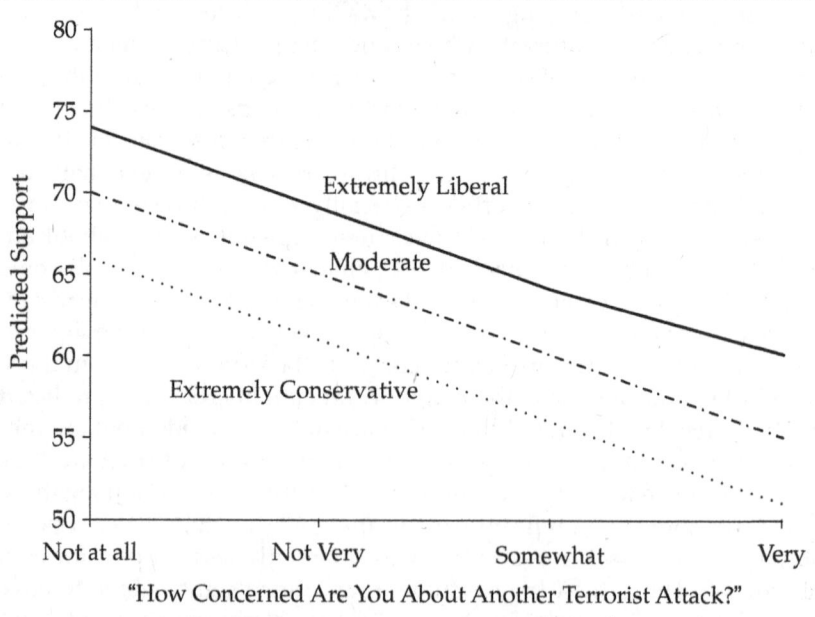

Source: National Civil Liberties Survey (2001).

Figure 4.5 Race, Ethnicity, Sociotropic Threat, and Support for Civil Liberties, 2001

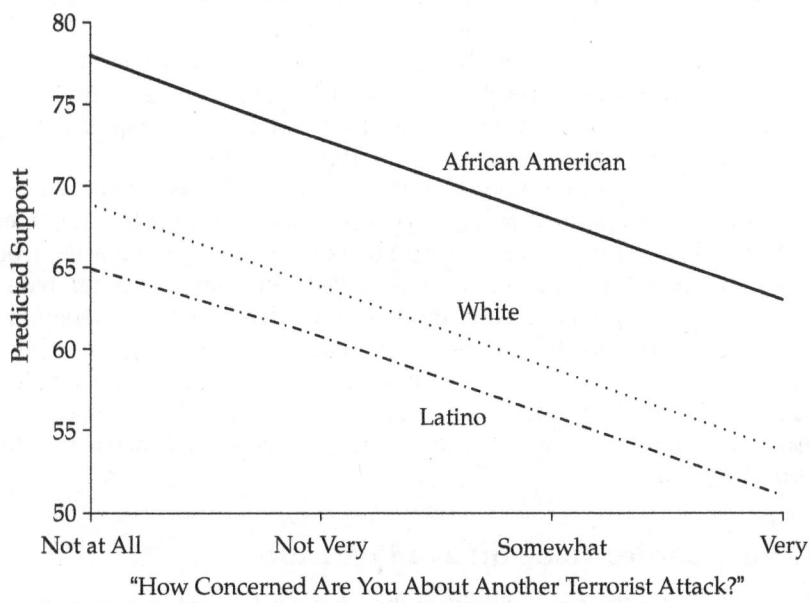

Source: National Civil Liberties Survey (2001).

creases with their perceptions of sociotropic threat. Far from wishing to commit constitutional suicide, in the face of a terrorist threat, both liberals and conservatives endorse granting greater authority to the state. Indeed, liberals who are very concerned about the possibility of a future attack support fewer civil liberties positions than conservatives who are not at all concerned do.

Although figure 4.5 shows that at all levels of sociotropic threat African Americans support civil liberties more than whites do, it also reveals the fundamental similarity between Latinos and whites in support for civil liberties among those who express some or significant concern about another attack. I again find that, regardless of race or ethnicity, people are more willing to exchange civil liberties for security if they are more afraid. The amazing story here is that blacks at all levels of sociotropic threat were more protective of civil liberties than whites and Latinos, but were still willing to cave in to their threat to a certain degree. Also, whites and Latinos reacted very similarly, or at least responded very similarly, to the same level of threat. Such differences are not statistically significant given the small samples sizes for Latinos, but clearly at all levels of threat Latinos were less protective of civil liberties than blacks.

It is clear from these findings that the decision to concede civil liberties is a complex one. In the context of the attacks of September 11, sociotropic threat combines with other factors to determine the extent to which citizens are willing to acquiesce to political authorities. Thus, to understand the support for civil liberties one must also understand the nature of threat, trust in the political authorities, psychological insecurity or dogmatism, political ideology, and race. Later on, in chapter 7, I will add another important variable: political partisanship.

To answer a question I posed at the beginning of this chapter, American citizens were indeed willing to concede their support for civil liberties in exchange for greater security. Such behavior can be expected from a nation that has never been exposed to the level of anxiety generated by the attacks of September 11. If another attack were to occur, depending on the severity and the number of casualties, citizens might not be as willing to cave in to the sense of threat. Too much has happened since September 11 that would make citizens wary of initial acquiescence. In the next chapter I explore whether the initial decision to concede civil liberties was sincere.

Civil Liberties Trade-off as a Predictor

I now consider the possibility that the causal relationship between support for civil liberties and political trust might flow in the opposite direction of what might be expected. That is, choosing between civil liberties and security might lead people to question their support of political authorities and possibly intensify their sense of vulnerability. Having to make such a decision might be uncomfortable for some. Furthermore, from a methodological standpoint, what we think of as cause and effect might come into question, given that all reactions are measured contemporaneously. As a result, the initial cause and effect might become blurred and the error associated with the prediction of the trade-off decision might in turn become correlated with the political trust measure.

I explore this nonrecursive relationship between the support for civil liberties and political trust. A simultaneous equation model was used to estimate the nonrecursive aspects of the trade-off between civil liberties and security and political trust. The goal of simultaneous equations and instrumental variables approach is to identify a set of predictor variables closely associated with the trade-off decision but unrelated to the error term and use it to estimate the model. Using a set of general democratic norms items that tapped support for freedom of speech, the right against self-incrimination, the rights of a person suspected of treason, and respect for different political beliefs, the model predicting trust was re-estimated with the normal set of independent variables. The substantive question here is the extent to which the choice between civil liberties and security influences trust in government. The results of this exercise suggested that trade-off decision was not a significant predictor of political trust.[12]

Conclusion

Threat and trust do not simply lead to favoring one set of values over another. Instead, they interact with one another to determine support for civil liberties versus security. The effect of trust in political authorities on support for civil liberties is conditioned by a sense of sociotropic threat—concern that the country will come under another terrorist attack—more than personal threat. However, at every level of trust in the federal government, an increased sense of threat leads to a greater willingness to concede some civil liberties for security and order. Attitudinal measures, such as political ideology, national pride, and social trust, influence how citizens react to the government's efforts to combat terrorism. These attitudes may either promote or weaken support for civil liberties. Civil liberties may suffer, for example, when the emotional appeals of patriotism favor order and security.

However, the level of support for civil liberties is not entirely contemporaneously determined. In addition to feelings of national pride and interpersonal trust, prior beliefs, such as political ideology, play a role even in crisis. So does group experience. Though they are just as patriotic as other Americans, African Americans' distrust of government and their history of struggle for civil rights leads to a greater support for civil liberties in the wake of the terrorist attacks. When concern about another terrorist attack is moderate to high, African Americans are substantially more supportive of civil liberties than either whites or Latinos.

The relations between threat, trust, and civil liberties that I observe reflect a picture taken shortly after September 11, at a time when the visual images of the events were played and replayed in the mass media and in people's minds. A year and a half after the attack, however, it was very rare to see pictures of the World Trade Center or the Pentagon in flames on television, yet the war on terrorism continues. Unpredictable events will provide the empirical reality that answers some of the questions about willingness to trade civil liberties for security in the future. If public anxiety about another terrorist attack wanes over time, will political and social attitudes remain fixed because of the recentness of the national trauma, or will they change as well? If another major attack were to occur, would some of the changes that have been observed intensify further—such as increased trust in government, patriotic fervor, or greater interpersonal trust—or might the direction of change reverse if people lose confidence in the government's ability to protect them, or if they begin to seek scapegoats among certain groups of people? These are, of course, just a few of the plausible future contexts in which support for individual rights might be tested. They remind us not to assume that the immediate post–September 11 experience forecasts how people will resolve the balance between civil liberties and security in the future. The chapters that follow attempt to address such questions.

Chapter 5

Acceptable Consequences

IN THE last chapter, I showed that America citizens conformed to theoretical expectations, drawing on normal value preferences and contextually driven perceptions to make sense of the choice between liberty and security. Under a heightened sense of threat and vulnerability, many individuals either adopted new positions or acquiesced to government policies in a way that seemed to contradict their normal system of political beliefs. Political liberals, normally protective of civil liberties, began to reflect the preferences of political conservatives under a heightened sense of threat. Similarly, individuals normally less trusting and suspicious of political authorities began to reflect the preferences of those most trusting of political authorities. Exposure to threat upset many of the normal protections of civil liberties to favor order and security. Would individuals continue to compromise their values if they were made aware of the consequences associated with their threat-induced preferences? Persuasive arguments can be made on both sides of the civil liberties for security trade-off issue, and the consequence of either extreme choice cannot be tolerated for long.[1]

The extent to which a heightened sense of threat pressured people to acquiesce, or to adopt preferences they would not normally support, raises important questions about the flexibility and validity of the newly derived value preferences. If the willingness to trade civil liberties for security is based on emotional reactions to the new threat, then the decision, with all of its implications, may not be completely thought through. Instead, value preferences may be only temporary, reflecting a momentary reaction that subsides with diminishing threat. However, if the decision is based on reasoned and informed judgments, in which the consequences are understood, the newly formed preferences may reflect a real change in attitudes and have more profound implications for democracy. Thus, though understanding the situational support for civil liberties is important, the extent to which citizens can be persuaded to moderate their opinions after deeper reflection of the consequences of their choices provides critical insight into attitudes in context. After a sober second thought, do citizens still maintain their initial choices in the trade-off between civil liberties and security?

In this chapter I assess the short-term stability of trade-off decisions by simulating an aspect of a political debate. Rather than treating the survey response as an inexorable attitude, I presented survey respondents with the consequences of their initial opinion, in the form of counterarguments, to determine the extent to which they either maintain or change their initial positions. These counterargument experiments (or quasi-experiments) were designed around three important issues raised in the context of the terrorist attacks and the subsequent Patriot Act I: first, the indefinite detention of noncitizens; second, making it a crime to belong to or contribute money to terrorist organizations; and, third, racial profiling. The extent to which people find the consequences of their trade-off decisions acceptable has tremendous implications for the enduring effects of the attacks. I proceed by examining the persuasibility approach and the basis for civil liberties decisions. Because a substantial percentage of respondents did change their opinions, I use the model developed in chapter 4 to understand the malleability of the trade-off between civil liberties and security.

Simulating Political Debate

Incorporating persuasibility experiments within a public opinion survey has been said to mimic aspects of a political discussion or debate (Kinder and Sanders 1990; Sniderman and Grob 1996). Survey respondents were asked penetrating questions to place them in uncomfortable positions, in which their expressed views were not considered final or unimpeachable. Risking offending and rubbing survey respondents the wrong way, as in real political discussions, persuasibility experiments are analogous to a seemingly polite political discussion with a stranger who challenges certain opinions with the hope of changing them. Simulating political debate in a survey takes shape when persuasibility experiments go further, offering circumstances in which respondents may not have considered certain viewpoints or the consequences of their initial beliefs. Political debate involves the exchange of viewpoints, information, and the shortsightedness of opposing opinions. As Paul Sniderman and his colleagues (1996) suggest,

> politics is about argument. It is about getting people who start off on one side of an issue to join your side or at least to leave theirs. And part of what it means to say there is a politics of rights is to say that the positions people take on questions of rights are subject to challenge. People attempt to persuade others. They attempt to induce them to qualify, give up, even reverse the positions they have taken. Where people start off politically matters,

but what counts is where they wind up after the pushing and shoving of political argument. (55)

Donald Kinder and Lynn Sanders (1990) also maintain that "by examining the kinds of alterations in reports of opinion that are induced by variations in question wording that mimic the rival frames prevailing in elite discourse, we can learn about how changes in public opinion are induced by changes in the setting beyond the survey, in the ongoing, everyday process of democratic discussion" (75). Considering that the discussion of the consequences of conceding civil liberties for greater security was stifled following the terrorist attacks, other than legal challenges by the American Civil Liberties Union (ACLU) and National Lawyer's Guild (NLG), the challenge to individual choices I construct reflect exposure to various arguments, both for and against.

Several studies using the persuasibility approach have advanced our thinking about support for civil liberties. Gibson (1998b) explores the extent to which Russian citizens were willing to moderate their views on whether members of their most hated groups could run for public office. A sizable number of Russians, 67 percent, supported banning the group from the ballot, but Gibson treated this first response as an "opening bid" from which to delineate the boundaries of tolerance. After the initial question, those giving an intolerant response were presented with three tolerant counterarguments, that the government should not be allowed to decide who has rights, that it is unfair to allow some and not others on the ballot, and that it is necessary to express views openly so that they can see they are wrong. The initially tolerant were presented with three intolerant arguments, that the hated group would destroy democracy as it came to power, that its ideas would offend people, and that it would not follow electoral rules. As in a political debate, individuals were not allowed either intolerant or tolerant expressions. Overall, few of the initially intolerant people moderated their position (between 10 and 24 percent), though a sizable portion of the initially tolerant did (between 45 and 50 percent). Such political discourse among Russian citizens revealed a degree of asymmetry, in which tolerant opinions were more pliable than intolerant opinions. This would become a consistent finding in persuasibility experiments.

Simulating political discourse through persuasibility experiments was also applied in South Africa, another society becoming acclimated to democratic expectations. In this setting, Gibson and Gouws (2003) asked an initial question about support for local authorities in banning members of their most disliked group from making a speech in their community. South Africans were almost evenly divided in their support for banning the speech. A series of random counterarguments challenged these initial attitudes. Supporters of banning the speech were confronted with arguments that authorities cannot be trusted to decide who has rights, that it is unfair to allow some and not others to speak, and that the disliked group should be able to express its views openly so that people could see that they were wrong. Opponents of banning the speech were confronted with arguments that their most disliked group would destroy democracy if it came to power, that its ideas would hurt people, and that the opposing audience might become violent. The findings are typical in that it was easier to talk people into intolerance than tolerance. People who at first responded intolerantly were less likely to change (13 to 24 percent) than those who first responded tolerantly (36 to 49 percent).

However, Sniderman and his colleagues (1996) found different results when they confronted Canadian respondents with counterarguments about reactions to laws against writing and speech that promoted hatred toward racial or religious groups. Initially, 74 percent of Canadians supported laws prohibiting written or spoken expressions of racial hatred. When challenged by the "possibility that it results in less freedom of speech about important public issues," almost half of the respondents suggested that they would change their position. Almost as many (43 percent) of those initially opposed to banning expressions of racial hatred supported it when confronted with the counterargument suggesting that not having such laws "would result in more racial and religious prejudice." Thus, on both sides of the civil liberty issue, individuals were willing to reconsider their initial attitudes.

These and other persuasibility experiments indicate that where people start off in their support of certain types of civil liberties is very important, but equally relevant is the extent to which they can defend their positions, and where they end up after having their views challenged. But a debate on civil liberties and security in the context of the terrorist attacks can be expected to be different from debates on other political issues. People, to a certain extent, had to be careful of what they said, or else face serious threat of investigation. Because certain attitudes may have been perceived as unpatriotic and anti-American, people were less willing to talk candidly about their beliefs, especially if they were critical of political authorities and its policies. Although this compelled many people to be silent, expressions that conformed to and supported the Bush administration were licensed, which ultimately exaggerated the nature of support.

The Persuasibility of Civil Liberties Attitudes

Individual liberty and freedom are diminished under a heightened sense of insecurity and threat in favor of conformity and acquiescence to political authority. Gibson (1998b) and Kuklinski and his colleagues (1991) suggest that the diminished support for individual liberty, and greater concern for protection, is a normal response to both threat and emotional information that accompanies threatening situations. Consistent with judgments made under emotional duress (Lerner and Keltner 2000), individuals aroused by a sense of threat became concerned with reducing their threatening situation. They may not fully process all relevant information and may fail to fully appreciate the consequences of their opinions. An overriding fixation with relieving anxiety means that other issues, such as beliefs about democratic norms, remain dormant unless activated by further deliberation over rights. Individuals under heightened threat may also endorse greater restrictions on civil liberties based on affective rather than cognitive information, and because people tend to weigh potentially negative consequences more heavily than positive.[2] By contrast, if people rely less on their emotions and more on a reasoned assessment of their civil liberties and personal security concerns, a different decision, usually more supportive of civil liberties and tolerance, is likely. This is supported by both laboratory-based (Butler and Mathews 1983; Mathews and MacLeod 1986) and survey-based research (Marcus et al. 1995; Peffley, Knigge, and Hurwitz 2001). For instance, Peffley and his colleagues (2001) demonstrate that greater consideration of competing values leads to greater acceptance and protection of civil liberties. George Marcus and his colleagues (1995) show that people who are told to pay attention to their feelings protect civil liberties significantly less than those who are told to pay attention to their thoughts. When asked to attend to their feelings, subjects focus on their immediate needs for security and react intolerantly. When asked to attend to their thoughts, subjects consider the benefits of protecting civil liberties, superseding their natural instinct to be intolerant (82). Marcus and his colleagues (1995) also show that individuals who are less committed to democratic principles are more open to persuasive messages than those who are more committed. Presumably, when asked to deliberate further on the implications of their initial responses, people's thoughts are more likely to come into play than their feelings.

I do not disagree with this conceptualization of emotion and its implications for attitudes toward civil liberties, but it may be limited to low-threat situations. Clearly, emotions trigger changes in cognitive processing, by which new information cannot reverse support for restrictions on civil liberties. But I am not sure whether individuals willing to consider new information in threatening situations will automatically support civil liberties—particularly in high-threat situations such as that in America after September 11. Given the intense and emotional reactions to the threat of terrorism, and that initial attitudes toward civil liberties are driven by affective considerations, requiring citizens to deactivate their sense of threat and fear may be an insurmountable task (LeDoux

1996). Because it is difficult to shut down a sense of threat, counterarguments may lead respondents to dwell even further on their insecurity. It is also possible that deeply reflecting on their sense of threat would simply remind people why they chose their initial security or civil liberties positions in the first place.

Moreover, if deliberation invites citizens to focus more on their sense of threat and fear, concerns for personal security might be expected to outweigh support for civil liberties. In support of this view, Kuklinski and his colleagues (1991, 22) assert that "reason need not always yield a more tolerant, just, or fair society." When asked to concentrate on the consequences of their civil liberties decisions, respondents consistently expressed less support for civil liberties. Exploring the qualitative statements of their survey respondents, the researchers attribute the results to the notion that when people think about the consequences, even with respect to general principles, they typically dwell on the negative, which reduces their enthusiasm for expanding civil liberties.

The literature provides important details to develop specific hypotheses regarding threat and the processing of civil liberties decisions. I expect that, especially in the context of September 11, reconsidering initial attitudes is likely to lead to more intolerance and less support for civil liberties. In contrast to previous experimental research, in which threat perceptions are generally low or only hypothetical, the September 11 attacks were real and caused widespread fear and concern among Americans. I do not expect a reconsideration of baseline responses on whether to support civil liberties or greater security to lead automatically to greater support for civil liberties. The graphic images of airplanes crashing into buildings left an indelible imprint on peoples' minds that, at least during the time of our survey two months later, was difficult to forget. Threat and fear among American citizens were not experienced only vicariously or at a great distance: the attacks occurred on American soil and thousands of innocent people were killed. Subsequent anthrax deaths in the fall of 2001 created widespread concern about bioterrorism and risks associated with such normally mundane activities as opening the daily mail. Unlike most other conflicts Americans have faced, the context created a greater opportunity for threat to be real.

However, as discussed in chapter 4, alienated groups such as African Americans can be expected to perceive threat and concessions to civil liberties differently from the dominant culture. When asked to further consider the trade-off between civil liberties and personal security, African Americans are expected to dwell on protecting civil liberties more so than other groups. Blacks are more likely to experience hostility and violence from society and the government, denied access to economic and political power, and deprived of equal rights and civil liberties. They are more likely to perceive the government and those who run it as disingenuous and untrustworthy, because of significant discrepancies between the values espoused by the political system and their own status. In short, I expect that, as the level of threat increases among blacks, support for civil liberties will increase as well.

The Meaning of Response Inconsistencies in Survey Experiments

My primary interest is in the direction of change in responses to civil liberties questions in survey experiments when respondents are presented with the consequences of their initial preferences. Interpreting change in survey responses is not straightforward. Philip Converse (1964) proposes that respondents who change their positions over time hold no convictions, but instead express random responses or nonattitudes. Under the assumption that the length of time between surveys is irrelevant to assess the extent of consistency, respondents are charged with having no real preferences if they offer different opinions on an issue in successive surveys.

Similarly, John Zaller (1992) suggests that inconsistencies result from differences in the accessibility and salience of information at the moment of the survey, which may be influenced by the survey itself. According to Zaller and Stanley Feldman (1992, 610), "individuals typically do not develop 'true attitudes' of the type that opinion analysts routinely assume, but possess a series of autonomous and often inconsistent reactions to the questions asked by pollsters." People possess multiple and often conflicting opinions, and any change may be a function of a combination of chance and accessibility of beliefs at the moment of the survey. Christopher Achen's (1975) and Robert Erikson's (1979) measurement error interpretation shifts the blame for response instability from respondents to the survey questions. Simple survey questions may not adequately capture complex attitudes. Alvarez and Brehm (2002) suggest that the nonattitudes and sampling perspectives may be somewhat overstated, because individuals can render reliable opinions based on predispositions.

Although these explanations for discrepancies in responses remain important, inconsistencies in survey responses, in which attitude change occurs over a matter of seconds (as opposed to months in the early response effects literature, or years in Converse's analyses), should be more meaningful and less susceptible to non-attitudes. I base this expectation on the idea that people strive for consistency in the context of a single conversation or interview, and hence, to the extent that there is a bias in asking people the same or similar questions in the same interview, the direction of the bias is likely to be against change. Because respondents are likely to be aware of potential discrepancies in their responses when they occur over a matter of seconds, they are also likely to understand when their responses conflict. Even if respondents' opinions are uninformed, or answers come off the top of their heads without much thought, there should also be a strain toward consistency.

However, the argument that all change in survey experiments is meaningful can only be taken so far. The normal approach in experimental designs in surveys involves presenting new information to respondents, so there is usually no way of knowing how respondents would have answered if they had been asked the same question with full information initially. In this situation, response change in reaction to new information or a counterargument may not merit being treated as persuasion. In this analysis, I do not claim that the respondents are being persuaded by new information, because this would entail a more sophisticated measurement strategy. Rather, I present additional information and counterarguments to examine the extent to which individuals defend their initial positions. That is, I ask how stable the responses to choices about civil liberties and personal security are when respondents are presented with information that challenges their initially stated beliefs.

Research Design

My approach to measuring the instability of responses utilizes counterarguments to assess the extent to which respondents modify their initial answers about civil liberties. Although understanding whether respondents changed their answers is interesting, I am mainly concerned here with the direction of change after counterarguments. A challenge to responses in the form of counterarguments can make people defensive and push them further to an extreme, lead them to moderate their position, or have no effect at all. The counterarguments were framed to show respondents the implications of their beliefs about the trade-off between civil liberties and personal security. A potential weakness to counterargument experiments is the difficulty in determining whether people on one side of an issue changed because their positions were more pliable or because they were confronted with stronger counterarguments. It is partly for this reason that this analysis relies on several experiments rather than one. But, it is important to note that in the context of the September 11 attacks, this expectation is probably unreasonable, given that certain types of expressions were tolerated more than others. As I alluded to earlier, people who were willing to trade civil liberties for security definitely had an advantage over those defending civil liberties because of the framing of information in the media and by political authorities.

Because survey respondents are not randomly assigned to counterarguments, quasi-experimental designs most appropriately describe my approach. Random assignment of the treatment or stimuli need not be seen as a necessary component of experimental designs (Kinder and Palfrey 1993). To be sure, the trade-off between the added control against greater theoretical leverage in the model should be weighed very carefully. James Gibson, Gregory Caldeira, and Lester Spence (2002) argue that theory should be given considerable weight in experimental designs and that nonrandom assignment is beneficial when theory necessitates an initially dedicated or baseline condition, such as questions involving tolerance and legitimacy.[3] To understand the extent to which individuals can be talked into or out of certain decisions, it is critical to know their initial opinions. Otherwise, respondents could feel compelled to defend positions they do not support, or to "accept" a position already held. The consequence of such an approach would render all such cases useless: one cannot talk another person out of an opinion they do not hold or into a position they already support. Thus, if exposure to counterarguments were random, such cases would be rendered useless and have to be discarded from the analysis, further reducing the number of respondents in the data.

However, as mentioned, attempting to persuade people to accept different positions may backfire, especially in the context of terrorist attacks. According to the psychological reactance theory (Brehm 1966), the extent to which individuals perceive a certain level of threat to believing what they want to believe creates a desire to reaffirm the threatened attitude. People, in a sense, will rebel against having certain beliefs questioned or being made to feel as if their answers were invalid. The saying that for every action there is an equal and opposite reaction may pose a problem for this type of survey experiment. As the level of threat increases from coercive pressure, individuals will become more reactant. Reactance entails either reasserting freedom by maintaining initial preferences, or altering initial preferences away from the position advocated in the message (boomerang effect). Attempting to moderate initial preferences may cause individuals to stake out more extreme positions. I do not discount the discomfort that counterarguments may pose for individual respondents, but many of the studies supporting the boomerang effect involve very heavy-handed tactics at persuasion. High-pressure social influence tactics are clearly counterproductive, but challenging opinions in a public opinion survey is probably at the lower end of the constrained behavior continuum. Of course, the amount of reactance depends on how much of a threat individuals perceive from having their opinions questioned.

Experiment 1: Crime to Belong to Terrorist Organization

Shortly after the September 11 attacks, both Americans and noncitizens with ties to Arab, Muslim, and Middle Eastern countries and organizations came under suspicion. Many were detained and arrested for alleged ties to organizations said to support terrorism, and with the casting of this broad net, several credible links in the United States and abroad to terrorist organizations were publicly identified. The Patriot Act made it a crime for people to belong or contribute to any organization the U.S. attorney general deemed a terrorist organization, or have links to an international terrorist organization. With echoes of the attorney general's list from the McCarran Act of 1950, this component of the Patriot Act raised the risk that many innocent persons would be judged guilty by association. Under the law, detaining citizens and deporting noncitizens who assisted in the lawful activities of a group the government claimed was a terrorist organization was permitted. The law removed the presumption of innocence for those under investigation, making it easier for the government to conduct surveillance on those suspected of violating conspiracy laws.

To capture general support for this issue, all survey respondents were asked whether it "should be a crime to belong to or contribute money to any organization that supports terrorism." Reflecting more of a quasi-experimental approach, an immediate follow-up question or suggestion challenged their initial support.[4] If respondents initially selected personal security over supporting civil liberties on detaining noncitizens, they were presented with the counterargument: "Suppose, in doing this, people would be judged guilty by association rather than by a crime they may have personally committed." Those who accepted civil liberties over personal security were presented with a different counterargument: "Suppose people who contribute to these organizations actually are supporting the activities and goals of terrorist organizations." Although there are probably other ways and information individual citizens can use to justify their positions, these counterarguments most likely reflect the most significant and straightforward rationalizations individuals use to defend their positions. That is, for many supporters of civil liberties, the danger in making it a crime to associate with organizations that support terrorism involved the possibility of being accused of a crime by mere association and the ambiguity of who and what evidence would define a terrorist organization. For those concerned about security, the danger was that many people could be indirectly abetting terrorists and organizations sympathetic to attacks against America.

Experiment 2: Indefinite Detentions

Indefinite detentions without a writ of habeas corpus were not approved as part of the Patriot Act, though they had been included in the initial proposal. However, arresting and detaining citizens and noncitizens were critical components of the government's efforts to prevent future terrorist attacks. Using material witness statutes, or charges related to visa or immigration status, detentions initially involved arresting people within the United States on immigration violations, denying them legal representation, and withholding their names from the public. After the invasion of Afghanistan, many individuals captured on the battlefield were detained and later transferred to Guantánamo Bay.

Similar to the previous experiment, survey respondents were asked initially "whether the government should be able to arrest and detain noncitizens indefinitely if they are suspected of belonging to a terrorist organization." Those who affirmed this were presented with a counterargument reminding them of the civil liberties position: "Suppose this means that many innocent people could be locked up for a long time without ever being charged with a crime." A response initially supporting civil liberties was challenged by this suggestion: "Suppose there were strong suspicions that these people are terrorists and detaining them would prevent them from committing other crimes." Again, these counterarguments simulate the actual justifications used to defend initial civil liberty tradeoff decisions. Objections to indefinite detentions of a suspected terrorist centered on the risk of innocent people being arrested based only suspicion, that is, the possibility of detaining innocent people. Based on sometimes inadequate and weak evidence, many people were detained for long periods after the September 11 attacks. At the same time, however, many were willing to tolerate such a risk. For them, not detaining highly suspicious individuals would be tantamount to supporting terrorism.

Experiment 3: Racial Profiling

Before the September 11 attacks, as I have said, racial profiling, directed largely at African Americans, was seen by many as racist. After an extended campaign by civil rights and civil liberties organizations, it fell from favor, and law enforcement officials around the country were trained to avoid it. However, after the attacks, the federal government recast racial profiling as part of a general profiling of prospective terrorists. Because the perpetrators of the September 11 attacks were all Middle Eastern, citizens perceived to have a Middle Eastern background and who matched other characteristics or behaviors that raised suspicions came under great scrutiny. Although intended to single out individuals with terrorist ties, the new guidelines led to many innocent citizens being questioned, searched, or harassed.

Respondents initially supporting personal security over civil liberties by accepting racial profiling were presented with the suggestion: "Suppose this means racial profiling leads to unequal treatment of people just because of their race or national origin." Those who selected civil liberties over personal security were presented with a justification for personal security: "Suppose people from certain racial or ethnic backgrounds were more likely to commit crimes." These counterarguments rest on individual perceptions of equality and fairness, issues that have been traditionally contested in the debate over racial profiling. The concern for security is challenged by equality whereas the concern for civil liberties is challenged by the idea that certain ethnic groups were associated with terrorist activities.

The Effects of Counterarguments

The three embedded experiments span the spectrum of security and civil liberties support found in the answers to this series of questions. In the first wave of the National Civil Liberties Survey, when asked about the racial profiling of people based on their race and ethnicity, 82 percent preferred to protect civil liberties (see figure 2.1). However, only 51 percent preferred protecting civil liberties over supporting indefinite detentions of noncitizens for greater personal security, and only 28 percent considered it a crime to belong to a terrorist organization. Because a different process seems to underlie the initial attitudes in the constructed experiments, I expect each experiment to also be driven by different processes and explanations. However, the extent to which the effects are consistent across the experiments reveals an important influence of the context of the terrorist attack.

My plan is to first show the marginal change in response to the consequences of their initial attitudes and then show a model exploring the direction of response change. According to table 5.1, many respondents moved in a civil liberties direction after the counterarguments, but respondents were far more likely to move in a security direction. When I challenged respondents who initially expressed security attitudes on whether it is a crime to belong to a terrorist organization, 48 percent did not alter their beliefs, and 15 percent acceded to the counterargument by moving in a civil liberties direction (see question 1a in table 5.1). However, a remarkable 37 percent of those who already favored a security position said that they would be even more likely to support detaining noncitizens indefinitely after the counterargument. On the other side of the issue, of those people who initially supported civil liberties, 14 percent became more supportive after the counterargument, 31 percent did not change their position, and 55 moved in a security direction. Such an asymmetry in attitude shifting, in which it is easier to talk people into security positions, is consistent with the previous literature (Gibson 1998b; Peffley, Knigge, and Hurwitz 2001; Sullivan et al. 1993). In the experiment concerning the indefinite detention and arrest of noncitizens, among those who initially chose a security position, 41 percent did not

Table 5.1 Distribution of Civil Liberties Counterarguments, 2001

Initial Position	Counter-arguments	Less Democratic	No Difference	More Democratic
1. Crime to belong to terrorist organization; guilt should not be determined by association.				
a. Crime to belong to terror organization (security)	Suppose people were judged guilty by association rather than by a crime they committed	36.7 (349)	48.4 (460)	14.9 (142)
b. Innocent (civil liberties)	Suppose people are actually supporting terrorists activities	54.9 (217)	31.4 (124)	13.7 (54)
2. Noncitizens suspected of belonging to terrorist organization should be detained indefinitely; no one should be held for long without being formally charged with a crime.				
a. Detained as long as it takes (security)	Suppose innocent people could be locked up for a very long time without being charged with a crime	17.2 (111)	40.8 (271)	42.0 (263)
b. Oppose detaining noncitizens (civil liberties)	Suppose detaining them would prevent them from committing other crimes	43.1 (313)	33.8 (245)	23.1 (168)
3. Law enforcement should be to stop or detain people of certain racial or ethnic backgrounds; racial profiling harasses innocent people just because of their race or ethnicity.				
a. Allow racial profiling (security)	Suppose this leads to unequal treatment of people just because of their race or national origin	38.8 (83)	49.1 (105)	12.2 (26)
b. Oppose racial profiling (civil liberties)	Suppose people from certain racial or ethnic backgrounds were actually more likely to commit crimes	14.4 (163)	70.3 (798)	15.3 (174)

Source: National Civil Liberties Survey (2001).

change in response to the counterargument, 42 percent supported civil liberties more, and 17 percent supported their initial security position more. But, unlike the previous experiment, exposure to the counterargument among this group of respondents generated support for civil liberties. By contrast, citizens who started from a civil liberties position were more likely to change their positions than those who first chose security. Only 34 percent maintained their initial positions, but 43 percent were less committed to civil liberties after the counterargument. The question on racial profiling elicited an initially overwhelmingly civil liberties response, and the resistance to and direction of change in response to counterarguments reflected a consistent concern for civil liberties. Racial profiling is an easier policy option for civil libertarians to uphold when challenged than arguments about belonging to a terrorist organization and indefinite detention. Among the few who initially supported racial profiling, 49 percent continued to do so, but 12 percent were less likely to support it after the counterargument. Citizens who started off supporting civil liberties were more likely to maintain this attitude in the face of counterarguments. Although most respondents (82 percent) did not at first support racial profiling, differences in support for it emerged when people were asked to think about the implications of their initial answers. Overall, the consequences of value preferences mattered more to respondents who initially defended liberty than they did to respondents who initially defended security. Consequences that restrict civil liberties are more tolerable than consequences that limit order and security.

Consistent with what might be expected from psychological reactance and a boomerang effect, many respondents tended to adopt more extreme positions, away from the intended goal of the follow-up questions. In the first experiment, 37 percent of the group initially supporting security became more supportive following the democratic counterargument, whereas only 14 percent of the group initially supporting civil liberties became more supportive. Similarly, in the racial profiling experiment, 39 percent of the security group became more concerned about security, and 15 percent of the civil liberties group became more concerned about civil liberties. This situation is somewhat reversed in the terrorist organization experiment, however. Whereas 17 percent of the security group adopted that position, 23 percent of the civil liberties group strengthened their stance. One might conclude that opinions harden to the extent that respondents find the follow-up questions impolite or threatening. Because psychological reactance has been linked to a dogmatic belief system—open-minded people tend to be more easily persuaded than dogmatic people—I am able to examine this alternative hypothesis directly. More precisely, people who are dogmatic are also resistant to influence and persuasion (Rokeach 1960) and intolerant of disagreement (Palmer and Kalin 1985).

Several tables are presented on the effects of dogmatism, ideology, race and ethnicity, and sociotropic threat on the counterarguments. I am interested in showing how dogmatism, liberals, conservatives, blacks, Latinos, whites, and people under different types of threat react to the consequences of their initial trade-off decisions. Table 5.2 reports responses to counterarguments by levels of dogmatism. Because dogmatism is closely intertwined with support for civil liberties, assessing the extent of reactance (and the boomerang effect) is not straightforward. Dogmatists who began supporting security could legitimately continue to do so in the face of a civil liberty counterargument, regardless of how they felt about the task. However, high dogmatists starting off defending liberty, but not caving in to the security counterargument I take as a clear sign of reactance. Reactance, just to recap, is when the intended persuasive message has the opposite effect. Change, however, is also an important component of reactance. If these assumptions are reasonable, I conclude that there is no discernable pattern in reactance as an alternative hypothesis. For instance, in panel 1b, 17 percent of the high dogmatists, versus 18 percent of medium dogmatists and 14 percent of low dogmatists, accepted the civil liberties position over the security counterargument about whether it is a crime to belong to a terrorist organization. Similarly, in panel 2b, 22 percent of high dogmatists who initially supported civil liberties in the indefinite detention experiment supported them even more in response to the security counterargument, versus 23 percent of medium dogmatists and 18 percent of low dogmatists. The same is also true for those who initially held civil libertarian positions on racial profiling. High dogmatists were only slightly more likely to reject the counterargument in panel 3b. Although there is no hard evidence of reactance, high dogmatists are otherwise not very different from low and medium dogmatists.

One of the most striking features of ideological differences in the reactions to trade-off decisions in table 5.3 is that many respondents would probably change their opinions in a political debate, but a large part of this change would not involve adopting different beliefs. Political liberals who might have taken uncharacteristic positions following the September attacks were not likely to reverse them, even when their views were challenged or they suddenly abandoned their initial stances. In table 5.3, liberals, moderates, and conservatives responded similarly to counterarguments challenging their initial civil liberties decisions, but liberals appeared to be on foreign ground. Those who started off supporting the security position on whether it should be a crime to belong to a terrorist organization became further entrenched in their support of security after the follow-up question. Liberals, moderates, and conservatives all became more extreme. This was unexpected, especially among political liberals, given that the counterargument was written to push re-

Table 5.2 Effects of Dogmatism on Counterarguments, 2001 (Percentages)

	Security	No Change	Democracy	Net Change	N
1a. Initially supported security on crime to belong to terrorist organization					
Low dogmatism	34	47	19	52	251
Medium dogmatism	40	51	9	53	325
High dogmatism	44	36	20	59	236
$x^2(4) = 10.15; p = .038$					
1b. Initially supported civil liberties on crime to belong to terrorist organization					
Low dogmatism	65	21	14	80	128
Medium dogmatism	63	25	12	67	129
High dogmatism	57	26	17	63	108
$x^2(4) = 18.66; p = .001$					
2a. Initially supported security on indefinite detention					
Low dogmatism	16	42	41	57	160
Medium dogmatism	13	43	43	57	290
High dogmatism	17	36	47	62	221
$x^2(4) = 5.63; p = .228$					
2b. Initially supported civil liberties on indefinite detention					
Low dogmatism	46	36	18	65	252
Medium dogmatism	44	33	23	70	248
High dogmatism	46	32	22	67	192
$x^2(4) = 14.92; p = .005$					
3a. Initially supported security on racial profiling					
Low dogmatism	2	4	48	51	68
Medium dogmatism	12	45	43	56	70
High dogmatism	22	55	23	47	67
$x^2(4) = 7.81; p = .100$					
3b. Initially supported civil liberties on racial profiling					
Low dogmatism	10	79	11	23	338
Medium dogmatism	11	75	14	27	402
High dogmatism	20	64	15	41	335
$x^2(4) = 30.72; p = .000$					

Source: National Civil Liberties Survey (2001).
Note: Because the initial dogmatism is a scale ranging from 1 to 5, it was reduced to a three-category measure to simplify the analysis: Low is identified as the scale score ranging from 1 and less than 2.5, medium is greater than 2.5 and less than 3.5, and high is greater than or equal to 3.5.

spondents in a democratic direction. It would seem that liberals, who normally support civil liberties, would be able to offer a greater defense than moderates and conservatives. A larger percentage of political conservatives took more extreme positions, as expected, but political liberals who started off supporting civil liberties caved in to the counterargument and moved toward supporting security.

As for the indefinite detention of suspected terrorists, I show that liberals and conservatives were willing to moderate their positions in the direction of the counterargument, but that political liberals did not appear overly receptive to civil liberties arguments, and that political conservatives did not appear to be overly receptive to security arguments. Thus, this issue seems to favor neither conservatives nor liberals. On the racial profiling question, those who started off supporting racial profiling could be moved by arguments against it. Political liberals and moderates showed a greater sensitivity to the civil liberties counterargument: 43 percent of liberals and 47 percent of moderates accepted it. However, those who were opposed to racial profiling resisted attempts to move them to support a security position. Racial profiling also seems to be a moot issue for political ideology after September 11.

The next issue I examine is the effect of race and ethnicity on the various counterarguments in table 5.4. Blacks differed from whites and Latinos in their reactions to counterarguments challenging their initial attitudes. Among those who started off supporting security on the terrorist organization question, blacks and whites were less likely to stake out more extreme positions (panel 1a). Among those who started off supporting civil liberties, blacks tended to be more resistant than whites and Latinos to counterarguments, though change was substantial across all groups. On the indefinite detention of suspected terrorists, blacks who initially backed security became more extreme in their support for this issue than whites and Latinos did. Among those who started off backing civil liberties, Latinos became more supportive of the democratic position than blacks and whites did. I surmise that the detention issue is more likely to be sensitive among minority groups. Racial and ethnic differences exist in the debate over racial profiling. Latinos who started off supporting racial profiling were more resistant to democratic counterarguments than blacks and whites were (panel 3a), and whites tended to be more receptive to the democratic argument. Compared to individuals who started off backing civil liberties on racial profiling (panel 3b), they were not as likely as they were in previous experiments to change in response to the counterarguments.

Threat also seems to work mysteriously. Based on table 5.4, with the exception of one instance, high levels of threat do not generally seem to make security appeals more attractive. That is, individuals under high and medium threat who started off opposing the criminalization of

(text continues on p. 107)

Table 5.3 Effects of Ideology on Counterarguments, 2001 (Percentages)

	Security	No Change	Democracy	Net Change	N
1a. Initially supported security on crime to belong to terrorist organization					
Conservative	50	37	13	54	324
Moderate	30	49	20	49	354
Liberal	40	47	14	52	134
$x^2(4) = 8.41; p = .078$					
1b. Initially supported civil liberties on crime to belong to terrorist organization					
Conservative	60	28	12	64	100
Moderate	58	23	19	70	144
Liberal	69	20	11	70	86
$x^2(4) = 5.63; p = .228$					
2a. Initially supported security on indefinite detention					
Conservative	19	41	41	59	254
Moderate	17	34	49	58	232
Liberal	8	51	41	60	86
$x^2(4) = .48; p = .976$					
2b. Initially supported civil liberties on indefinite detention					
Conservative	44	36	20	63	200
Moderate	54	28	18	71	295
Liberal	32	44	24	59	141
$x^2(4) = 10.45; p = .034$					
3a. Initially supported security on racial profiling					
Conservative	21	50	29	45	95
Moderate	2	51	47	53	84
Liberal	12	45	43	61	19
$x^2(4) = 7.61; p = .107$					
3b. Initially supported civil liberties on racial profiling					
Conservative	16	70	14	34	344
Moderate	12	75	13	28	433
Liberal	11	74	15	24	207
$x^2(4) = 8.10; p = .088$					

Source: National Civil Liberties Survey (2001).
Note: To simplify the analysis, political ideology was collapsed from a five-category (that is, very conservative, conservative, moderate, liberal, and very liberal) measure to a three-category measure.

Table 5.4 Effects of Race and Ethnicity on Counterarguments, 2001 (Percentages)

	Security	No Change	Democracy	Net Change	N
1a. Initially supported security on crime to belong to terrorist organization					
African American	45	29	25	52	166
Latino	25	41	34	54	108
White	41	46	12	49	573
$x^2(4) = 7.51; p = .111$					
1b. Initially supported civil liberties on crime to belong to terrorist organization					
African American	56	34	10	60	115
Latino	65	10	24	64	32
White	62	24	13	72	208
$x^2(4) = 11.87; p = .018$					
2a. Initially supported security on indefinite detention					
African American	18	31	51	68	110
Latino	16	25	59	57	88
White	15	43	43	57	413
$x^2(4) = 12.04; p = .017$					
2b. Initially supported civil liberties on indefinite detention					
African American	45	36	19	61	185
Latino	54	4	42	72	61
White	47	34	19	67	424
$x^2(4) = 11.58; p = .021$					
3a. Initially supported security on racial profiling					
African American	45	38	18	63	19
Latino	6	51	43	47	27
White	11	51	38	50	156
$x^2(4) = 5.89; p = .207$					
3b. Initially supported civil liberties on racial profiling					
African American	19	60	21	33	278
Latino	8	85	7	36	119
White	13	73	13	27	650
$x^2(4) = 6.73; p = .151$					

Source: National Civil Liberties Survey (2001).

Table 5.5 Effects of Sociotropic Threat on Counterarguments (Percentages)

	Security	No Change	Democracy	Net Change	N
1a. Initially supported security on crime to belong to terrorist organization					
Very concerned	41	44	15	52	333
Somewhat concerned	36	47	17	50	410
Not very concerned	40	47	13	51	92
Not at all concerned	45	38	17		29
$x^2(4) = 3.53; p = .740$					
1b. Initially supported civil liberties on crime to belong to terrorist organization					
Very concerned	61	22	17	71	120
Somewhat concerned	63	25	12	69	179
Not very concerned	67	22	11	59	49
Not at all concerned	41	19	40		15
$x^2(4) = 13.26; p = .039$					
2a. Initially supported security on indefinite detention					
Very concerned	18	35	46	63	268
Somewhat concerned	12	44	44	57	271
Not very concerned	19	47	34	48	62
Not at all concerned	3	52	45		19
$x^2(4) = 10.78; p = .095$					
2b. Initially supported civil liberties on indefinite detention					
Very concerned	50	27	23	70	218
Somewhat concerned	46	37	18	63	356
Not very concerned	47	40	13	63	90
Not at all concerned	35	15	50		26
$x^2(4) = 11.97; p = .063$					
3a. Initially supported security on racial profiling					
Very concerned	10	50	40	52	71
Somewhat concerned	16	48	36	50	99
Not very concerned	4	62	34	49	26
Not at all concerned	0	27	73		9
$x^2(4) = 2.12; p = .908$					
3b. Initially supported civil liberties on racial profiling					
Very concerned	16	68	16	37	35
Somewhat concerned	11	77	12	22	128
Not very concerned	12	47	17	30	403
Not at all concerned	36	47	17		405
$x^2(4) = 29.27; p = .000$					

Source: National Civil Liberties Survey (2001).

membership in terrorist organizations were more likely than individuals under low threat to accept security counterarguments (panel 1b). However, threat, regardless of the level, seemed to make security counterarguments more palatable for criminalizing membership in terrorist organizations (panels 1a and 1b). Threat moved respondents to accept security positions among those who started off from supporting civil liberties on indefinite detention (panel 2b), but among those who started off supporting security, threat increased receptivity to civil liberties counterarguments (panel 2a). On the question of racial profiling, threat makes those who started off supporting it less supportive (panel 3a). It seems, however, to have no effect on counterarguments among those who initially oppose racial profiling.

In short, simulating political debate in the context of a public opinion survey seems to be only the beginning to understanding reactions to the terrorist attacks. After people answered survey questions, they were willing to change their views systematically, following their political ideology, racial and ethnic experiences, perceptions of threat, and a host of other variables I chose not to include. However, in the following analysis, I seek to control for a variety of those other variables to understand why individuals might find the consequences of their initial position more or less acceptable.

Predictability of Alteration in Trade-off Decisions

I expect the possible undoing of initial answers through counterarguments to be related to the same mix of factors that influenced the initial trade-off decision discussed in chapter 4. My main interest in this part of the analysis is to understand if being exposed to the consequences of their initial value preferences matters, and if so, in what way. Because the dependent variable now has three discrete categories (1 = change in a democratic direction, 0 = no change, and −1 = change in a security direction), ordered-probit is used to estimate the effects of the theoretical model developed in chapter 4 on the ordinal ranking of the response categories from each experiment. With the comparison category set as the middle category or 0 (no change), a significant positive coefficient indicates an increased probability of supporting the civil liberties counterargument and a significant negative coefficient indicates an increased probability of supporting the security argument. Because of the possible confounding effects of including blacks and whites in the same equation, I analyze them separately.[5] Latinos are excluded from this part of the analysis because of small cell frequencies.

Based on the ordered-probit analyses in tables 5.6 and 5.7, my expectations concerning the effects of threat on the alteration of civil liberties responses are generally supported. Although each experiment has some idiosyncratic aspects and I have included only three, there is consistency across the experiments. My overall interpretation of these findings is that mere exposure to the consequences of initial value preferences does not automatically lead to civil liberties positions. Instead, a sense of threat may compel initial civil libertarians to dwell further on their sense of vulnerability, as many respondents switched from civil libertarian to security positions after the counterarguments. I would speculate that in the context of the terrorist threat to America, when respondents were asked to reflect further on their opinions on the fundamental issue of trading off security for civil liberties, further processing of information evoked images of the tragedy of September 11. After hearing the consequences of their initial security attitudes on whether it should be a crime to contribute money to organizations suspected of supporting terrorism, for white respondents, the higher their sense of personal threat, the less supportive of restrictions on civil liberties they became.[6] This finding is consistent with that of Kuklinski and his colleagues (1991) on the differences between the affective and cognitive bases of threat and fear. Whereas the initial response may have been driven more by affect than reflective thought, when challenged to reflect on their initial answers, the respondents—continuing to focus on the source of anxiety—moved even further away from civil liberties. This is impressive, given that the counterargument was intended to moderate their initial baseline responses.

On the other side of the issue, neither personal nor sociotropic threat among white respondents influenced their willingness to moderate initial civil-libertarian positions after hearing the consequences of strict adherence to civil liberties. The level of threat does not lead to moderation of initially staked-out positions. Among whites who initially supported a security position on the indefinite detention of noncitizens, personal threat remained a critical determinant. Consistent with the results from the previous experiment, a sense of personal threat leads to greater support for security, or a more extreme position among respondents who started off favoring detaining citizens suspected of terrorism indefinitely. Threat does not seem to moderate, but attenuate the consequences for certain respondents.

In column three of table 5.6, pertaining to racial profiling, personal threat continues to compel white respondents to back off from their initial civil liberties position after hearing about the consequences of adhering to that position. Despite supporting civil liberties initially, whites who continued to dwell on their sense of threat became more supportive of racial profiling. Threat is not related to changing positions of respondents who initially supported civil liberties. Results of a similar ordered-probit analysis for African Americans are reported in table 5.7. Although the re-

Table 5.6 Ordered Probit Analysis of Counterarguments on Survey Experiments, 2001 (Whites Only)

Independent Variables	Terrorist Organization		Detaining Citizens		Racial Profiling	
	Initially Pro-Security	Initially Pro–Civil Liberties	Initially Pro-Security	Initially Pro–Civil Liberties	Initially Pro-Security	Initially Pro–Civil Liberties
Sociotropic threat	.02 (.09)	−.30* (.16)	.10 (.10)	−.14 (.10)	.03 (.17)	.00 (.08)
Personal threat	−.19** (.08)	−.04 (.14)	−.23** (.09)	−.11 (.09)	−.34* (.15)	−.06 (.07)
Political trust	−.16* (.07)	−.07 (.15)	−.01 (.08)	−.10 (.10)	.15 (.14)	.22 (.07)
Dogmatism	−.13* (.06)	.01 (.10)	.05 (.07)	−.01 (.07)	−.12 (.11)	−.02 (.06)
Self-reported ideology	.11 (.07)	.12 (.14)	.09 (.08)	.14 (.09)	.33 (.18)	.20** (.07)
Education	−.02 (.05)	−.15 (.09)	−.08 (.06)	−.16** (.06)	−.10 (.10)	−.11** (.05)
Age	−.02 (.03)	.09 (.05)	.01 (.03)	−.05 (.03)	.08 (.05)	.07** (.03)
Female	.47** (.11)	.54** (.20)	−.01 (.12)	−.02 (.12)	.82** (.22)	.08 (.10)
X²	35.81	15.88	9.24	22.40	32.11	27.94
Pseudo R²	.03	.04	.01	.03	.11	.03
N	535	189	383	396	148	603

Source: National Civil Liberties Survey (2001).
Note: Dependent variable: change in civil liberties direction. 1 = civil liberties response, 0 = no change, −1 = security response. Standard errors in parentheses.
*p < .05; **p < .01.

sults suggest that it was appropriate to analyze blacks in separate equations, they also confirm my expectations. Whites may have the luxury of thinking mainly about the source of threat from the attacks, but blacks may perceive multiple threats in a national crisis—the threat from terrorism and from the government itself—and support civil liberties more strongly. To be more exact, among African Americans who initially opposed treating contributions to terrorist organizations as a crime, a heightened sense of sociotropic threat led to greater support for civil lib-

Table 5.7 Ordered Probit Analysis of Counterarguments on Survey Experiments (African Americans)

Independent Variables	Terrorist Organization		Detaining Citizens		Racial Profiling	
	Security	Civil Liberties	Security	Civil Liberties	Security	Civil Liberties
Sociotropic threat	−.01 (.15)	.66** (.19)	−.28 (.21)	.32** (.13)	—	.08 (.11)
Personal threat	.58** (.18)	−.74** (.20)	−.32 (.18)	.07 (.15)	—	.42** (.12)
Political trust	.07 (.15)	−.26 (.17)	.36 (.20)	.28* (.13)	—	−.54** (.12)
Dogmatism	.19 (.13)	.13 (.16)	−.07 (.15)	.11 (.13)	—	−.35* (.10)
Self-reported ideology	.26 (.15)	−.10 (.20)	.27 (.18)	−.05 (.14)	—	−.29** (.12)
Education	.30** (.11)	−.99** (.20)	−.14 (.16)	.16 (.11)	—	−.09 (.09)
Age	−.30** (.07)	.07 (.09)	−.23* (.11)	.01 (.06)	—	−.06 (.05)
Female	−.66** (.25)	−.76* (.32)	.03 (.27)	−.22 (.20)	—	−.33** (.17)
X²	42.65	49.57	29.22	19.80		71.53
Pseudo R²	.14	.28	.17	.01		.17
N	142	94	92	157		233

Source: National Civil Liberties Survey (2001).
Note: Dependent variable: change in civil liberties direction. 1 = positive civil liberties response, 0 = no change, −1 = positive security response. Standard errors in parentheses.
*p < .05; **p < .01.

erties after a counterargument that, in effect, reminded them of actions that law enforcement officers could take. The significant and positive coefficient suggests that African Americans, rather than moderating their positions in the face of sociotropic threat, became even more committed to civil liberties on hearing the consequences of strict adherence to civil liberties. This relationship must be regarded with some circumspection, however. The coefficients of measures of personal threat suggest that a heightened sense of personal threat leads to moderate support for civil liberties regardless of where one begins. This result is the only instance in which this happened. I rely on the two remaining experiments to clarify.[7]

In the experiment challenging responses to the indefinite detention of citizens, a heightened sense of sociotropic threat among African Americans led to greater support for civil liberties. Blacks also displayed stronger support for civil liberties after a counterargument challenged their initial position. Similarly, in the racial profiling experiment, and again after a counterargument, a heightened sense of threat also led to greater support for civil liberties. Taken together, these results suggest that whites and blacks respond very differently to a heightened sense of threat. Although an increased sense of threat compelled both groups to adopt more extreme positions in survey experiments designed to moderate their baseline responses, they changed in opposite directions. Whites were more concerned about personal security, and blacks more about civil liberties.

Conclusion

Citizens' initial reactions to the trade-off between civil liberties and personal security are not always maintained after a second thought, but the expectation that a sober second thought translates to greater support for democracy and civil liberties needs revision. Second thoughts may not be sober second thoughts, but instead, in many cases, may evoke emotion-laden memories of the horror of September 11 and the threat of more powerful political authorities taking away constitutional rights.

Relying only on the initial choices that people make between civil liberties and personal security, one would conclude that the terrorist attack and government efforts to combat it have only a modest effect on transforming American society. If initial reactions were driven mostly by affective considerations, such as a sense of threat and vulnerability, trust in government, and patriotism, the preference for personal security over civil liberties might be only temporary. As the threat of terrorism subsides, so should the rally effects on trust in government and patriotism, and so too, perhaps, the willingness to cede rights to the government for the sake of greater security against terrorism. That after further consideration and a direct challenge to their antidemocratic beliefs, some people became even more willing to concede civil liberties, however, suggests a more serious threat to support for those liberties. It is easier to talk people into abandoning support for civil liberties than for security. Personal security concerns are probably anchored to more accessible and affective reactions to threat and a sense of vulnerability. Those who are already committed to a pro-security position become even more extreme in their personal security concerns after deliberation, despite efforts to dissuade them. Just how enduring these responses are requires considerably more attention. But there is little support for the idea that discussion and deliberation will lead people toward more moderate positions. Although the initial positions of African Americans on the civil liberties questions are also affected by their sense of threat, those with a greater sense of threat of terrorism are less likely to concede civil liberties for security, because blacks are concerned about both the threat from terrorism and the threat from government itself. This effect only grows as their civil liberties position is challenged. Again, differences in race and ethnicity are discussed in much greater detail in chapter 8. The chapter that follows deals in more detail with the idea of the "second thought," and its implications not only for bringing people to more moderate positions.

Chapter 6

Civil Liberties in an Evolving Context

THE SOBER second thought approach I used in the last chapter captured an important aspect of attitude stability: the extent to which individual citizens were willing to defend their security or civil liberties positions when confronted with the consequences of their initial preferences. In response to information challenging their attitudes, many respondents hardened their positions instead of moderating them, though respondents who initially preferred civil liberties were more likely to moderate their preferences than those who initially preferred security. This asymmetry is understandable, given the heightened sense of threat after the attacks of September 11, and my confrontational approach. But it implies that, over time, citizens might accept arguments favoring security and cave in to requests from political authorities. If this is now the "new normal" and the way people think about the trade-off between civil liberties and security, then the September 11 might have permanently weakened support for liberal democracy.

Whereas the response change in the persuasability approach discussed in chapter 5 took place in a matter of seconds, a long-term approach to assessing the stability of responses involves analyzing those same respondents at different points in time, but over a much longer time interval. With two additional panel waves of the national survey over three years, this chapter examines how individual citizens, and American society as a whole, might have changed over time.[1] The analysis centers around the belief that support for civil liberties is largely situational, and as the political and social context changed following the attacks, so did the clash over values. I argue that a heightened sense of threat and vulnerability, without the requisite trust in political authorities, diminishes the willingness to cede civil liberties. A new normal is likely to involve American citizens becoming accustomed to a sense of vulnerability, but not necessarily a willingness to sacrifice civil liberties for security.

Anticipating a New Normal

After the attacks, and efforts by political authorities to provide safety and security, American citizens were expected to adjust to a new way of life. The new normal involved getting used to excruciatingly long waits, pat-downs, and greater security in airports, sporting events, and concerts. Family members, friends, and neighbors were to be appreciated more and not taken for granted. Fast-paced hectic lives were to become more relaxing and enjoyable. More important, American citizens would have to adjust to greater limitations on their civil liberties and freedoms, through greater surveillance and monitoring of communications, racial and ethnic profiling, stricter immigration rules, and greater scrutiny of reading habits and financial records. A great deal of this monitoring would be unnoticeable. The public would also have to stomach violations of international laws protecting prisoners from abuse and torture.[2] However, because no other attacks occurred on American soil—except the brief anthrax scare, which many suspected was domestic—and as Americans returned to their routines, the new normal looked a lot like the old. People stopped giving to charities and volunteering. American flags displayed in front of homes and patriotic bumper stickers disappeared. Church attendance returned to pre–September 11 numbers, and old animosities resurfaced. Nevertheless, by many accounts, the attacks left an indelible imprint of vulnerability on American citizens. Correspondent Lisa Anderson of the *Chicago Tribune* observed that

> Of all the changes in all the 9/11-related statistics amassing day by day, one of the greatest, and perhaps most lasting, is the abrupt introduction of Americans to feelings of insecurity, fear, and vulnerability to terrorism on their soil. In the space of hours, Americans learned for themselves what people in so many other countries have known for years: No one truly is safe from terrorism. The attacks on the World Trade Center and the Pentagon did what the bombings in Oklahoma City in 1995 and at the World Trade Center in 1993 failed to do: galvanize a country grown complacent about its security and its role in the world. ("Changed Lives," *Chicago Tribune*, March 10, 2002, 1)

Following this line of thought, American citizens were expected to think differently about the world and no longer feel isolated from world problems, to mature, in some sense, and to take greater interest in U.S. policies and their effects on foreign citizens. That Americans would no longer be complacent about world events and possess a seemingly healthy concern about the risks of terrorism was a good thing. But political and social life can be quite precarious under a sustained sense of threat and vulnerability. In many respects, it is tantamount to becoming used to acquiescing to political authorities and accepting restrictions on civil liberties and freedom. Thus, a new normal characterized only by a greater sense of threat (chapter 4), can potentially lead to other changes, such as increased patriotism, intolerance toward dissimilar social groups (chapter 9), and, of course, a willingness to concede civil liberties for greater security. Although the threat of terrorism will likely lead to extra vigilance, the new normal might have dangerous consequences, especially if citizens under a sustained sense of threat vulnerability are prepared to continue to trade civil liberties for security. Knowing how this story has unfolded in the years since the attacks of September 11, I question the extent to which threat by itself can sustain the choice of security over liberty.

Expectations for Change

Support for freedom and liberty has been generally thought of as situational and dependent on context. We know from previous analysis that ardent supporters of freedom and liberty in one instance can become their opponents in another. This is a major theme throughout this book. People ordinarily protective of civil liberties can be made to accept restrictions on civil liberties, and vice versa. But, though there are clearly no absolutes, the changing political and social environment should shape the direction and magnitude of change in the trade-off between civil liberties and security. Different contexts give rise to different civil liberties issues and value conflict, but the contexts determine support for civil liberties to some extent, as previous research suggests.

In the first panel analysis of civil liberties decisions, James Gibson (2002) asks a fundamental question about how support for civil liberties among Russian citizens was affected by the changing political, social, and economic context during an uncertain democratic transitional period. Using the least-liked group approach to measure support for civil liberties in 1996 and 1998, Gibson found that Russian citizens were basically intolerant and that support for civil liberties was moderately stable. Although the percentage of Russians who would not tolerate their political enemies dropped from 79 percent in 1996 to 72 percent in 1998, the correlation between the civil liberties measures was very strong ($r = .40$), and 29 percent changed their positions. Despite the growing political chaos and uncertainty during the transitional period, perceptions of threat also remained stable. Greater support for civil liberties was seen as increasing a sense of threat. Most noteworthy, however, was the somewhat limited ability of cross-sectional explanations of tolerance to predict future tolerance. Although support for civil liberties was influenced much more by contemporaneous than by lagged factors, contextual factors, such as economic evaluations, meant little for civil liberties. Perceptions of threat increasingly explained support for civil liberties. Social disorder was seen as exacerbating feelings of threat, which in turn undermined political tolerance and support for democratic institutions (Gibson 2002, 316).

In a different democratic transition environment, Gibson and Gouws (2003) turned to South Africa to consider the extent of commitment to and durability of civil liberties decisions. Many South Africans, like the Russians, had little experience with liberal democratic norms and their applications. Both systems experienced the dismantling of oppressive governmental restrictions, and in South Africa the history of racial oppression and apartheid continued to influence support for civil liberties for groups that suffered under that system. Comparing least-liked measures of tolerance over a year and a half, Gibson and Gouws (2003) revealed incredible intolerance among South Africans. In 1996, 42 percent expressed tolerance toward their most threatened group, and this remained steady a year later in 1997. But underlying this aggregate-level stability was considerable individual-level movement. Reflecting a degree of asymmetry, 64 percent gave consistently tolerant responses, and 46 percent gave consistently intolerant responses. South Africans who more strongly supported civil liberties had more consistent attitudes than their counterparts. Broken down by race, the analysis uncovered a dramatically different story about stability and change in support for civil liberties. White South Africans basically developed more stable perceptions of civil liberties over time but their support was more directly connected to exogenous factors, such as crime. They were sensitive to changes in their environment, which held important consequences for perceptions of threat and tolerance. Black South Africans, on the other hand, had less stable attitudes and were also likely to be influenced by exogenous factors, such as crime or quality-of-life issues.

These two studies, spanning different societies and political experiences, nearly make up for the dearth of civil liberties panel data because they reveal components of civil liberties judgments that could not have been understood in cross-sectional analyses. First, aggregate measures of civil liberties can mask individual movement to support civil liberties. Support for civil liberties is mutable: connected to a larger set of beliefs about democracy and institutions, it nonetheless changes with the social and political context. Although it is almost impossible to determine this from aggregate measures, the staunch defender of freedom and liberty can become its antagonist, and vice versa. This view is consistent with one of the major themes of this book: that people support and defend democratic values most strongly when it is easy and convenient, but less when costs are tangible, such as tolerating a certain amount of vulnerability and uncertainty. Second, the origins of cross-sectional support for civil liberties, and the changes in support for civil liberties over time, are derived from the same explanations. Exogenous and societal factors may come into play in important ways, but, for the most part, changes in tolerance and civil liberties decisions are constrained by the environmental or situational factors in which they originated. Because the trade-off decisions made after the September 11 attacks are integrally connected to threat, political trust, patriotism, ideology, and racial perceptions in the cross-sectional analysis, understanding changes in those decisions should revolve around those factors as well. This may indeed be an oversimplification, but if we know what drives the decision to trade civil liberties for security and vice versa in the first place (chapter 4), then it is fairly straightforward to hypothesize that when those underlying drives change, so does the outcome of the decision. The model I use to assess change in the political environment therefore begins with cross-sectional explanations.

Research Design

Recall from the description of the data in chapter 1 that, respondents in my national survey conducted from November 2001 to January 2002 were also interviewed in two follow-up sessions. In the first (second-panel wave), conducted from January to May 2003, 679 first-wave respondents were interviewed a second time (46.9 percent of 1,448 first-wave respondents) and a new national sample was conducted (n = 1,284, 41.1 percent response rate). In the second (third-panel wave), conducted from July to November 2004, 342 of both first- and second-wave respondents and 811 second-wave respondents were interviewed again. Another new sample was conducted simultaneously, resulting in 960 respondents (49.4 percent response rate).

Following Donald Campbell and Julian Stanley (1963), the new national samples were intended to assess the internal validity of the panel results. Campbell and Stanley identified several threats to internal validity that could challenge substantive conclusions based on panel results, such as maturation, testing, and mortality.[3] Following the first-wave interviews, respondents may have become sensitized to questions about terrorism and politics that would bias their second-wave responses. Panel attrition can also bias second- and third-wave responses if there is a systematic reason for respondents not participating, such as interest and education. The mean differences in the dominant explanatory and demographic variables by panel participation are reported in appendix B. If the hypothesis is that panel participants are driven by a greater sense of threat, distrust, and support for civil liberties, this hypothesis is rejected. Although there are small differences between respondents who refused to participate in the first follow-up interview and respondents who agreed, the differences are not statistically significant. Support for civil liberties does not vary by participation. First-wave respondents who refused to participate in a follow-up survey were more personally threatened by the terrorist attacks than those who did participate. As is common in panel analyses, significant demographic differences were significant as well. Second-wave panel respondents also had less education, were younger, and were more likely to be white.

Because continued participation requires more time, interest, and stable residence, I suspected that the differences between the first and second waves would be somewhat magnified between the second and third waves. This seems to be the case when looking at the mean differences for new participants in the second wave who refused to participate in subsequent waves. This time, respondents who refused indicated higher levels of sociotropic and personal threat, and tended to be more conservative. As with the first- and second-wave differences, the demographic differences were also significant and should be controlled for in subsequent analyses.

Enduring Support for Civil Liberties

The analysis of change begins by examining the percentage of respondents who chose to protect civil liberties over enhancing security in the three waves. Panel A of table 6.1 shows the aggregate percentages for the individual items that comprise the trade-off scale for each wave. Based on the percentages across all three waves, reactions to policies in the three years following the attacks were highly stable in the aggregate; Americans' decisions concerning the trade-off between civil liberties and security did not change much. Most of the change is trivial and insignificant. Because the new interviews conducted simultaneously with the follow-up interviews differ little on most items, it is reasonable to assert that the results across the panels are not because of testing effects or panel attrition. If these findings hold up, it would be truly remarkable, because neither the passage of time nor the variety of events taking place after the terrorist attacks would be major consequences to the trade-off decision. Yet these are only aggregate results, which might mask individual movement.

Two civil liberties items in particular show a good measure of change (greater than 5 percent over three years): detaining noncitizens indefinitely and allowing teachers to criticize the government. Both measures move significantly toward supporting civil liberties. Slightly over half of the country (51 percent) supported detaining noncitizens indefinitely immediately after the attacks, but a year later, preference for civil liberties increased by 6 percent. A year after that, in 2004, it increased by 4 percent—a 10-percent rise over two years. I believe that when the indefinite detention of noncitizens was first discussed as a measure to combat terrorism, Americans only vaguely understood the policy and its implications. They were probably not aware that American citizens could also

Table 6.1 Analysis of Civil Liberties Trade-offs by Panel Waves

Panel A. Civil Liberties Responses

	Wave 1	Wave 2			Wave 3		
		Panel	New Case	t	Panel	New Case	t
Abstract	55	50	50	−.39	54	42	1.59
Identification cards	46	42	46	−.73	42	41	−2.23*
Guilt by association	28	25	24	.68	25	27	.86
Detain noncitizens	51	57	57	1.22	61	62	−1.52
Racial profiling	82	81	81	.48	80	85	1.17
Teachers criticize	38	50	47	−1.98*	53	48	−2.32*
Search and seizure	75	77	73	3.48**	74	74	−1.30
Wiretapping	65	61	60	.72	67	61	−.12
Nonviolent protest	90	92	88	2.85**	90	93	−.38
Total N	1,450	679	1,284		349	954	

Panel B. Cross-Tabulations by Wave 1 and Wave 2

	Wave 2					
Wave 1	High Security	Low Security	Moderate	Low Civil Liberties	High Civil Liberties	N
High security support	54	11	31	3	0	35
Low security support	21	22	43	8	5	134
Moderate	4	24	43	23	7	114
Low civil liberties support	3	7	38	30	21	229
High civil liberties support	2	1	9	21	67	163

$X^2(16) = 380.76$, $p = .000$

Source: National Civil Liberties Survey (2001, 2002).
Note: The civil liberties measure is the percentage of supportive responses on the nine civil liberties items. To simply the interpretation, the civil liberties measure was divided into five equal categories: 1 to 20 is high security support, 21 to 40 is low security support, 41 to 60 is moderate support, 61 to 80 is low support, and 81 to 100 is high support.
*p < .05; **p < .01.

be caught up in such a predicament, denied other legal rights, such as the right to legal representation, and possibly jailed for more than three years.[4] Others may have understood the issue, but nonetheless acquiesced to a popular presidential administration. However, as the detention policy unfolded, the frame of reference for American citizens should have also changed. Similarly, following the 9/11 attacks, more people supported teachers teaching loyalty and patriotism than criticizing the government. Over time, this support declined by 12 percent in the second wave, and by an additional 3 percent in the third wave, until 50 percent supported teachers' ability to criticize the government. Although there were many cases in which teachers were fired or reprimanded for making unpatriotic comments, American public and media attention on them was minimal. I suspect that, because this issue touches on a fundamental freedom of speech issue, the increased support reflects a broader move toward civil liberties.

The analysis of individual-level preferences in panel B of table 6.1 captures remarkable movement. One year later, individuals at both extremes of the trade-off decision were less likely to change their preferences than other respondents. More intensely held preferences, one way or the other, are more difficult to change. But the change is not symmetrical: 67 percent maintained their preference for civil liberties versus 54 percent for security. From the first to the second wave, 31 percent of respondents strongly favoring security switched to a moderate position, compared to only 9 percent of those strongly favoring civil liberties. Similarly, 43 percent switched from a low to a moderate security preference a year later, compared to 38 percent in the civil liberties camp. This direction of long-term movement contradicts the short-term results noted in chapter 5, in which intolerant or security preferences were less likely to change in response to counterarguments. With more time and a changing political climate, people found it easier to maintain their support for civil liberties than for security.

Between the two extremes, change in civil liberties trade-offs is almost evenly divided between civil liberties and security, but overall people became more protective of civil liberties than of security over time. Individuals who took a moderate position on the trade-off issue were more likely to change their positions than remain steadfast (43 percent), but those who did change were almost as likely to adopt a security (24 percent) as a civil liberties (23 percent) position. People rarely switched extremes; change was more incremental than dramatic. These findings were unexpected, and whether they reflect random change or can be explained by the shifting political climate is the next question I address.

Persistent Threat Perceptions

As the distance from September 11 increased with no other major attacks by foreign terrorists on American soil, the level of sociotropic threat and personal threat might reasonably be expected to diminish. Because there were reasons for American citizens to be optimistic and less anxious, they would be able to recover, albeit with a new appreciation of their vulnerability. The Taliban government and al Qaeda insurgents in Afghanistan, considered dominant sponsors of terrorism and Islamic fundamentalism, were handily defeated. Captured enemy combatants and al Qaeda operatives, instead of being released to foment further hatred and attacks against the United States, were held indefinitely at Guantánamo Bay, Cuba. Although the war with Iraq would require a sustained effort, the sitting Iraqi government was defeated and Saddam Hussein eventually captured—effectively crippling if not eliminating the country as a serious terrorist base. On the domestic front, law enforcement appeared to effectively uncover potential terrorist sleeper cells. In creating the Department of Homeland Security, the federal government was perceived as better prepared to deal with the threat of terrorism. Cities and local governments developed new procedures for emergency preparedness. Without the usual bickering, political leaders in Congress also conveyed a degree of calmness and civility, interacting with a new spirit of cooperation.

However, at the same time that American citizens found cause to be hopeful, they found many more reasons to remain anxious. Many events that were expected to make people feel safer had the opposite effect. As mentioned in chapter 1, individual reactions to threat were somewhat irrational in that they did not match the likelihood that people themselves would be involved in a terrorist attack. This was perfectly reasonable, however, given that the government and the media told them to be afraid and behaved as if there were reasons to be. The terror alert system, a color-coded warning system introduced in March 2002 to notify the country of heightened risks of terrorism, reminded people of their vulnerability and had the potential to stoke their fear.[5]

Additionally, government behavior and Bush administration policies that were supposed to make people safe, at least in the long term, had the short-term effect of making them more afraid. The unilateral invasions of Afghanistan and Iraq angered former allies and exacerbated tensions between them and the United States,[6] because the actions were seen as consistent with the type of policies that led to the hatred toward the United States that had contributed to the terrorist attacks in the first place. Americans saw themselves as basically standing alone in the fight against terrorism. Although the war in Iraq brought down a long-standing threat to the United States, it incurred U.S. casualties and was perceived as creating more terrorists throughout the Middle East. Osama bin Laden continued to elude capture, and threatened more attacks on American citizens through videotaped messages. Terrorist attacks abroad in Madrid, London, and Bali also reminded Americans of the continued threat.

In short, though there were reasons for citizens to feel both safer and more vulnerable, the framing of the terrorist threat by political authorities and the media had greater import than events intended to reduce perceptions of threat. A heightened sense of fear, anxiety, and threat is difficult to deactivate, especially when the dominant message is that the country continues to face serious threats. I do not expect perceptions of sociotropic threat to diminish significantly, and it is probably reasonable to expect that people became more threatened over time. Either way, sociotropic threat should remain high. As to personal perceptions of threat, American citizens as a whole did not exhibit this to any significant degree following the attacks. Given that no further terrorist events occurred except for the anthrax mail attacks, I do not expect personal threat to increase. The government always faces a dilemma in that talking to the public about preparedness may have an unintended consequence of raising concerns about an attack.

I analyze changing threat perceptions against this background. The reality, perhaps not surprisingly, is more complex than theoretical expectations. In panel A of table 6.2, I first compare the percentages of the combined "very concerned" or "somewhat concerned" responses to the individual threat items across the three waves of the survey. Beginning with sociotropic threat—the concern that the country as a whole will be attacked— there was a larger decline between the second and third waves than the first and second waves. Following the terrorist attacks, 85 percent were concerned that another attack would occur within the next six months. This level of concern declined slightly in the second wave.

The personal threat items fall considerably short of the level of concern pertaining to sociotropic threat, but because of the short-term events surrounding personal risk and vulnerability, the personal threat items show greater variability. This marks a critical difference between sociotropic and personal threat. Although sociotropic threat might be considered long-lived, personal threat is short-lived. People may find it easier to fear things beyond their immediate control.

In almost every instance, personal threat declined over the three years. The proportion of respondents who were "somewhat concerned" or "very concerned" about opening their mail declined from 33 percent in the first wave to 9 percent in the third; this is understandable, given the lack of a subsequent attack after the anthrax scare in the fall of 2001. Concern about being in tall buildings also declined, from 37 to 35 percent in wave 2, to 29 percent in wave 3. The concern over food and water safety declined from 46 percent in Wave 1, to 43 percent in wave 2, to 41 percent in wave 3. By contrast, the percentage who expressed concern about being in large crowds or stadiums did not decline from its initial level. I attribute this to events that occurred abroad after September 11, such as the terrorist attack in Bali (October 12, 2002), or perhaps a concern about possible retaliation by al Qaeda or Saddam Hussein for the at-

Table 6.2 Analysis of Threat Perceptions by Panel Waves (Percentages)

Panel A. Threat Responses

	Wave 1	Wave 2 Panel	Wave 2 New Case	t	Wave 3 Panel	Wave 3 New Case	t
Sociotropic threat	85	84	81	.48	80	79	.93
Flying in airplane	49	58	48	4.29**	40	48	−2.24**
Opening mail	33	17	27	−5.12**	9	21	−3.06**
Safety of food and water	46	43	52	−4.29**	41	49	−2.79**
Being in tall buildings	37	35	41	−3.93**	29	38	−2.62**
Being in stadiums or crowds	42	48	52	−2.99**	42	45	−.71
Mean personal threat	2.25	2.12	2.34	5.29**	2.09	2.24	2.91**
Total N	1,450	679	1,284		349	954	

Panel B. Cross-Tabulations by Wave 1 and Wave 2

	Wave 2 Threat Perceptions				
Wave 1 Threat Perceptions	Not at All Concerned	Not Very Concerned	Somewhat Concerned	Very Concerned	N
Not at all concerned	36	18	27	18	22
Not very concerned	13	34	38	15	82
Somewhat concerned	1	14	61	24	343
Very concerned	1	2	35	62	229

Source: National Civil Liberties Survey (2001, 2002).
Note: To simplify the analysis, response categories "Very concerned" and "Somewhat concerned" are combined in panel A.
$x^2(9) = 237.48; p = .000$

tack on Iraq, which began while the second wave was in the field. Moreover, concern for flying on an airplane increased in wave 2 by 9 percent, but by the third wave this was 9 percent lower than the immediate reaction following the September 11 attacks. Along with no airplane-related attacks or crashes occurring, the strict security measures in airports and by the airlines are probably linked to this reduced threat. In the end, when combining the personal threat items into a single index minimizes the idiosyncratic component of each item, I found that the sense of personal threat declined significantly over the three waves of the survey.

Panel B presents the cross-tabulations of sociotropic threat in the first and second waves. Based on these results, the aggregate responses obviously masked a great deal of movement among respondents. To the extent that panel participants changed, they became more threatened in the second wave. From the first to the second wave, 62 percent remained "very concerned" about another attack on the United States, and 61 percent remained "somewhat concerned." Relatively few who were concerned about another attack had a complete change of heart: 35 percent of those "very concerned" became "somewhat concerned," but 24 percent of those "somewhat concerned" became "very concerned."

However, more movement is evident among respondents who were initially not concerned about another attack. From the first to the second wave, 36 percent remained "not at all concerned" and 34 percent remained "not very concerned." Forty-five percent of respondents who were initially "not at all concerned" and 53 percent who were "not very concerned" became more concerned by the second wave. Of the respondents who were initially "not at all concerned," 45 percent became more so by the second wave, and of those initially "not very concerned," 53 percent did. Testing effects for sociotropic threat across the panel waves cannot account for the sizable change we see among individual respondents.

The question remains, however, whether these results reflect the levels and change in prevailing public opinion in the country over time, or whether instead they are at least to some degree a methodological artifact. Three survey organizations, CNN/USA Today/Gallup Poll, Pew Research Center, and CBS News, asked a version of the sociotropic threat question in national surveys. Illustrated in figure 6.1, these polls reveal an interesting pattern of sociotropic threat over time.[7] There was a consensus across survey organizations on the level of threat immediately following the terrorist attacks. Whereas CBS News, CNN/USA Today/Gallup, and my results showed 85 percent of the U.S. public was threatened by another attack, Pew Research Center reported 73 percent. I cannot show the immediate decline in threat that all of the polling organizations show after the attacks and the general pattern reflected in their results, but by the anniversary of the attacks the level of threat increased. My second wave results show a very slight decline (83 percent), but only the CBS News polls show a similarly high level (80 percent). During this time, CNN/USA Today/Gallup report the lowest level of threat (62 percent) and the Pew polls report a higher level (73 percent). However, by the time of my third wave, the level of sociotropic threat across the survey organizations dramatically diverged. I continued to show a high level of threat around 80 percent, but the nearest CBS News poll reported 71 percent and the CNN/USA Today/Gallup poll reported 51 percent.

That I show consistently higher levels of perceived sociotropic threat than the Gallup, CBS News, and Pew polls is probably due to several factors. First, my surveys were all about terrorism and civil liberties, beginning with the "informed consent" that solicits the participation of the re-

Figure 6.1 Sociotropic Threat Measures Over Time

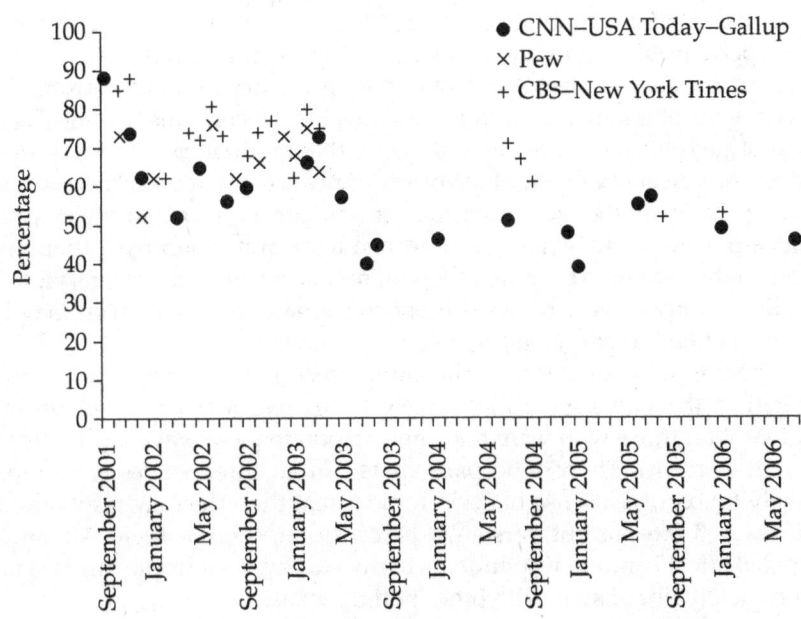

CBS–New York Times Poll:
How Likely Do You Think It Is that There Will Be Another Terrorist Attack in the United States Within the Next Few Months? (Very Likely and Somewhat Likely Combined)

USA Today–Gallup Poll:
How Likely Is It that There Will Be Further Acts of Terrorism in the United States over the Next Several Weeks? (Very Likely and Somewhat Likely Combined)

Pew Research Center:
How Worried Are You that There Will Soon Be Another Terrorist Attack in the United States? (Very Worried and Somewhat Worried Combined)

Source: Author's compilation of data from CNN–USA Today–Gallup Poll, Pew Research Center, CBS–New York Times Poll.

spondents in a survey "about events that have taken place since September 11."[8] Although the questions about perceptions of threat were at the beginning of my questionnaire, respondents may have been self-selected to some degree based on their being more concerned about terrorism than the average person. Second, the volatility in levels of sociotropic threat shown in the Gallup, CBS News, and Pew Surveys may be partly a product of the fact that the surveys are typically in the field just a few days and are subject to the short-term influences of the news of the day. It may also be affected by survey content and question order. I can only speculate that if respondents are cued to think about the threat of terrorism, perhaps by previous questions in a survey and a reference to specific events, they are more likely to say they are worried about terrorism—even without taking into account the possible effects of the historical context of each survey. Third, another factor that might increase the reported levels of perceived threat of terrorism in my second and third wave surveys is their multiwave character. Respondents who were interviewed in an earlier survey may have been primed to be more concerned about terrorism the next time they are called for an interview, or those interviewed in a previous wave who were more concerned about terrorism may be more inclined to participate in a subsequent wave.

There is some evidence of the latter effect. Respondents who participated in the panel were more likely to express a sense of sociotropic threat than those who were first-time respondents in wave 2 (84 percent vs. 81 percent). Those who participated in all three waves were more likely to express a sense of sociotropic threat than the new respondents in wave 3 (86 percent versus 78 percent). So, though there is a small "panel effect" among respondents to my survey, sociotropic threat is not completely out of sync with other polling results.

Among several factors discussed in chapter 4, sociotropic threat is the most important one affecting the trade-off between civil liberties and security, though it is quite possible for other motivations, such as political trust, to overshadow threat. Sociotropic threat and support for civil liberties seem to move in different directions one year after the attacks. For different reasons, the durability (and slight increase) in sociotropic threat should have translated into a greater willingness to concede civil liberties for security, but instead individuals came to support civil liberties more rather than less—contradicting theoretical expectations. I suspect that such a divergence will weaken the relation between the trade-off decision and sociotropic threat, though I do not expect it to change direction—that is, as threat increases, so will the willingness to trade civil liberties for security.

Because the relation between support for civil liberties and sociotropic threat has been uncommonly powerful throughout this book and in the political tolerance literature, I consider their relation with the panel data in a simple two-variable model at each time point. Figure 6.2 shows the correlations in the simplified model of the dynamics of civil liberties trade-offs and sociotropic threat. Consistent with previous analyses, civil liberties trade-off decisions are stable across the three years following the attacks. Sociotropic threat is relatively stable as well, but less so than support for civil liberties. Although the correlation between them dimin-

Figure 6.2 Correlations Between Civil Liberties and Sociotropic Threat Across Panel Waves

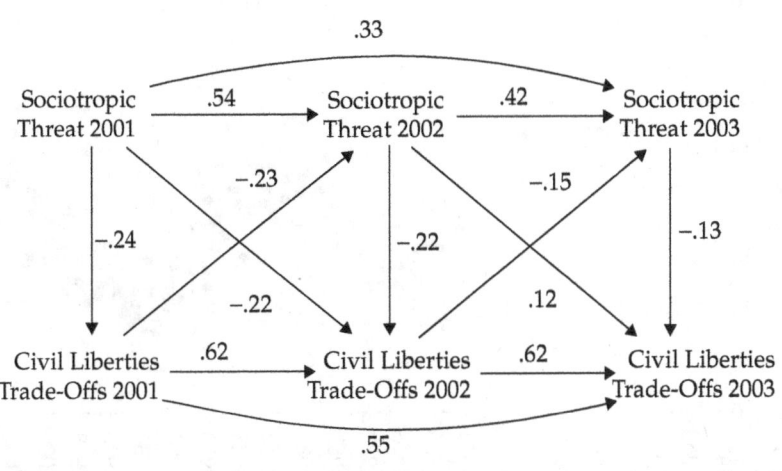

Source: Author's compilations.

ishes over time, it remains relatively strong. In the immediate aftermath of September 11, the bivariate correlation is −.24. The sign is in the right direction, but it declines to −.22 in 2002. Two years after the attacks, it declines again to −.13. A similar weakening role of threat can also be seen in the lagged correlations with support for civil liberties. Thus, departing from the cross-sectional analysis in chapter 4, the bivariate relationship between sociotropic threat and civil liberties using panel data suggests a much weakened relation. Which of the remaining factors will be able to account for the increased support for civil liberties?

Declining Trust

Whereas threat and vulnerability were the most dramatic consequence of the September 11 attacks, by far the most dramatic change in the years that followed involved the declining trust in political authorities and the support for President Bush in particular. As noted in chapter 4, the immediate aftermath witnessed a general acquiescence and unprecedented increase in political trust, despite cynicism toward government about the 2000 presidential elections (Price and Romantan 2004). As illustrated in the monthly percentage of political trust in figure 6.3, not since the Kennedy administration in the mid-1960s has political trust breached 60 percent. Domestic issues, dissatisfaction with the Vietnam War, and Watergate in the late 1960s and early 1970s began a gradual decline in trust

Negative Liberty

Figure 6.3 Political Trust Over Time

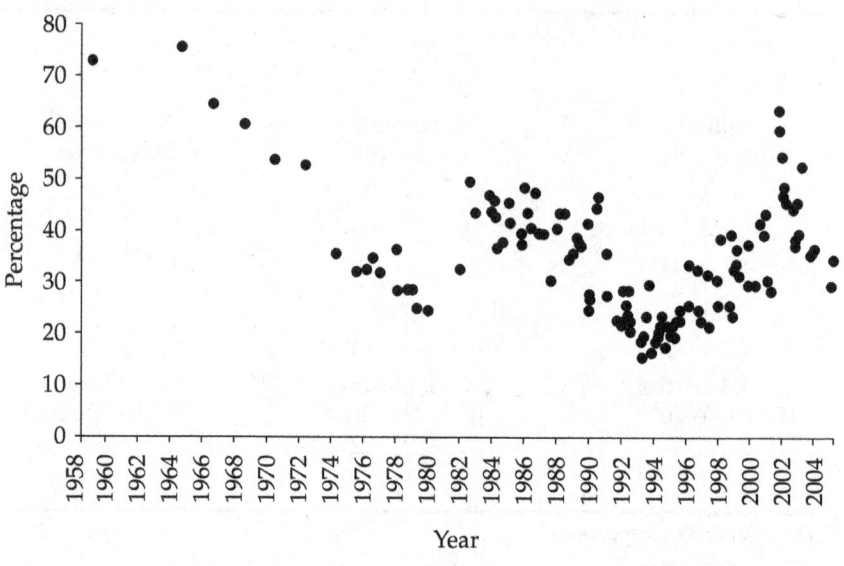

Source: Author's compilations from Gallup polls.

that bottomed out in 1980. It recovered briefly with the first Reagan administration, but by the end of the 1980s it was in another downturn. By 1994, it was at its lowest level since the measure had been introduced, but afterward fluctuated without fully recovering. Polling data taken in March 2001 indicated that 30 percent of American citizens said they trusted the government "just about always" or "most of the time." After the attacks, Gallup data indicated that 65 percent trusted the government. This tide of good will was short lived. By December 2001, polling data revealed that trust in government had declined to 49 percent. This decline is supported by my data as well, in which 51 percent of American citizens trusted the government. The high level of political trust, which it ultimately could not sustain, gave the government considerable flexibility in conducting the antiterrorist campaign. The increase in trust was a direct result of the terrorist attacks and the decrease was a reaction to governmental efforts to provide for the safety and security from terrorism, such as the Patriot Act and the challenge to civil liberties.

The attacks of September 11 reflect an incredible period of partisan and ideological depolarization, in which individuals placed greater faith in the government and expected the government to protect them in turn. Because of their sense of threat and patriotism, people were probably willing to give the government the benefit of the doubt; likewise, the decline in trust over time is tied to the perceived ability of government to provide safety and security. Given that political trust is directly related to the evaluation of the government's performance, the events and behavior that reminded individuals of their continued sense of vulnerability also led them to doubt political authorities and the Bush administration. This is exactly what I found in examining the relation between sociotropic threat and political trust. As threat increased, individuals trusted political authorities more. However, over time, this relationship diminished: people who were most threatened by the attacks remained threatened, but their trust in government declined. The neat relation between political trust and threat following the attacks thus became misaligned. This is to be expected, given events such as the release of the 9/11 Commission report and the false pretenses under which President Bush invaded Iraq.

Across the three-wave interviews, trust in the federal government declined over time (see table 6.3). The largest decline occurred between the second and third waves, but over all three, political trust declined from the initial 51 percent who said the government in Washington could be trusted "almost always" or "most of the time" by 14 percent. The new samples conducted alongside the follow-up interviews indicate that testing effects or panel attrition may have influenced this decline in political trust.

The aggregate decline in trust is also reflected in individual responses. In panel B of table 6.3, individuals on the low end of political trust were more stable in their opinions than those at the high end. At both extremes, however, an almost equal percentage of respondents moved in opposite directions, potentially canceling the movement: 26 percent of respondents who never trusted government remained in the same position by the second wave, but 48 percent softened their position by trusting some of the time, and 26 percent by trusting most of the time. Likewise, 28 percent of respondents who always trusted government in the first wave did not change, but 49 percent moderated by trusting most of the time in the second wave, and 23 percent by trusting some of the time. The most unequal movement is toward less trust, with 38 percent of those who trusted the government most of the time in the first wave switching to some of the time in the second. Given these explanations, decline in trust in the government, more than sociotropic threat, should contribute to a decline in people's willingness to cede civil liberties to the government to fight terrorism.

Panel C in table 6.3 shows the relationship between another aspect of trust: perceptions of whether government is run by a few big interests or for the benefit of all. It is clear that whereas people who consider it run by a few big interests are more consistent across the first two waves (83 percent), a smaller percentage of those who consider it run for the benefit of all are (67 percent). I take this as further evidence of the decline in

Table 6.3 Analysis of Political Trust by Panel Waves, 2001 and 2002 (Percentages)

Panel A. Political Trust Measures

	Wave 1	Wave 2 Panel	Wave 2 New Case	t	Wave 3 Panel	Wave 3 New Case	t
Trust government to do what is right	51	47	48	1.66	46	36	−2.02**
Government run for the benefit of all	52	42	48	2.03*	42	43	1.36
Total N	1,450	679	1,284		349	954	

Panel B. Wave 1 and Wave 2 of Cross-Tabulations of "Trust Government to Do What Is Right"

Wave 1 Trust Perceptions	Wave 2: Never	Wave 2: Some of the Time	Wave 2: Most of the Time	Wave 2: Always	N
Never	26	48	26	0	27
Some of the time	3	73	23	1	291
Most of the time	1	38	54	7	290
Always	0	23	49	28	57

Panel C. Wave 1 and Wave 2 Cross-Tabulations of "Government Run for the Benefit of All"

Wave 1 Trust Perceptions	Wave 2: Government Run by a Few Big Interests	Wave 2: Government Run for the Benefit of All	N
Government run by a few big interests	81	19	284
Government run for the benefit of all	33	67	284

Source: National Civil Liberties Survey (2001, 2002, 2004).
Note: For "trust government to do what is right," "Always" and "Most of the time" are combined in Panel A.
$x^2(9) = 203.27$; $p = .000$ for Panel B.
$x^2(9) = 139.07$; $p = .000$ for Panel C.

support for the political authorities or the incumbent administration a year after the attacks.

Change in Patriotism

As mentioned in earlier chapters, the country saw a renewed sense of pride and patriotism following the attacks of September 11. These sentiments created a new sense of national identity. Because this faith was more emotional than evaluative, it should be quite durable and capable of absorbing negative evaluations of government. As American citizens return to their routines, it can be expected to be a part of what I have called the new normal. Because patriotism is more symbolic of the country and the national community, it is not expected to follow the ebbs and flows of the government the way that political trust and presidential approval do. As presented in table 6.4, an overwhelming percentage of American citizens were proud to be American following the attacks and in subsequent waves. Following the attacks, 78 percent said they were "very proud" to be an American and 14 percent said they were "proud." Very few indicated that they felt no pride. A year later, the combined percentage expressing pride declined by 4 percent, and a year after that, it remained very high (87 percent). Individual change (panel B) indicates that few respondents became less prideful over the first two years.

There are different ways to interpret these results. My take is that, perhaps due in large part to the war in Iraq and support for American troops, American citizens were able to separate their sense of pride from their feelings about political authorities.

Explaining Change in Panel Responses

To assess the explanations of individual change in the trade-off decision, a dependent variable of change is created by taking the difference between the percentages of civil liberties responses in the second wave and the first wave. This measure is repeated using the appropriate items for change from the second and third waves. A positive value indicates increased support for civil liberties. Following the theoretical rationale developed in chapter 4, the independent variables include perceptions of sociotropic and personal threat, as well as change in the level of trust in the government and in national pride. A set of control variables is also included (race, ethnicity, age, gender, and education).

Table 6.5 reports OLS regression results for the first- and second-wave panel and the second- and third-wave panel. The panels analyze the same respondents, though many refused to participate in successive interviews, and others could not be recontacted. Nevertheless, for the sizable number who participated in my study, the results follow expectations. First, the previous level of support for civil liberties is a counter-

Table 6.4 Analysis of Patriotism by Panel Waves (in Percentages)

Panel A. Proud to Be an American

	Wave 1	Wave 2 Panel	Wave 2 New Case	Wave 3 Panel	Wave 3 New Case
Very proud	78	74	72	72	70
Proud	14	14	17	17	18
Somewhat proud	9	9	8	8	7
Not very proud	2	2	3	3	5
Total N	1,450	679	1,284	349	954

Panel B. Cross-Tabulation of Proud to Be an American by Wave 1 and Wave 2

Wave 1 Pride Perceptions	Wave 2 Pride Perceptions				
	Not Very	Somewhat	Proud	Very Proud	N
Not very	45	27	0	28	11
Somewhat	12	50	21	17	34
Proud	1	21	40	38	97
Very proud	1	4	9	87	509

Source: National Civil Liberties Survey (2001, 2002, 2004).
Note: To simplify the analysis, "Not very proud" and "Not proud at all" were combined to form four categories for Panel A.
$x^2(16) = 502.69$; $p = .000$ for Panel B.

weight to subsequent support for civil liberties. A higher previous level is associated with a decline in support for civil liberties over time. Individuals who previously valued security over civil liberties become more likely to support civil liberties in the future, and vice versa. In other words, people were likely to moderate their views over time.

Second, as expected, change in sociotropic threat did not produce a statistically significant influence on change in the trade-off decisions. Although a previous sense of sociotropic threat made people more concerned about security than civil liberties in the third wave, sociotropic threat lost its power to predict change. In these analyses, sociotropic threat and the trade-off decisions were only moderately related, and appeared to evolve in different directions. Threat tended to increase slightly over time, but respondents who were probably most threatened initially began to moderate their security positions more than those who had held civil liberties positions.

Third, higher initial trust in government, as well as increasing trust in

Table 6.5 OLS Regression Coefficients of Explanations of Change in Civil Liberties Trade-Offs

	Change from Wave 1 to Wave 2	Change from Wave 2 to Wave 3
Civil liberties (wave 1 or 2)	−.43** (.04)	−.43** (.05)
Sociotropic threat (wave 1 or 2)	−.37 (1.28)	−2.84 (1.73)
Change in sociotropic threat	−.39 (1.25)	−2.06 (1.55)
Political trust (wave 1 or 2)	−3.11** (.51)	−1.46* (.70)
Change in political trust	−.87 (.53)	−2.37** (.73)
Patriotism (wave 1 or 2)	−2.56 (1.60)	−1.36 (1.80)
Change in patriotism	−2.64 (1.49)	−1.30 (1.90)
Ideology	−.47 (.77)	−3.29** (.99)
African American	5.16* (2.78)	8.55* (3.65)
Latino	3.45 (2.89)	−14.00** (5.51)
Female	−2.53 (1.62)	5.70** (2.09)
Constant	55.57** (8.69)	60.50 (10.37)
R^2/adjusted R^2	.25/.23	.33/.30
Root MSE	18.17	16.37
N	520	275

Source: National Civil Liberties Survey (2001, 2002, 2004).
*p < .05; **p < .01.

government over time, is associated with a greater willingness to trade civil liberties for greater security. Both regression coefficients are large and statistically significant. As a result, political trust plays a more important role in the extent to which people were willing to change their trade-off decisions. Among the explanatory factors, political trust declined the most over the three years after 9/11.

Fourth, despite significant reductions in the sample proportion of African Americans in the subsequent waves, race continues to be a very important factor shaping support for civil liberties. The positive coefficient for blacks indicates that, everything else being equal, they were more likely than whites to support civil liberties more strongly a year later. This overwhelming support is consistent with findings in chapters 4 and 5. By the third panel wave, blacks are no longer distinctive, but again, some caution should be used, given the reduced number of black panel respondents.

Overall, the major factors accounting for the level of support for civil liberties in the cross-sectional analysis reported in chapter 4 are also important in accounting for change in support for civil liberties over time. Perhaps the most telling result of our examination of longitudinal change in support for civil liberties, however, is that change in sociotropic threat does not have nearly the impact of change in political trust. Another way to look at the relative strength of the various explanations is to compare the standardized variables across each period. Table 6.6 reports the standardized OLS coefficients for each cross-section. Several important conclusions can be drawn from this table. Consistent with the noted results, sociotropic threat and trust were the two most important explanations of the trade-off decision in the immediate aftermath of the attacks (chapter 4). A year later, sociotropic threat and political trust declined significantly in importance, being surpassed by political ideology and patriotism. In 2004, however, although ideology and patriotism retained their relevance, trust regained its potency and sociotropic threat remained significant, but not as powerful in the immediate aftermath.

Table 6.6 Cross-Sectional Determinants of Civil Liberties Trade-Offs (Standardized Regression Coefficients)

	Wave 1	Wave 2	Wave 3
Sociotropic threat	−.17**	−.05**	−.08**
Personal threat	−.05	−.07	.03
Political trust	−.19**	−.06**	−.16**
Ideology	−.17**	−.22**	−.25**
Patriotism	−.17	−.16**	−.17**
African American	.10**	.10*	.08**
Latino	−.04	.02	−.01
Gender (1 = female)	−.02	−.02	−.12**
Education	.07	.03**	.05*
	N = 1226	N = 1671	N = 1509

Source: National Civil Liberties Survey (2001, 2002, 2004).
*p <. 05; **p < .01.

The Patriot Act

Although the focus has been on the underlying civil liberties issues that the Patriot Act raised, an interesting question is how effective citizens perceived the act in combating terrorism. Do the factors that drive the trade-off decision also drive the explicit support for the act? Despite President Bush's having signed the act into law on October 26, 2001, no survey questions addressed this issue in the first wave of the data.

I included a question on the effects of the Patriot Act on security in the two subsequent surveys. From the distribution of responses to this question, shown in figure 6.4, few people thought that the act itself would decrease their security. Although 31 percent thought it would have little impact, twice as many (62 percent) thought it would heighten security. This is a ringing endorsement, despite the problems that some citizens have with certain aspects of the legislation. The Patriot Act was viewed positively and as increasing security against terrorism. Despite the controversy, which involved allegations of civil rights abuses and a desire in the Bush administration to make certain temporary provisions permanent, perceptions of effectiveness remained high. There was only a 4 percent decline in the perceived effectiveness of the Patriot Act from 2002 to 2004. Thus, though people were willing to move to a more civil libertar-

Figure 6.4 Perceptions of Effect of Patriot Act on Security, 2002 and 2003

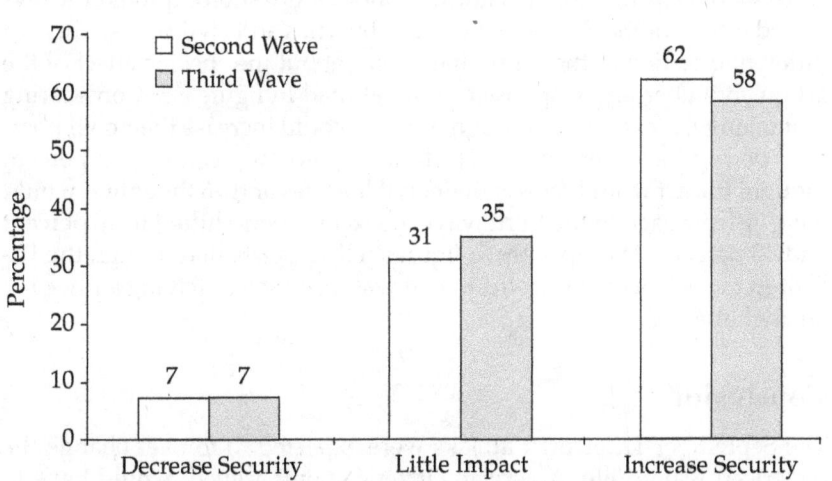

Source: National Civil Liberties Survey (2002, 2003).

Figure 6.5 Perceptions of Effect of Patriot Act on Civil Liberties, 2002 and 2003

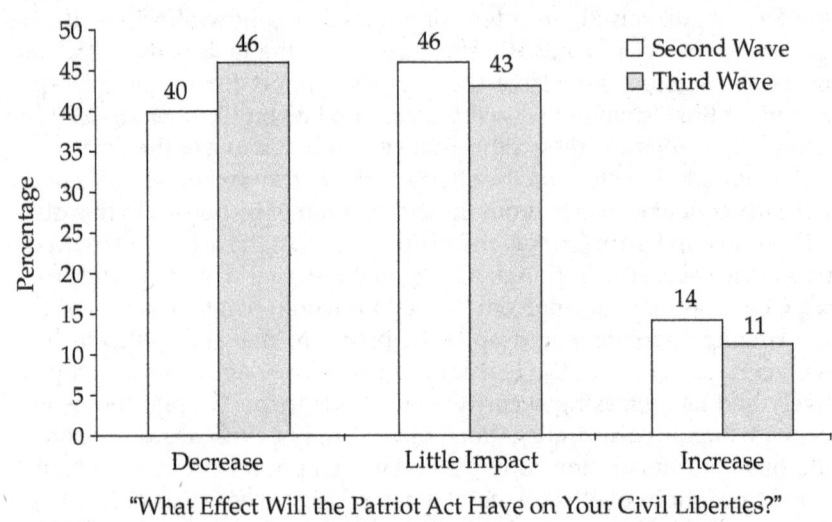

"What Effect Will the Patriot Act Have on Your Civil Liberties?"

Source: National Civil Liberties Survey (2002, 2003).

ian position after the attacks, support for the Patriot Act faltered only slightly.

To shed some light on this finding, another question explored the perceived effects of the Patriot Act on civil liberties and civil rights. This is a different question in the sense that it asks about the specific effect of the act on civil liberties. Responses are illustrated in figure 6.5. Considering that relatively few people thought the act would increase their civil liberties, perceptions were basically divided into two camps: 40 percent thought the act would reduce their civil liberties and 46 thought it would have little impact. In the third wave, these numbers shifted to 46 percent and 43 percent. The story these figures tell suggests that though the Patriot Act was perceived as effective, it was also seen as having a price tag on civil liberties.

Conclusion

The September 11 terrorist attacks were expected to forever change the American way of life. American citizens, many argued, would have to get used to a new normal, in which their well-being would be connected to that of the rest of world, and in which they would have to tolerate greater limitations on their civil liberties and freedom. I show that this story is partially correct. Americans have become more sensitive to the outside threats the country faces, and this perception (sociotropic threat) has remained quite stable. Not only did the attacks lead to intense feelings of vulnerability, but many of the events intended to reduce the threat of terrorism in the long term also increased their sense of vulnerability in the short term. America now lives with a certain understanding of risk and vulnerability. "The new normal," according to a *USA Today* article two years after the attacks, "can recognize terrorist risks, without being paralyzed by them" ("A New Normal, Post-9/11," September 10, 2003, A-11).

Despite this, American citizens are not as willing to cede their civil liberties for greater security as they were immediately after the attacks. Though aggregate support for civil liberties changed only slightly in the three years after the attacks, individual citizens showed considerable movement. Those who initially supported enhancing security over protecting civil liberties were more likely to moderate their positions. What has also changed is the potency of the underlying factors that influenced trade-off decisions. Although perceptions of threat have lost some of their potency, political trust became more important in determining support for civil liberties. Clearly, it takes both a heightened sense of threat and trust in political authorities for Americans to be willing to give up civil liberties for a long period, even in times of a national crisis.

Chapter 7

Spiral of Silence: Partisan Orientations in a Climate of Threat

IN THE discussion so far, ideology has been an important consideration in understanding how individuals responded to the terrorist attacks of September 11. For the most part, political conservatives were more willing than moderates and liberals to concede freedom for greater security. But chapter 4 suggested that when exposed to a heightened sense of threat, liberals and moderates began to resemble conservatives in valuing security over civil liberties. The broader political discourse at the time reflected a similar ideological convergence among Democrats, who appeared to tolerate restricting civil rights and liberties—political values they have faithfully defended.[1]

Democrats and, to a lesser extent, political moderates would have had to ignore their traditional civil libertarian values to acquiesce to the administration's policies increasing safety and security, though dissenting by supporting democratic and constitutional values would have been seen as disloyal and unpatriotic. Whether Democrats shifted their political views by supporting issues they would not ordinarily support or simply remained silent, the effects of political trust and patriotism raised important questions about the utility of traditional partisan orientations in structuring individual reactions. By examining the behavior of political partisans in the context of the 9/11 attacks, I attempt to provide some insight into this "spiral of silence" (Noelle-Neumann 1993)—the unwillingness to voice objections to policies that seem to receive overwhelming endorsement, and that would portray the objectors in a highly unfavorable light.

How important were traditional partisan orientations in helping individual citizens understand the trade-off between civil liberties and personal security? Under normal circumstances, partisanship, beyond its close association with political ideology, is extremely useful in structuring political behavior and helping individuals make sense of politics. But how stable and meaningful are partisan positions when individuals are exposed to a heightened sense of threat, and when patriotism, trust in political authorities, and the nature of politics become especially one-sided? I argue that traditional partisan orientations lose their ability to structure civil liberties decisions during periods of ideological depolarization because they become misaligned with traditional partisan preferences. Threat may be involved, but other factors, such as a sense of patriotism, should take on added importance. As politics repolarize with increasing levels of political distrust, partisan orientations regain their predictability and realign with political ideology. Several competing explanations, however, such as the nature of change and partisans' ability to hold discordant political preferences, need to be addressed as well.

Conceptualizing Party Identification

The questions I raise in this chapter assume a conceptualization of party identification that allows simultaneously for discordant political preferences and a certain degree of partisan stability. These requirements are at odds with the traditional view of party identification, which suggests that people have deeply held psychological orientations or enduring attachments to political parties (Campbell et al. 1960).[2] Acquired through early political socialization, identification with a political party, for the most part, is expected to survive the ebb and flow of elections and campaigns, societal events, and lifestyle changes. Partisan attachment is so critical in understanding politics that Angus Campbell and his colleagues (1960) argue that, "identification with a party raises a perceptual screen through which the individual tends to see what is favorable to his orientation. The stronger the party bond, the more exaggerated the process of selection and perceptual distortion will be" (133). Discordant information is essentially ignored, because party identification is seen as almost impervious to change, except in extreme circumstances. This makes party identification primarily an exogenous variable to the electoral process and societal events, and a base or core orientation to politics: Democrats are more likely to vote for Democratic candidates and view the policies of Democratic administrations more favorably than those of Republicans, and vice versa. It has been the standard against which most attitude change is considered.

This traditional view of party identification has come under increasing attack, but its most limiting aspect involves its unresponsiveness to political events. The revisionist critique of the psychological attachment points out that party identification does change, that individuals do hold discordant political views, and that political events and increased information can indeed modify political orientations. According to Morris Fiorina (1981), party identification should be seen as a "running tally" of past evaluations of the performance and policies of political parties. Although initial socialization experiences may influence party identification, "as time passes, as the citizen experiences politics, party id comes more and more to reflect the events that transpire in the world" (90). Party identification is both a cause and consequence of political attitudes. Discordant political views may exist to the extent that unflattering information may be a part of the tally of information, but they may not outweigh positive evaluations. Party identification is stable to the extent "that political parties favor the same sides of various socioeconomic cleavages over time, and its citizens find themselves in the same socioeconomic circumstances over time" (91). Individuals are likely, however, to update their partisan orientations if party positions become inconsistent, new political and social issues arise, or their own circumstances change.

The revisionist conceptualization of partisanship is attractive in its ability to reflect the dynamics and dissonance of partisanship, but its malleability can only be taken so far. In a period of depolarization immediately following the terrorist attacks, when Democrats viewed the Bush administration's policies more favorably,[3] a running-tally conceptualization of partisanship seems too malleable, as it is probably unreasonable to expect individuals to shift their allegiance in response to rally events (Norrander and Wilcox 1993). Nevertheless, I do not want to abandon this view, because it does allow partisans to hold discordant ideological views that an overly rigid and strict psychological attachment conceptualization disavows.

There is a neat solution, in that both views of party identification can work together. Donald Green, Bradley Palmquist, and Eric Schickler (2002) synthesize them to capture both the dynamics and stability of partisanship. As people develop affinities and attachments to political parties akin to their attachments to religious and social groups, they continue to evaluate and use information. Discordant political views can be expected to arise because party identification outlasts negative and unflattering information. Individuals can become aware of deficient and negative aspects of their group attachments without changing them. Partisan attachments shape the way individuals evaluate political candidates and policies, but "seldom does the political environment change in ways that alter how people think of themselves or their relationship to significant social groups" (23). Green and his colleagues maintain that "people may assimilate new information about the parties and change their perceptions of the parties without changing the team for which they cheer" (8). Building on this synthesis, individual preferences can be changed, but the way people think about political parties is slow to do so. As with any other form of political or social attachment, partisanship provides self-esteem and becomes a part of a person's self-concept. Like an attachment to a social group, a partisan identity helps individuals structure their thoughts about the world, political events, and political candidates. Affinity for one's political party and enmity for the opposing one can be expected to fluctuate with one's agreement with the party positions, performance, and representatives. As a necessary first step, I will determine whether party identification behaves according to expectations. After the attacks, did party identification change, like a running evaluation of party performance, or did it remain relatively stable, like a form of psychological attachment?

The Stability of Party Identification

The extent to which party identification is stable and responsive to short-term political and social events has been somewhat controversial. My measures of macro-partisanship and time-series analyses of aggregate levels of partisanship paint a different picture of partisan stability than analyses based on panel data do. This is not the first time that the political behavior of respondents has differed in the aggregate from individual-level behavior (Davis 2000; Davis and Davenport 1999; Kramer 1983).[4] Studies of macro-partisanship suggest that changes in party affiliation, usually based on Gallup party affiliation, are related to short-term factors, such as the economy, consumer sentiment, presidential approval, and political events, such as wars and international crises (MacKuen, Erikson, and Stimson 1989). The basic argument is that the more popular a sitting president, the more attractive it is to be affiliated with his party. As party affiliations change according to political evaluations, they are viewed as more malleable. Analyses of party identification of panel data, on the other hand, show incredible stability, challenging the revisionist conceptualization. As with other ecological issues, the difference between aggregate and individual-level analyses probably reflects different processes, though Paul Abramson and Charles Ostrom (1994) have argued that it may be an artifact of measurement.

My interest lies with micro-partisanship, but I also draw on aggregate data to contextualize the micro-level results.[5] Previous studies using panel data have found very high levels of partisan stability. Converse (1964), analyzing data from 1956, 1958, and 1960, and Converse and Gregory Markus (1979), analyzing data from 1972, 1974, and 1976, find that individual partisanship remained fairly consistent in tracking the same individuals over time. Individual partisanship did move, but very slightly. Kent Jennings and Markus (1984) show that, among their parental sample (taken in 1965, 1973, and 1982), party identification was highly stable. The correlation between party identification from 1965 to 1973 was .67; from 1973 to 1982, .70. Party identification was more stable than other political and personal orientations, such as civic tolerance, political trust, political knowledge, self-confidence, and church attendance. Over time, it became more stable. Tom Rice and Tracey Hilton (1996) show across a variety of panel studies, such as the Kent Jennings and Gregory Marcus (1984) data and the NES Panel Studies of 1956, 1980, and 1992, that a large percentage of respondents do not shift their partisanship across three panel waves, and most who do move no more than three contiguous places on the scale. Only a few can be said to have changed their partisan stripes. The analogy of individuals as "tethered by a loyalty" has been used to describe individual-level change in partisanship (Rice and Hilton 1996). In a different form of analysis examining the same measure across different waves, the correlation between before and after measures of party identification was .86 (Dreyer 1973). Abramson and Ostrom (1994) report a similar stability in party identification using a four-wave panel survey. Using the traditional SRC measure of party identification ("generally speaking"), 74 percent of respondents remained consistent across four waves. Even though the Gallup poll ("as of today") was less stable than the SRC measure, it too showed unexpected stability: 61 percent in the four-wave survey and 74 percent in a three-wave survey. Abramson and Ostrom argue that most of the change is a function of respondents moving into and out of the independent category, as opposed to partisans changing affiliation.

I assess party identification against this background of stability. My expectations for the stability of party identification and affiliation following the September 11 attacks are somewhat ambiguous. From one perspective, it would seem that the incredible popularity of President Bush at the time, the rise in political trust, a heightened sense of threat, and a surge in patriotic sentiments could shake independents and Democrats from their partisan orientations. The terrorist attacks are the type of cataclysmic event commonly viewed as capable of shifting party affiliations. If there were any reason to switch partisan orientations, even temporarily, the most horrific attack on American soil by foreign terrorists might be one. On the other hand, given the prior polarization and ideological differences between the political parties, abandoning traditional orientations is no simple task and should not be taken lightly. What people have to accept, and what they become if their allegiances do change, have to be weighed against their willingness to change. The context of September 11 was more than the attacks; it also involved restricting civil liberties, diminishing the rights of citizens, and denying that U.S. foreign policy facilitated hatred abroad—issues that Democrats would try to capitalize on in the 2004 presidential election. This did not necessarily create a climate conducive to partisan conversion. On the contrary, to the extent that Democrats perceived the immediate post-9/11 atmosphere as incompatible with their values, political conversion was highly unlikely. With a heightened sense of threat and patriotism, Democratic partisans were simply willing to suffer in silence, acquiesce, and tolerate a certain amount of dissonance to solve the pressing problems facing the country. Partisans can, and frequently do, support opposing party positions without feeling pressure to change their attachments.[6] Despite prior polarizing views, Democrats operating from a variety of motivations (such as fear, threat, patriotism) could be expected to support the policies of a Republican president, and their willingness to acquiesce need not be interpreted as acceptance or conversion. As mentioned, it could have been simply tolerance, or fear of being seen as un-American, as disloyal, or as weak. Meanwhile, their existing partisan orientation may have strengthened. This is what might be expected from terror management theory (chapter 4).

Figure 7.1 uses monthly Gallup data to show the change in party affiliation from January 2001 to January 2006. As Abramson and Ostrom (1994) have shown, we should expect some volatility from the Gallup measure. At first glance, the figure gives the appearance of instability as both Democratic and Republican identifiers bounce around. However, swings in party affiliation following the attacks are relatively small—usually within sampling error—and short-lived. Early in Bush's first

Figure 7.1 Monthly Party Affiliation

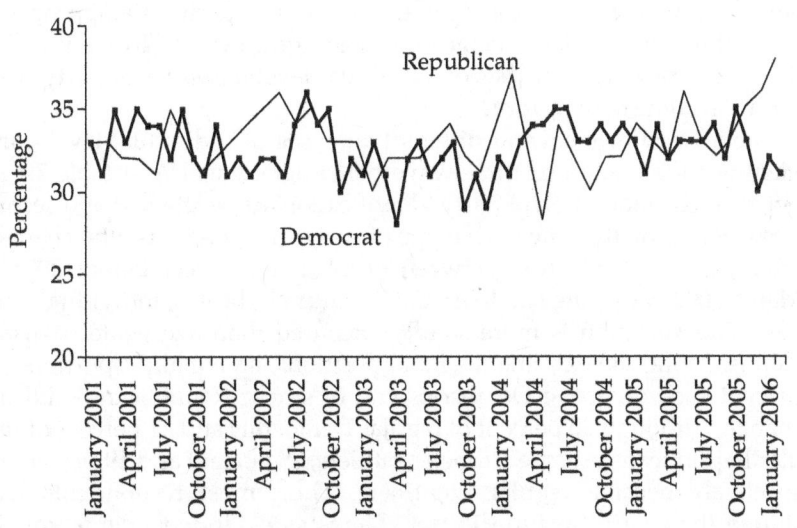

Question: "In Politics, as of Today, Do You Consider Yourself a Republican, a Democrat, or an Independent?"

Source: Author's compilation of data from Gallup Poll.
Note: Each point represents an average of monthly surveys.

term, Democrats and Republicans were almost evenly matched, with Democrats holding a slight advantage until the attacks. The percentage of Republican identifiers increased after the terrorist attacks, but this seemed to last for a year, until the war in Iraq. The increase in Republican identifiers after the attacks was drawn from independents, because the percentage of Democratic identifiers appeared to increase.[7]

Reflecting a lack of support for the war in Iraq, the percentage of Democratic identifiers increased as the percentage of Republican identifiers decreased. With the capture of Saddam Hussein, the percentage of Republican identifiers increased as that of Democrats declined. Capturing Hussein brought the greatest benefits to Republicans, but, again, this increase did not endure. Democrats and Republicans appeared to return to some imaginary base level of support. Heading into the 2004 presidential election, Republicans would have a slight advantage over the Democrats, except for a brief period in April 2004.

Thus, though party affiliation seems responsive to short-term events, the terrorist attacks did not produce a large swing. The monthly data reflects that Democratic identifiers did not shift their party affiliation in response to the attacks, but did rally to events, such as the war in Iraq. Where some scholars see instability, I see stable but responsive party identification. Outside of the major events, change in partisanship appears small and random, within the sampling error of the national surveys from which the percentages are drawn. It is perhaps inappropriate to attribute such small changes to meaningful events. To what extent does cross-sectional analysis of individual-level measures of party identification confirm this story?

Table 7.1 shows several different analyses of individual-level party identification using our three-wave panel data. Panel A in table 7.1 reports a cross-tabulation of party identification across the first and second wave. Based on this, the percentage of survey respondents who changed their party identification between October and December of 2001 to March 2002 was quite small. As the literature indicates, individual-level party identification is more solidly anchored than aggregate partisanship is. Along the extreme diagonal positions, an equal proportion—71 percent each of strong Democrats and of strong Republicans—did not change. Although 20 percent of regular Democrats and 21 percent of regular Republicans became strong identifiers, 25 percent and 19 percent respectively became regular identifiers. Thus, most respondents who shifted their partisanship did not change sides. Independents, for the most part, remained independent (83 percent), and those who changed were almost evenly divided among Democrats and Republicans. This is extremely strong evidence that partisanship did not change after the September 11 attacks.

Panel B in table 7.1 provides additional evidence of the stability of

Table 7.1 Analysis of the Stability of Party Identification, 2001, 2002, 2004 (Percentages)

Panel A. Cross-Tabulation of Wave 1 and Wave 2 Partisanship

Wave 1	Wave 2					
	Strong Democrat	Weak Democrat	Independent	Weak Republican	Strong Republican	N
Strong Democrat	71	25	3	1	1	126
Weak Democrat	20	50	24	4	2	118
Independent	2	6	83	7	1	149
Weak Republican	2	9	22	46	21	87
Strong Republican	0	1	9	19	71	103

Panel B. Partisan Stability Across All Waves

Stable	52
Absolute movement = 1	23
Absolute movement = 2	14
Absolute movement = 3	5
Absolute movement = 4	4

Panel C. Partisan Stability by Wave Comparisons and Correlations

	Wave 1 to Wave 2	Wave 2 to Wave 3	Wave 1 to Wave 3
Stable	66	68	63
r	.83**	.80**	.81**

Source: National Civil Liberties Survey (2001, 2002, 2004).
$x^2(16) = 832.86$; $p = .000$ for Panel A.
**$p < .01$.
Note: This analysis is based on the five-category partisanship measure. The percentage of stable identifiers and the correlation across waves increase if a three-category partisanship measure is used.

partisanship. Taking advantage of my three-wave panel, respondents are classified by the total distance they move on the party identification question across all three waves. For instance, if a weak Democrat in the first wave moved to being independent in the second, and then to a weak

Republican in the third, the absolute movement is two spaces. If a strong Republican in the first wave moved to a weak Republican in the second wave, but did not move in the third, the absolute amount of movement is one space. The least movement is zero, which indicates no change over the three waves, and the highest absolute movement is eight, for which a strong partisan would have to adopt the opposing extreme in each wave. Based on this analysis, 52 percent of all survey respondents maintained a consistent party identification on the five-category measure across the three waves, whereas 23 percent moved only one response category. I interpret this as a clear sign of partisan stability in party identification.

Approaching stability from a different perspective, panel C in table 7.1 breaks down consistency by wave comparisons, giving the correlation across waves. Consistent with the previous analyses, 66 percent of all respondents maintained their party identification from the first to the second wave. In the year after, 68 percent of all respondents maintained a consistent party identification from the second to the third wave. Over three years, 63 percent of all respondents maintained a consistent party identification. The correlations between partisanship across the three waves are also important. From the first to the second wave, partisanship correlated at .83, a .80 correlation from the second to the third wave, and a .81 correlation from the first to the third wave.

In short, despite a highly tumultuous period, I find high levels of partisan stability, comparable to previous analyses of panel data conducted in a period of relative quiescence. Perhaps in response to a heightened sense of threat, patriotism, and political trust, Democrats were willing to tolerate a certain amount of dissonance and discordant political views. Pressure from the political establishment to change political affiliation, however, was minimal. I turn next to the issue of political and ideological depolarization, in which Democrats, rather than changing their political views, simply supported more discordant and heterodox positions. Such unharmonious state should have been extremely uncomfortable.

Republican Stability, Democratic Depolarization and Repolarization

The election of George W. Bush in 2000—one of the most highly contested presidential elections in American history—has been connected to the increasing level of ideological and party polarization of the American electorate. It took several weeks and the Supreme Court to resolve the issue[8] and deepened the country's political divisions. Mindful of the intense divisions the election created, President Bush came into office promising to unite the country. In his victory speech delivered to the Texas House of Representatives nearly a month after the election (on December 14, 2000), he proclaimed,

The spirit of cooperation I have seen in this hall is what is needed in Washington, D.C. It is the challenge of our moment. After a difficult election, we must put politics behind us and work together to make the promise of America available for every one of our citizens. I am optimistic that we can change the tone in Washington, D.C. I believe things happen for a reason, and I hope the long wait of the last five weeks will heighten a desire to move beyond the bitterness and partisanship of the recent past. Our nation must rise above a house divided. Americans share hopes and goals and values far more important than any political disagreements. Republicans want the best for our nation, and so do Democrats. Our votes may differ, but not our hopes. I know America wants reconciliation and unity. I know Americans want progress. And we must seize this moment and deliver. Together, guided by a spirit of common sense, common courtesy and common goals, we can unite and inspire the American citizens. ("It Is a Charge to Keep, and I Will Give It My All," *USA Today*, December 14, 2000, 4A)

As his leadership style and policy preferences developed, Bush's promise of uniting a divided nation fell short in practice. His administration was seen by Democratic and moderate voters as making an insincere effort to appeal to centrist voters. Its policies on taxation, national security, social issues, the environment, and business appealed instead to his conservative base. According to a Republican congressman quoted in the *Washington Post*, the disagreement ran deep: "We are not just opponents or rivals now. We are enemies, with every fight being zero-sum" (Jim Hoagland. "The Price of Polarization," May 5, 2005, A25).

An alternative perspective describes Democrats as too rigid in their response to overtures by the president and unwilling to compromise. For their part, Democrats found attempts at compromise unacceptable, and consistently pushed for larger concessions. To compromise would be to give the president credit, and the general perception was that more was to be gained from opposing him. In the same *Washington Post* article, a Democratic congressman suggested that there was no common ground: "Compromise is seen as weakness by many of your constituents, and by all of your potential opponents in the next primary." However the ideological and partisan polarization under Bush will eventually be understood, political divergence is not a recent phenomenon. Although the threat of terrorism and international crises might have temporarily depolarized independents and Democrats, the normal course for the two major parties in American politics leans toward increasing ideological polarization. Several scholars have investigated the causes of this in the electorate. DiMaggio, Evans, and Bryson (1996) show that while American society has not converged across a variety of issues (such as feelings toward the poor, abortion, aid to minorities) and across groups (such as region, race, and educational attainment), political parties have increasingly become more polarized. Democrats and Republicans see the world differently, and as a result, the political parties are likely sources of social conflict. Fiorina and his colleagues (2005) suggest that though the claims of a cultural war and an increasingly polarized American electorate are exaggerated, political parties have become more polarized. Liberal Republicans and conservative Democrats, it is argued are now rare breeds. It is also attributed to the growth in partisan polarization to the realignment of southern whites, who were once Democrats but are now more likely to be conservative Republicans, leaving the Democrats more liberal. Also, people change their political views to match their political parties, so that discrepancies between party and ideology are diminished. Research by Edward Carmines and James Stimson (1981) demonstrates that the transformation of racial issues into government activism in the 1950s led African American voters to support the Democratic Party and, over time, conservative white southerners into the Republican Party. According to Alan Abramowitz and Kyle Saunders (1998), American society beginning in the Reagan era has undergone a secular realignment reflected in the increased ideological polarization of the two major parties. They argue that the ease with which Democratic and Republican parties during the Reagan and post-Reagan eras separated themselves along policy preferences realigned both parties along ideological lines. The Reagan administration's pursuit of ideological policies, such as tax cuts, increased military expenditures, and reductions in domestic social programs, is argued to have increased ideological polarization among party leaders and activists. Further dividing the nation was Newt Gingrich's Contract with America, which allowed Republican candidates across the country to run as "members of a party team committed to enacting broad ideological legislative programs" (637). This made it easier for citizens to recognize differences between the parties' positions, and choose a party on the basis of its proximity to their own ideological position. Geoffrey Layman and Thomas Carsey (2002) found that increasing polarization occurred among stronger partisans, who are more attentive to and reflect the polarized positions of political leaders. They argue that "in recent decades, the choice increasingly offered to voters is one between a Republican party taking consistently conservative positions on social welfare, racial, and cultural issues and a Democratic party that is consistently liberal on all three agendas" (788).

To illustrate the extent of party polarization, I analyzed the presidential approval series by partisanship using ABC News/Washington Post polls for four years following the attacks. In addition to presidential approval, these polls asked a series of questions about Bush's handling of the war on terrorism, the war in Iraq, and the economy. Unlike party affiliation, I expect presidential evaluations among both Democrats and Republicans to respond to major events, such as the September 11 attacks, the war in Iraq, and the capture of Saddam Hussein, but for parti-

Figure 7.2 Presidential Approval By Partisanship

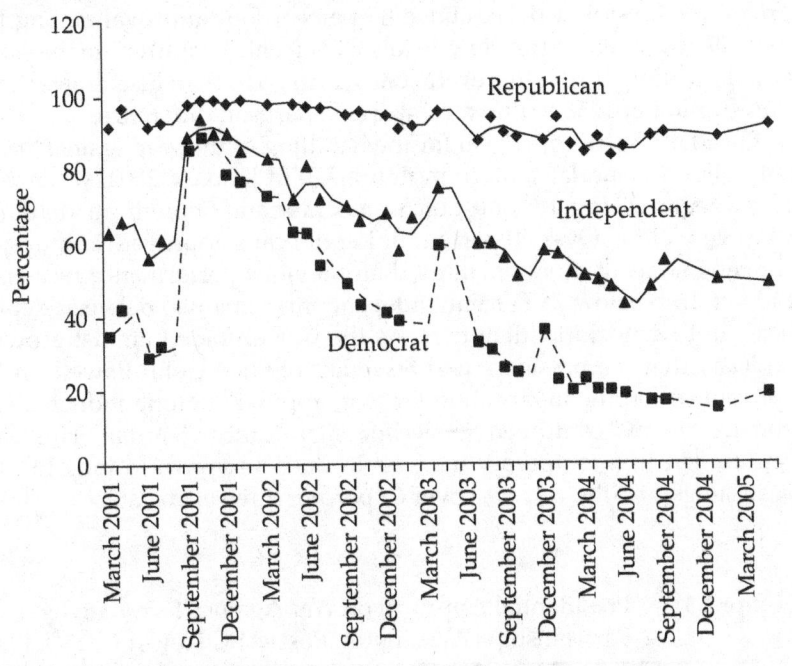

Source: Author's compilation of data from Washington Post–ABC News Poll.

sans to basically repolarize. Figure 7.2 shows President Bush's monthly approval ratings by partisanship in the months leading up to the attacks, and for three years afterward. Following the 2000 presidential elections, partisan identifiers were understandably highly polarized in their opinions of President Bush. Given the contentiousness of the election, there was no reason to be cooperative. In June 2001, 30 percent of Democratic identifiers approved of Bush, and 92 percent of Republican identifiers and 59 percent of independent identifiers approved of him. Although issues such as the economy and tax cuts exacerbated partisan differences, the 2000 election figured prominently in the level of partisan polarization. The attacks of September 11 led to a depolarization or rally effect among Democratic identifiers, but this level of support was only temporary (Jacobson 2005). Although the initial approval of the president was well over 90 percent among Republicans and more than 80 percent among Democrats, approval among Democratic identifiers fell off fairly quickly, as if they were turned off by the president's initial rhetoric and framing of the attacks. The pace of declining approval reversed briefly with the invasion of Iraq on March 20, 2003, but this reprieve did not last long. By September 2004, Republican identifiers retained very high approval for President Bush, above 85 percent, but approval among Democrats was at its all-time low, below 20 percent. To appreciate the extent of polarization during this event, one has to go back to Eisenhower's administration in 1956 to find a comparable partisan difference.

President Bush's approval for the handling of the war against terrorism follows a similar pattern in figure 7.3. In January 2002, when ABC News began asking this question, Democratic and Republican identifiers were very close. Over 80 percent of Republicans approved, and despite showing signs of more volatility than previous performance measures, did not drop below 75 percent. Independents remained between Republican and Democratic identifiers. As the war unfolded amidst growing criticism that the president and Secretary of State Colin Powell misled the country on the justification for war, approval among independents and Democrats continued to decline significantly. Saddam Hussein's capture led to a temporary increase in Bush's approval rating but the partisan gap on the war was over 65 percent three years later.

Figure 7.3 Presidential Approval on War Against Terrorism by Partisanship (Washington Post–ABC News)

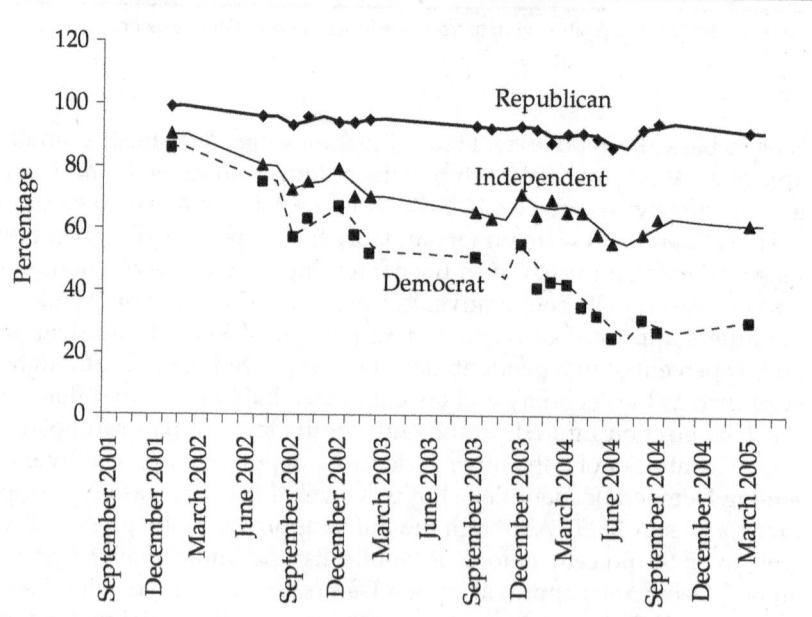

Source: Author's compilation of data from Washington Post–ABC News Poll.

Figure 7.4 Presidential Approval on War in Iraq By Partisanship (Washington Post–ABC News Polls)

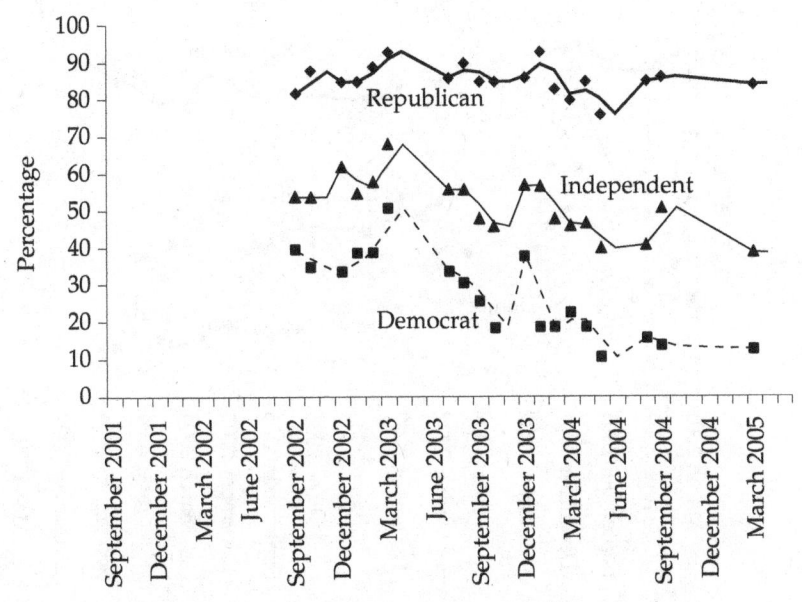

Source: Author's compilation of data from Washington Post–ABC News Polls.

Indicative of the partisan disagreement on the invasion of Iraq, a large gap existed initially between Republicans' and Democrats' perceptions of the president's handling of the war with Iraq. As figure 7.4 suggests, Republicans were highly supportive of Bush's handling of the Iraq war and they did not appeared to be phased too much by the allegations of the false pretenses of going to war or the capture of Saddam Hussein. Among Democrats, as the time wore on their initially lukewarm support for Bush's handling of the war deteriorated, though there was a temporary increase in response to Saddam Hussein's capture.

Partisan perceptions of President Bush's handling of the economy (figure 7.5) continue the previous patterns. Despite claims that the attacks created the economic recession, they actually occurred in the middle of a recession and during ongoing collapses in both business investment and the stock market. Although the process leading to recession can be traced to 2000, the attacks of September 11 exacerbated it by undermining consumer confidence and producing joblessness. It was estimated that from September to December of 2001, the economy lost more than 1 million jobs. Democrats' approval briefly increased after the at-

Figure 7.5   Presidential Approval on the Economy (Washington Post–ABC News)

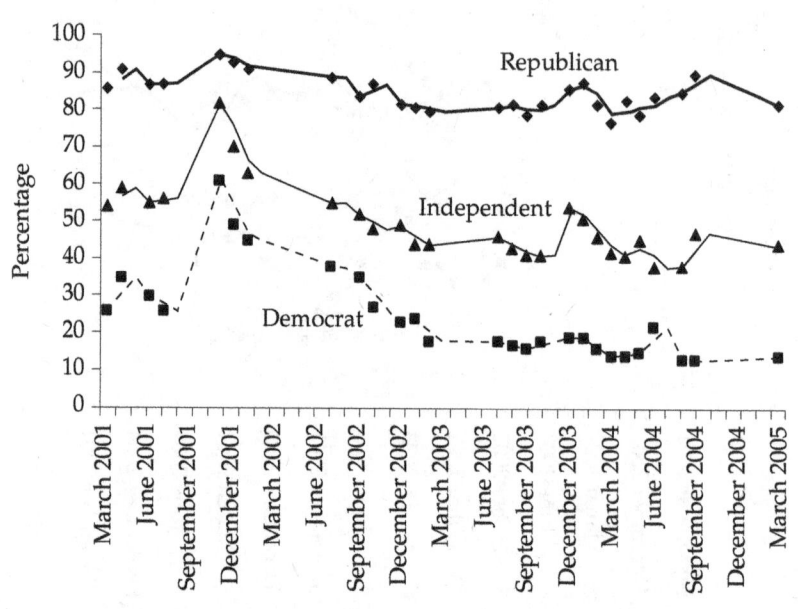

Source: Author's compilation of data from Washington Post–ABC News Poll.

tacks, though it was considerably less than the level of general presidential approval or perceptions of handling of the war in Iraq. Thus, issues not directly connected to terrorism temporarily benefit from Democratic willingness to rally around the president following the attacks. Republicans continued to overwhelmingly approve of the president. Political independents rallied somewhat, but this was also short-lived. Neither the war in Iraq nor the capture of Saddam Hussein translated into positive perceptions of the economy. By January 2003, Democrats were solidly polarized, with less than 20 percent approving of Bush's economic performance.

These graphs support the general conclusion that while Republicans hardly wavered in their support for President Bush, Democratic identifiers depolarized following the terrorist attacks, but this was extremely short-lived. Immediately, perceptions of presidential performance began to decline, eventually culminating in extreme partisan polarization. I now turn to how individual-level partisanship and ideology may have been shaped by the context of threat.[9]

The Relationship Between Ideology and Partisanship

An explicit theme of this book is that under heightened senses of threat, political trust, and patriotism, individuals can be expected to adopt positions they would not ordinarily take. Because political partisans adopted heterodox views after the attacks instead of changing their affiliations, I now investigate the individual-level component to partisan and ideological depolarization: the extent to which depolarization occurred among individuals, and the factors that led to it. As I have emphasized, periods of partisan and ideological depolarization are rare. Ideological preferences and partisan attachments should move together (Sharp and Lodge 1985), and more sophisticated citizens are better able to connect them (Box-Steffensmeier and DeBoef 2001). For much of the electorate, the concepts liberal and Democrat, and conservative and Republican, are interchangeable, but for many others, partisan and ideological belief systems are not mutually reinforcing, and events like the terrorist attacks can temporarily misalign them. Whereas Republicans were able to maintain, or even strengthen, their ideological perceptions after September 11, Democrats adopted inconsistent political views. From one perspective, such an inconsistency among Democrats is not unusual. Political partisanship may simply mask a certain level of ideological confusion.

Because of its ideological homogeneity, the Republican Party is generally viewed as truly conservative. By contrast, the Democratic Party is seen as more ideologically divided; self-identified Democrats are more likely than Republicans to hold discrepant and heterodox ideological views (Carmines and Berkman 1994; Levitin and Miller 1979). A conservative segment among Democrats views parties, candidates, and issues in ways, given their partisan affiliation, that one might not expect. Previous explanations of heterodox political views point to a certain level of political apathy and a misinterpretation of ideological labels (Levitin and Miller 1979). Other explanations center around the possibility that conservative Democrats find it difficult to abandon their party affiliation because of the symbolic value of the groups associated with the party (Carmines and Berkman 1994). In the end, the discrepant views of conservative Democrats do not fall in line with their fellow partisans, and may dampen the uniformity and predictability of partisanship. However, as the events that temporarily dislodged existing ideological beliefs diminish and people return to traditional orientations, partisanship and ideology may recalibrate.

The behavior of political independents—who are frequently assumed to occupy a moderate political position between the two major parties—further weakens the expected monotonicity between partisanship and ideology. Although some evidence suggests that independents think of themselves as detached from political parties, their political behavior makes some scholars think of them as closet partisans (Dennis 1992) or unrealized partisans (Keith 1992). In the context of the terrorist attacks, independents would have found it difficult to maintain a moderate political position. Again, operating off a heightened sense of threat, a willingness to trust and acquiesce to the president, or a sense of patriotism, they could be expected to adopt more conservative political views, such as conceding civil liberties for personal security, than Democrats would.

According to panel A in table 7.2, there is moderate overlap between ideology and partisanship (tau b = .34), but Democrats, as expected, were more likely to hold discrepant ideological views. Among strong Republicans, 30 percent self-identified as "very conservative" and 62 percent identified as "conservative."[10] Among normal Republicans, only 7 percent self-identified as "very conservative" and 71 percent as "conservative." Inexplicably, 15 percent of Republicans self-identified as liberal. Political independents in context are not ideologically moderate, nor are they evenly divided among the political parties. Also tending toward conservatism following the attacks, only 16 percent of independents were moderates, and 32 percent liberal; 52 percent self-identified as conservative. As we saw in the aggregate analysis, the views of political liberals can be expected to moderate as the war on terrorism unfolds. Democrats show substantially weaker ideological allegiances. Among strong Democrats, 13 percent self-identified as "very liberal" and 43 percent as "liberal," but 10 percent did so as "very conservative" and 28 percent as "conservative." Continuing this inconsistent tendency toward conservatism, 45 percent of regular Democrats self-identified as "conservative." It is clear from this analysis that though the terrorist attacks did not dislodge individuals from their partisan attachments, Democrats tended to reveal discrepant political views.

To begin to understand the discrepancy between ideology and partisanship and the role that context plays, I developed a discrepancy measure by subtracting the five-response category ideology measure from the five-response category partisan measure. As in most traditional analyses of partisanship and ideology, the discrepancy measure assumes that both partisan and ideological responses are evenly spaced and comparable across the two measures. The measure ranges from 4 to –4. A positive value indicates someone who is more conservative than the Democratic affiliation suggests, and a negative value indicates someone who is more liberal than the Republican affiliation suggests. According to the mean of the value in panel B of table 7.2, the largest partisan-ideological discrepancy occurs among African Americans, who, though overwhelmingly identifying as Democrats, tend to think of themselves as more conservative than their party affiliation would suggest. This dis-

Table 7.2 Cross-Tabulation and Correlations Between Party Identification and Ideology

Panel A. Cross-Tabulation in Wave 1 (Percentages)

Partisanship	Very Liberal	Liberal	Moderate	Conservative	Very Conservative	N
Strong Democrat	13	43	7	28	10	255
Weak Democrat	8	38	9	43	2	249
Independent	5	27	16	47	5	301
Weak Republican	1	15	5	71	7	174
Strong Republican	2	4	3	62	30	186

Panel B. Mean Discrepancies

	Wave 1		Wave 2	
	Mean	SD	Mean	SD
Whites	−.05	1.14	−.19	1.16
African Americans	.85	1.39	.82	1.40
Latinos	.01	1.15	.42	1.38

Panel C. Correlations by Race

	Wave 1		Wave 2	
	r	p	r	p
All respondents	.39	.000	.41	.000
Whites	.41	.000	.49	.000
African Americans	.10	.097	.07	.201
Latinos	.49	.002	.09	.106

Source: National Civil Liberties Survey (2001, 2002, 2004).
Panel A Note: To simplify the analysis, initial seven-point scales were reduced to five-point scales in which leaning independents were treated as pure independents.
$x^2(16) = 286.34; p = .000$.
Panel B Note: This measure of discrepancy was derived by subtracting party identification from ideology. High positive values indicate party identification is more liberal than ideology.

crepancy also existed a year after the attacks. In the first wave, whites were slightly more liberal than their Republican affiliation suggested, but a year later, their liberal discrepancy increased. Partisanship among Latinos following the 9/11 closely matched their ideological identities. However, in the second wave, they developed a more conservative identity than expected from their Democratic affiliation. These findings are reinforced by the correlations in panel C. Although the correlation between ideology and partisanship is higher among whites than it is among Latinos, it is virtually nonexistent for blacks. Despite their overwhelming identification with Democrats, blacks are known to have conservative views across a variety of issues related to morality, homosexuality, gay marriage, and abortion.

Partisan-Ideological Discrepancy

What accounts for the discrepancy between ideology and partisanship? In the context of the terrorist attacks, what would compel Democratic identifiers or independent identifiers to think of themselves in conservative terms? This misalignment between partisanship and ideology has weakened over time as the political parties have become more polarized. Table 7.3 presents an OLS regression model predicting self-reported ideology for Democratic identifiers and independents.[11] To make up for not having a measure of political sophistication, political interest is added to the normal cast of explanatory variables. Research by Robert Luskin (1990) indicates a strong relationship between sophistication and political interest. Based on this analysis, the discrepant political views among Democrats and independents stem from a heightened sense of patriotism. Patriotism pulls Democrats in directions inconsistent with their political views, toward a more conservative identity. Expressions of patriotism among Democrats and independents were instrumental in altering how individuals perceived their political ideology. This finding also holds across panel waves. Education had a consistent effect among Democratic identifiers: the more highly educated were less likely to develop discrepant partisan and ideological identities. Race also continued to be a significant factor, as mentioned, with African Americans proving more conservative politically than their affiliation would lead one to expect.

Although the discrepancy explanation is useful and informs an aspect of the partisan and ideological depolarization following the September 11 attacks, it does not account for actual change in ideology among Democrats and independents. I have shown that the level of support that Democrats and independents were willing to give to the president and his policies did not last very long. Using panel data, I considered a number of factors, such as threat, patriotism, and political trust, which may account for the change in ideology among Democrats and independents. Republicans were not included because their ideological positions did not generally change after the attacks.[12] A sustained sense of threat should continue to support conservatism among Democrats and independents, but to the extent that threat declines, a conservative ideology should become less appealing. The level of patriotism should reflect a similar pattern. In the data, not only did the level of patriotism increase

Table 7.3 OLS Regression of Explanations of Self-Reported Ideology

	Wave 1		Wave 2	
	Democratic Identifiers	Independent Identifiers	Democratic Identifiers	Independent Identifiers
Sociotropic threat	.02	.11	−.02	.03
	(.06)	(.10)	(.05)	(.06)
Patriotism	.35**	.26**	.43**	.47**
	(.08)	(.09)	(.06)	(.08)
Political interest	−.11*	−.02	−.27	.13**
	(.06)	(.08)	(.07)	(.07)
Education	−.37**	−.09	−.18**	−.02
	(.05)	(.06)	(.05)	(.05)
Age	.02	.07	.02	.01
	(.03)	(.04)	(.02)	(.03)
Female	−.03	−.08	−.02	−.33**
	(.10)	(.12)	(.09)	(.10)
South	.30**	−.00	.06	.10
	(.10)	(.13)	(.10)	(.11)
African American	−.03**	.13	.15	−.32
	(.11)	(.12)	(.11)	(.22)
Latino	−.32	−.47	.41**	−.30
	(.17)	(.26)	(.13)	(.21)
Constant	2.14**	1.61**	1.93**	.60
	(.46)	(.49)	(.40)	(.46)
R^2/adjusted R^2	.21/.19	.11/.08	.20/.19	.13/.11
Root MSE	.98	1.01	1.06	1.06
N	471	292	616	439

Source: National Civil Liberties Survey (2001, 2002).
Note: The dependent variable is the self-reported ideology. High values on the dependent variable indicate strong conservative identification.
*p < .05; **p < .01.

after the attacks, fostered by other events, such as the invasion of Afghanistan and the war in Iraq, but continued patriotism also increased support for conservative appeals. However, unlike threat and patriotism, political trust changed in a way that did not support the president or other types of conservative appeals. Thus, relative to the effects of threat and patriotism, I expect the change in political trust to be a significant factor in repolarizing Democrats and independents. If Democrats and independents are willing to support the conservative policies of the president out of a sense of trust, it logically follows that a decline in trust should compel people to withdraw their support.

According to the regression coefficients of a model predicting the level of change from the first-wave survey to the second-wave survey for Democrats and independents, reported in table 7.4, this seems to be exactly what happened. Neither the change in patriotism nor the change in threat influenced the change in ideological positions among Democrats and independents. As political trust increased, so did Democrat and independent support for conservatism. As the level of trust decreased, so too did the support for conservatism.

Partisanship and the Civil Liberties Trade-off

Partisanship has rarely been connected to political tolerance and support for civil liberties. Sullivan and his colleagues (1982) consider the role of partisanship in pluralistic intolerance—the extent to which there is agreement on the number of groups to repress in society. Partisan differences in pluralistic tolerance convey a sense of which groups might suffer under "majority tyranny." In 1978, Democrats' most disliked groups were radical Right groups (38 percent), communists and socialists (33 percent), and New Left groups (13 percent). Republicans' most disliked groups were also communists and socialists (40 percent), radical Right groups (24 percent), and New Left groups (19 percent). Otherwise, partisanship has not been seen as an essential component of political tolerance.

My view is that the measurement of political tolerance has shown its usefulness. But because the least-liked-group measurement approach does not involve an evaluative component of government or political authorities, beyond abstract support for general democratic norms, there has been no theoretical justification for including partisanship above its overlap with political ideology. Not only would ideological reasoning be needed, but using partisanship would be redundant with ideology. Nevertheless, political partisanship should influence the decision to trade civil liberties for security because the decision involves transferring power to political authorities. When people consider the choice between civil liberties and security, they are explicitly deciding whether to relinquish their rights to the government. To many people, political authorities have real faces, represented by the president and his political party. Over and above ideological preferences and political trust, as mentioned, Republicans are likely to support the policies of a Republican adminis-

Table 7.4 OLS Regression Coefficients of Wave 1 to Wave 2 Change in Ideology

	Democratic Identifiers	Independent Identifiers
Ideology $_{t-1}$	−.40**	−.41**
	(.05)	(.07)
Change in political trust	.53**	.29*
	(.10)	(.14)
Political trust $_{t-1}$	.41**	.20
	(.12)	(.13)
Change in patriotism	.12	.16
	(.11)	(.14)
Patriotism $_{t-1}$	.09	.24*
	(.12)	(.12)
Change in sociotropic threat	−.03	.04
	(.09)	(.11)
Sociotropic threat $_{t-1}$	−.17	.05
	(.09)	(.13)
African American	.40**	.14
	(.16)	(.30)
Latino	−.06	−.44
	(.15)	(.43)
Constant	.27	−.54
	(.61)	(.63)
R^2/adjusted R^2	.38/.35	.23/.19
Root MSE	.81	.85
N	208	169

Source: National Civil Liberties Survey (2001, 2002).
*p < .05; **p < .01.

tration, and Democrats more reluctant. Partisanship was not included in my analysis of civil liberties (chapter 4) because I did not expect it to be meaningful in the immediate aftermath of the terrorist attacks and in context of the other variables it was up against. However, as ideological and issue preferences realign with partisan attachments, partisanship should regain its connection to the trade-off decision.

I analyze the bivariate relation between partisanship and the various civil liberties items following the attacks in table 7.5 (panel A). Partisanship is definitely related, at least in the bivariate case, to the trade-off between civil liberties and security. Democrats support civil liberties more

Table 7.5 Mean Level of Support for Civil Liberties Items, 2001, 2002, and 2003

Panel A. Civil Liberties by Partisan (Means)

	Wave 1	Wave 2	Wave 3
Strong Republican	51	43	49
Weak Republican	58	51	56
Independent	63	62	68
Weak Democrat	63	61	64
Strong Democrat	64	63	72
r	−.17**	−.19**	.28**

Panel B. Civil Liberties by Ideology (Means)

Strong conservative	51	45	52
Conservative	57	53	60
Moderate	60	57	64
Liberal	67	67	72
Strong liberal	74	73	79
r	−.26**	−.34**	−.35**

Panel C. Correlations

	Wave 1		Wave 2	
	Partisanship	Ideology	Partisanship	Ideology
All respondents	−.09	−.21	−.23	−.31
Whites	−.07	−.20	−.24	−.35
African Americans	−.08	−.10	.01	−.19
Latinos	.16	−.10	−.04	−.17

Source: National Civil Liberties Survey (2001, 2002, and 2003).
**p < .01.

than Republicans do, but even Republicans support civil liberties strongly. With the exception of strong Republican identifiers in wave 2 and wave 3, a majority of Republican identifiers have supported civil liberties. I do not wish to portray Republican identifiers as blinded by security concerns, because the data clearly suggest the opposite. Support for civil liberties over security boils down to degrees, whereby Democratic identifiers supported civil liberties more. Individuals who claim they do not identify with either party resemble Democratic identifiers more than Republican in their supporting civil liberties. Independents are generally considered as being somewhere between Democrats and Republicans, and on the trade-off issue this is probably true, but otherwise they are definitely closer to Democratic identifiers.

Did the relationship between partisanship and the trade-off decision become stronger over time? The largest increase in the support for civil liberties over time occurred among strong Democrats, where the mean level of support was 64 in wave 1 and the mean level of support was 72 in wave 3. Increased support for civil liberties was also registered among weak Democrats, and independents. Although the support for civil liberties declined among strong Republicans and weak Republicans in wave 2, by the third wave the mean level of support was almost the same as in wave 1. Thus, the mean level of support for civil liberties increased overall over time, but partisan identifiers moved at their own pace. This strength in relationship is also shown in the correlation coefficients.

The same analysis of the support for civil liberties is applied to political ideology in panel B. Here, too, the support for civil liberties reflects a matter of degree. With the exception of the strong conservatives in wave 2 (45 percent), conservatives should be thought of as supporting civil liberties, unlike security hard-liners. But, it is evident that liberals were more supportive of civil liberties and became even more so over time. The critical difference between political ideology and partisanship is that within each survey wave, ideology is stronger and provides greater structure for the trade-off decision. Panel C in table 7.5 shows the correlations among partisanship, ideology, and civil liberties. Confirming the previous results, support for civil liberties is more highly correlated to ideology than partisanship. The relationship strengthens in the second-wave.

In the immediate aftermath of 9/11, partisanship is not expected to matter much, because of the misalignment of partisanship and ideology. But I expect partisanship to become more influential in structuring trade-off decisions in subsequent panel waves. The unstandardized regression coefficients of two models are reported in table 7.6. Whereas the first model presents the analysis for all new respondents, the second presents it for panel respondents only. Both models support my expectations nicely. In the combined sample, partisanship appears inconsequential in the first wave, which I attribute to partisanship having a minimal influence in structuring views on the trade-off decision in the immediate aftermath of 9/11. In the second and third waves, however, the marginal impact of partisanship becomes statistically significant, though more powerful in the second wave. At the same time, the influence of political trust becomes more powerful in the third wave. Also, the influence of political ideology remains strong and significant. Other factors, such as so-

Table 7.6 Unstandardized Regression for Predictors of Civil Liberties and Security Trade-Offs by Panel Repondents, 2001, 2002, 2003

	New Panel Respondents			Panel Respondents		
	Wave 1	Wave 2	Wave 3	Wave 1	Wave 2	Wave 3
Partisanship	.40 (.55)	−3.00** (.63)	−2.01** (.64)	−.25 (.81)	−1.13 (.88)	−3.30** (1.04)
Ideology	−2.92** (.64)	−5.28** (.69)	−3.51** (.69)	−3.12** (.95)	−.34 (.99)	−3.04** (1.19)
Sociotropic threat	−6.33** (.88)	−.46 (.87)	−1.71** (.96)	−7.96** (1.28)	−5.27** (1.29)	−4.90** (1.83)
Political trust	−2.47** (.90)	−1.65 (1.02)	−4.41** (1.19)	−6.09** (1.36)	−8.14** (1.58)	−7.75** (2.07)
Patriotism	−5.72** (1.06)	−6.14** (1.17)	−5.56** (.99)	−4.61** (1.67)	−6.94** (1.52)	−4.69** (1.87)
African American	6.37** (2.03)	2.45 (2.28)	3.89 (2.71)	3.27 (3.64)	8.87** (3.57)	4.08 (4.13)
Latino	−3.34 (2.23)	.37 (2.56)	−3.48 (2.72)	−5.21 (3.52)	−5.23 (3.20)	−22.14** (6.17)
R^2/adjusted R^2	.14/.14	.20/.20	.21/.20	.16/.16	.18/.17	.23/.21
Root MSE	22.16	21.61	19.69	21.13	22.87	20.95
N	1138	944	713	577	567	296

Source: National Civil Liberties Survey (2001, 2002, 2003).
Note: Entries are standardized coefficients; t statistics are in parentheses.
*p < .01; **p < .05.

ciotropic threat and patriotism, lose some of their influence, but nonetheless remain quite important in structuring trade-off decisions.

This general pattern of effects is also confirmed by the analysis of panel respondents. Again, partisanship increases its structuring ability by the third wave. Political trust becomes more important and sociotropic threat becomes less so. The influence of patriotism increases in the second wave, but continues to be significant.

Conclusion

The question motivating this chapter involves the extent to which political partisanship structured individual reactions to the terrorist attacks of September 11, during a brief period of depolarization between the two major political parties. I have argued that with events such as the attacks, individuals are moved by their sense of threat, trust, or patriotism to take positions they would not ordinarily take, diminishing the influence of traditional orientations. This chapter showed that a sense of patriotism was instrumental in getting Democrats and independents to accept conservative positions. However, as the level of trust declined over time, Democrat and independent support for conservative policies significantly diminished. The clash over values was not nearly as intense for Republicans as it was for Democrats. Thus, adding to the theme of threat leading individuals to adopt uncharacteristic positions, partisans can be compelled by their sense of patriotism to support positions they would not ordinarily support. This is an important finding. Those with strong partisan and ideological convictions are not the norm. Because their political beliefs help define who they are, they do not easily adopt divergent views. When they do, they are likely to experience some dissonance, and as a result, they will seek ways to reduce such an uncomfortable position. In sum, for many Democrats and independents there was no way in the immediate context of the terrorist attacks to escape the discomfort of acquiescing to Republican-led policies.

Because of discordant political views, traditional partisan orientations were not very meaningful in structuring the trade-offs in the immediate aftermath of the attacks. Over time, as issue preference and political orientation realigned, partisanship becomes an important explanation of support for civil liberties, with Republicans supporting security over protecting civil liberties. This chapter also examined the extent to which partisanship changed. It was in fact very stable, and did not change much a year after the attacks. Democrats had no reason to change, given the extreme conservative rhetoric from the White House and the growing criticism of the Bush administration's security lapses and the war in Iraq. Democrats rallied to the president's conservative preferences not because they were more threatened by the attacks than Republicans were, but because of their sense of trust and patriotism. As their trust declined, they returned to the values of their partisan affiliation.

Chapter 8

Racial Reactions

RACE AND ethnicity have rivaled other factors, such as political trust and perceptions of sociotropic threat, in comprehending the effects of the September 11 attacks on individual attitudes. Although American citizens and political institutions appeared to acquiesce to political authorities to make the country safe and secure, they did not share equally in their willingness to concede civil liberties. As I showed in chapters 4 and 5, African Americans were much less likely than most other citizens to cave in to their sense of threat and vulnerability. When presented with the security consequences of their initial trade-off decision, blacks rejected them, remaining firmly committed to civil liberties and their personal rights. Because their long struggle for equality and civil rights involved their own experience with aspects of terrorism, and because of their sense of disaffection from the political system, it was reasonable for blacks to be sensitive to the human suffering that the attacks caused, yet, at the same time, guarded against the government's increasing authority and invasion of individual rights, both domestically and internationally (Stanford 2002). Whites and Latinos, on the other hand, rejected the antidemocratic consequences of their initial preferences and followed their concern for security.[1]

Because the trade-offs between civil liberties and security reflect only one aspect of the attachment to the political system (Easton 1965), in this chapter I turn to other dimensions of political support to better understand racial differences in the reactions to the attacks. Also motivating this analysis is the extent to which aggrieved citizens set aside their grievances against the political authorities when society is attacked (Sears and McConahay 1973). How much can African Americans be counted on to support the political system when an external enemy threatens it, and when their continued antagonism may represent another front on which the government might be diverted? Could they operate under what W.E.B. DuBois described in 1924 as a double motive, acquiescing to political authorities in times of national crisis both to prove their loyalty and to promote claims of equal citizenship (1924/1970, 32)?

Equally important questions are being raised about how other groups' perceptions of the political system change when the system is threatened. Does the willingness of members of the dominant culture to support political authorities reflect unquestioning loyalty, or are there limits to what political authorities can do in a national crisis? Does the level of acculturation among Latinos translate into blind devotion to the government, or do their senses of ethnic consciousness and inequality make them more critical? The terrorist attacks on America are a unique and meaningful context in which to examine the significance of race in political support. In such a context, the internalization of threat, perceptions of political authorities, and racial and ethnic distinctions have real consequences.

I argue in this chapter that though most citizens may have found the response to the terrorist attacks by political authorities comforting and reassuring, aggrieved groups, such as African Americans, may have felt less secure given their previous distrust of the government and commitment to civil rights. However, such feelings are expected to strengthen support for the political system generally, but not necessarily for political authorities especially on the heels of the 2000 presidential election. I believe that, for blacks, protection and security lie with the proper and unbiased functioning of the democratic system, as opposed to when the so-called rules of the game are not closely followed. It is the deviation from norms of equality and the due process of law that may give rise to a greater sense of anxiety and trepidation, which in turn leads to an even greater commitment to those norms.

Disaffection from the Political System

Racial differences in the trade-off decision in chapter 4 were grounded in the psychological reactions to a heightened sense of anxiety and threat. Consistent with those motivations, racial differences in perceptions of the broader political system when it is attacked should also be related to normal perceptions of the political system. Previous feelings about political authorities should not be simply forgotten when the country faces a national crisis; instead, both positive and negative, they should influence how and how much individuals acquiesce. Those deprived of equal political and economic participation in American society are not likely to strongly identify with the political system, and can be expected to have less sympathy toward it than other individuals do. Because political authorities are perceived as having ignored the democratic norms on which their claim to legitimacy rests, politically disaffected and disenfranchised citizens view leaders and institutions as illegitimate. Equally important, they are likely to see duplicity and hypocrisy in government actions and are less likely to respond to appeals to pull together with dominant groups and political authorities. Although the politically disaffected are likely to acquiesce to or remain silent before new measures to promote common defense, these new policies may be considered suspect. Clearly, political disaffection does not necessarily mean rejecting underlying system norms (Sears and McConahay 1973), not complying with governmental policies (Sears et al. 1978), or withdrawing support from the political system as a whole. However, resentment and frustration stemming from unjust treatment result in a lack of concern for political authorities who experience some of the negative consequences of their policies. People who think that they have been treated unfairly may be skeptical of political leaders, and of appeals to subordinate their individual or group rights in a crisis. Alienated citizens are also likely to see the same arrogance and imperialism in U.S. foreign policy that people in many other countries perceive. As a result, although politically alienated individuals may not actively undermine the government's efforts when it is faced with an international crisis and an external enemy, they are likely to experience a sense of relief when the government is attacked and society gets to experience what it is like to walk in their shoes.

African Americans

Following the attacks, blacks were observed to respond somewhat differently from other groups. Brian Gilmore cites one example:

> On the radio in the days after the bombing I heard many black Americans state that they felt bad for the victims, they felt violated, and they felt that America had to do something, but then some would add at the end of their comments statements about not feeling that deep sense of patriotism that most Americans feel. The kind of emotion that pushes you to put your hand over your heart, take your hat off when the National Anthem is played. The "God Bless America" brand of patriotism. They were Americans, but not quite as American as white Americans. They cried for the victims, but not necessarily for America. (2002, 27)

Like many American citizens, African Americans grieved, volunteered, rallied to President Bush, and contributed to relief efforts. Because foreign terrorists did not spare blacks, and because race did not appear to be a consideration in targeting airplanes to crash into the World Trade Center and the Pentagon, African Americans could easily imagine themselves as victims of terrorism. That is to say, blacks were not spared the pain of the terrorist attacks, because many perished in them or were directly influenced by them. Attesting to this sense of national identity and support for the victims, black leaders and the black press were quick to offer devotional support for the victims, and supported governmental restraint in responding to the perpetrators (Malveaux and Green 2002; Simmons and Thomas 2001). The most notable expression of caution involved Barbara Lee, a U.S. congresswoman from California, who cast the only dissenting vote authorizing presidential use of necessary and appropriate force against anyone involved in the 9/11 attacks.

Underlying such conciliatory and cautionary expressions, however, were African American experiences with aspects of terrorism, and a belief that America was responsible for fostering the hatred that led to the attacks. Previous experiences with government, specifically the extent to which they feel alienated or distrustful of the political system, can be expected to help African Americans make sense of their reactions when the political system is attacked. African Americans' reactions to the terrorist attacks are integrally connected to their level of disaffection from the American political system. Beginning in early childhood and intensifying through adulthood, African Americans grow up more politically alienated and distrusting than other citizens (Aberbach and Walker 1970). The political reality of black Americans—in which they experience hostility and violence from society and the government, are denied access to economic and political power, and are deprived of equal rights and civil liberties—yields a deep sense of resentment (Abramson 1983; Howell and Fagan 1988). Blacks are likely to perceive political authorities as disingenuous and untrustworthy because of significant discrepancies between the values that the political system espouses and their own status within that system. In times of national crisis, when the government needs citizens' support and compliance, the African American experience of unfulfilled promises and mistreatment is likely to be held against those in power.

In addition to the 2000 presidential election, which many blacks believed was manipulated to elect George Bush, the Bush administration also boycotted the UN World Conference on Racism in Durban, South Africa, citing offensive language against Israel and an unwillingness to consider possible reparations for American slavery. Many saw the conference, which took place a week before September 11, and Secretary of State Colin Powell's probable attendance as a symbolically significant and lost opportunity to begin a dialogue on the influence of racial discrimination, exclusion, and abuse.

If all this is true of African American feelings about the September 11 attacks, the results would echo Myrdal's observations concerning blacks' perceptions of World War II:

> But it is quite common that Negroes feel a satisfaction in the temporary adversities and want the War to become as serious a matter as possible to the white people in power. There have been reports that poor Negro sharecroppers in the South sometimes indulge in dreams of a Japanese army

marching through the South and killing off a number of "crackers." They do not want them to land in the North, though. And they certainly do not want them to stay. But much more common is a glowing ill-concealed satisfaction over the war adversities on various fronts. (Myrdal and Bok 1996: 1007)

Even though the social and political situation of African Americans has improved since Myrdal, they might have experienced a vicarious sense of satisfaction or retribution from the September 11 attacks. This is not the kind of satisfaction that makes people rejoice. It is instead probably best described as schadenfreude, or pleasure experienced from the pain of others. In this case it is the pain of political authorities and the government.

Latinos

Although there are many similarities between African American and Latino frustration with the American political system, the groups' political histories and experiences are very different. The Latino reaction is not likely to be tied as much to their sense of alienation or discrimination.[2] Recent research has begun to detail the complex political perceptions and values among Latinos (Davis and Silver 2004a; Pantoja, Ramirez, and Segura 2001; Shaw, de la Garza, and Lee 2000). Differences in the political values among Latinos seem to suggest that, though they often suffer from degrading experiences similar to those of blacks, the political orientations and core values of Latinos—particularly native-born Latinos—tend to be more closely aligned with the dominant culture (de la Garza et al. 1996). Like the pattern for European immigrants, the process of acculturation of Latinos is said to facilitate accepting certain political values, such as greater trust. On the other hand, their sense of consciousness from identifying with a larger distressed community, and from not being totally accepted as Americans, may lead to theirs being more of an outsider's than an insider's assessment of the political system (Fuchs 1990; Portes and Rumbaut 2001). As a result, political behavior among Latinos may reflect cross-pressure from balancing the demands of acculturation to American society and their identity with their country of origin (Jones-Correa 1998; Garcia 1987). As Rodolfo de la Garza et al. (1996) explains, naturalized citizens form an emotional attachment to the United States and its ideals, but an intense ethnic consciousness may work against supporting core American values.

I expect Latinos' perceptions of the terrorist attacks on America to be similar to those of the dominant culture because of acculturation, but at the same time to reflect a peripheral and critical view of the political system because of their own sense of alienation and ethnic consciousness. However, exposure to the threat of terrorism may intensify Latinos' attachment to the American political community. Of course, this argument may be time bound, given that the Immigration and Naturalization Service (INS) began to question the status of Latinos and immigrant communities in the months that followed the September 11. Stringent visa requirements and indiscriminant sweeps of workers in sensitive jobs, such as those in airports and border security, could also lead to greater resentment in the Latino community. Nevertheless, this expectation is supported by evidence, presented in chapter 4, showing that Latinos were more likely than whites and blacks to concede civil liberties for greater security. At each level of perceived threat, Latinos, like whites, showed a weaker attachment to civil liberties than blacks did. Research by de la Garza and his colleagues (1996) shows high support among Latinos for core American values of patriotism and individualism. Mexican Americans at all levels of acculturation who are U.S. citizens express patriotism at levels equal to or higher than whites. Elsewhere, de la Garza (1995) shows that Puerto Ricans expressed less support for civil liberties than whites did and more trust of government. However, native-born Puerto Ricans and whites were equally patriotic, trusting in government, and politically intolerant. Christopher Parker (2003) also shows that Latinos tend to be more blindly patriotic, to have an uncritical loyalty to the United States. Relying on perceptions among Puerto Ricans, de la Garza shows that, again like European immigrants, as succeeding generations Americanize, they continue to strongly support of U.S. society, but become more critical of the nation's social and political processes. Latinos also perceive less discrimination and trust the government more than African Americans do (Pew Hispanic Center/Kaiser Family Foundation 2002).

Dimensions of Support for the Political System

Several explanatory variables used throughout this book have been identified as important factors in perceptions of the political system. In *A Systems Analysis of Political Life,* David Easton (1965) argues that the persistence of a political system hinges not only on regulating the inflow of demands, but also on a minimal level of trust. But trust in the political system is multifaceted, relating to support for the political community, the authorities, and regime norms or principles. The political community can be thought of as citizens subject to the same government, authorities as the incumbents or officeholders, and regime norms as the core guiding principles or constitutional order, on the basis of which the system is commonly said to operate (Easton and Dennis 1969). Support for these three objects is considered essential for any political system to survive, especially in times of stress. I use Easton's distinctions in this analysis to reflect different but interrelated dimensions of affect toward the American political system. Because Pippa Norris (1999) considers Easton's dimensions too limited and that they should be expanded to include performance, political actors, and institutions, I also examine support for President Bush and perceptions of an American identity.

Specific hypotheses can be crafted from the theoretical explanations of racial differences and the dimensions of the political system. The reactions of blacks and Latinos are evaluated against those of whites (usually the excluded categorical value in the analyses). I use the behavior of whites to reflect the dominant culture and establish a baseline to measure racial differences. Blacks are hypothesized to be less trusting of political authorities, and, more important, exposure to threat is hypothesized to reduce that trust. They are also hypothesized to be more supportive of democratic norms and less attached to the national community. Latinos, on the other hand, are expected to mimic the behavior of whites, showing greater support for political authorities and the national community, and less for democratic norms. A heightened sense of threat should enhance support for the former and weaken support for the latter.

Trust in Political Authorities

The overwhelming support political authorities received in the immediate aftermath of the attacks (see chapter 6) was probably based more on a sense of hope that authorities would respond appropriately than on a sudden discovery of how trustworthy, honest, or responsive the government had been all along, especially following the 2000 presidential election. The decline in trust is probably connected to a simple lack of trustworthiness and honesty. When citizens thought of government in the context of the terrorist attacks, federal law enforcement, the attorney general, or the president were likely to be involved in their assessments.

The results of a model explaining political trust are reported in table 8.1. In the overall model, sociotropic threat is positively related to trust in the federal government: individuals under a heightened sense of threat place greater faith in government and, as expected, turned to it for security and protection. More revealing in this equation is the finding that Latinos trusted authorities significantly less than whites did, everything else being equal. Blacks, on the other hand, were virtually indistinguishable from whites on the political trust measure, but their level of trust (and mistrust for that matter) have different origins.

What about the effects of trust when people were exposed to threat? An important and at first perhaps a surprising finding, once the groups are disaggregated in the analysis, is the significant coefficient for sociotropic threat. As the level of perceived threat increased, trust

Table 8.1 OLS Regression Coefficients of the Determinants of Trust in Federal Government, 2001

	All	African American	White	U.S.-Born Latino
Sociotropic threat	.08**	−.14**	.17**	.08*
	(.03)	(.06)	(.04)	(.08)
Personal threat	−.02	−.12	−.06	.01
	(.03)	(.07)	(.04)	(.09)
Conservative ideology	−.01	−.10**	−.02	−.16**
	(.01)	(.03)	(.02)	(.06)
Female	.13**	−.23**	.11*	−.62**
	(.04)	(.10)	(.05)	(.13)
Education	.01	.04	−.01	.21**
	(.03)	(.06)	(.02)	(.07)
Age	.03*	.15**	−.00	−.04
	(.01)	(.03)	(.01)	(.04)
African American	−.10	—	—	—
	(.07)			
Latino	−.23**	—	—	—
	(.05)			
Born in United States	.06	—	—	—
	(.08)			
Constant	2.11**	2.37**	2.22**	2.22**
	(.14)	(.30)	(.15)	(.58)
R^2/adjusted R^2	.04/.03	.17/.15	.03/.03	.45/.41
MSE	.70	.76	.67	.55
N	1240	253	787	123

Source: National Civil Liberties Survey (2001).
Note: Standard errors in parentheses.
*p < .05; **p < .01.

in the federal government decreased among blacks but increased among whites. Thus, when the country faced a national crisis, blacks trusted political authorities less, and whites and Latinos gravitated toward them. Chapter 4 argued that during a national crisis, political authorities are likely to encroach on individual rights and civil liberties, which blacks are especially unwilling to concede. Whites, by contrast, place greater trust in political authorities to help assuage their fears. This could be based on a realistic assessment that providing greater support for the government will reduce threat.[3] Latinos similarly exposed to the threat of terrorism behaved more like whites. As their level of threat increased, so did their trust in government, but less than whites'.

A wellspring of trust exists among older African Americans, which

Figure 8.1   Predicted Trust in Federal Government, 2001

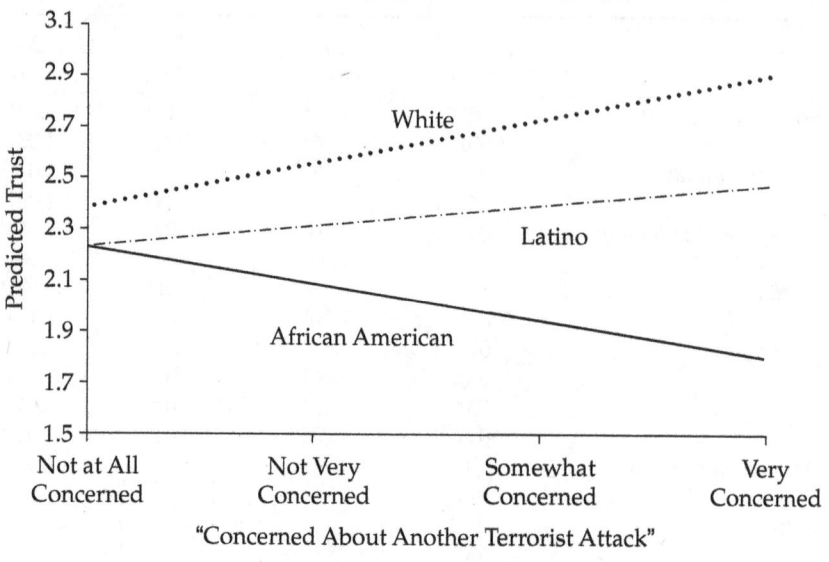

Source: National Civil Liberties Survey (2001).

perhaps harkens back to a period when blacks were more supportive of political institutions (see Gibson and Caldeira (1992). Higher levels of education are associated with greater political trust among Latinos, but not among blacks. Whether or not survey respondents were born in the United States did not affect their trust in the government. The most impressive result of this part of the analysis, however, is the difference between blacks, Latinos, and whites in the effect of perceptions of sociotropic threat on trust in government. As figure 8.1 shows, with each step up in concern about another terrorist attack on America, Latinos and whites put more trust in the government and blacks put less. The more strongly blacks sense the external threat of terrorism, the more guarded their support for the government is.

Because there is generally no greater object of political trust than the president, there is a question concerning the extent to which political trust captures an evaluation of President Bush. The vast majority of Americans rallied to the president in the immediate aftermath of September 11, 90 percent as reported in a Gallup survey. As can be seen in figure 8.2, President Bush's job performance was rated very high among all three groups in the National Civil Liberties Survey: 92 percent of whites, 88 percent of Latinos, and 77 percent of blacks supported him.

Figure 8.2 Presidential Approval, November 2001

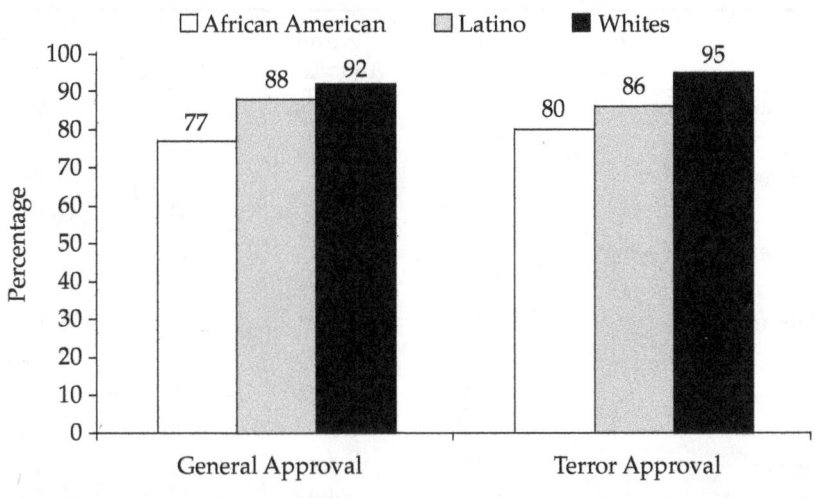

Source: National Civil Liberties Survey (2001).

This level is statistically significant: each group can be considered highly supportive. President Bush also received extremely strong support for his handling of the war on terrorism: 95 percent of whites, 86 percent of Latinos, and 80 percent of African Americans gave this rating. There is no significant difference between general approval of the president and of his handling the war on terrorism. Moreover, given the initial high level of approval, an interesting question is what caused individuals to rally around the president, even those who might have questioned his electoral victory in the 2000 election. Logit estimates of a model predicting support for Bush, reported in table 8.2, show that blacks were less likely to approve than whites were, everything else being equal. Latinos were not statistically distinct from whites. It is clear from this model that threat did not work to Bush's advantage early on. Partisanship, as opposed to political ideology (see chapter 7), and patriotism across all groups were the driving forces behind approval of the president immediately after the attacks. As with most rally events, people looked to the president for comfort and guidance and perhaps thought it their duty and obligation to support him.

It is worth noting that sociotropic threat among African Americans is significant and negatively related to the approval of President Bush. For whites and Latinos, it is positive but inconsequential. Taken together with the effects for political trust, it is again clear that blacks became

Table 8.2 Logit Coefficients of Model Predicting Bush Approval, 2001

	All	African American	White	U.S.-Born Latino
Sociotropic threat	.10	−.52*	.11	1.24
	(.17)	(.22)	(.25)	(1.05)
Personal threat	.03	.37	.29	−3.39*
	(.17)	(.34)	(.24)	(1.61)
Conservative ideology	.25**	.06	.35*	1.38
	(.11)	(.18)	(.16)	(.90)
Patriotism	.74**	1.03**	.88**	1.94*
	(.15)	(.36)	(.20)	(.99)
Partisanship	.45**	.97**	.37**	2.20*
	(.11)	(.33)	(.14)	(1.04)
Female	.32	−1.50**	.92**	.78
	(.23)	(.49)	(.33)	(1.52)
Education	−.24	−.01	−.10	−1.52**
	(.11)	(.25)	(.15)	(.69)
Age	−.08	−.02	−.12	02
	(.07)	(.14)	(.08)	(.57)
African American	−.70**	—	—	—
	(.32)			
Latino	−.29	—	—	—
	(.46)			
Born in United States	.79	—	—	—
	(.61)			
Constant	−1.98	3.34	−4.37**	−6.51**
	(1.04)	(2.05)	(1.22)	(6.75)
Pseudo R^2	.16	.17	.16	.70
N	1084	193	720	148

Source: National Civil Liberties Survey (2001).
Note: Standard errors in parentheses.
*p < .05; **p < .01.

more suspicious and less trusting as the sense of threat and vulnerability increased. I argue that such a finding is expected. A healthy sense of distrust has been a functional and integral component of the African American response to politics for some time.

Support for Democratic Norms

Support for the "operating rules and the rules of the game" conveys a different dimension of system support. According to Easton (1965), for decisions "to be accepted as binding, the members would need to accept some basic procedures and rules relating to the means through which controversy over demands was to be regulated and work out some ends that would at least broadly and generally guide the search for such settlements" (191). Support for democratic norms involves endorsing the rules of the political order and democratic governance. This dimension became especially relevant after 9/11, reflecting the extent to which commitment to fundamental values may be challenged in a crisis. Support for abstract democratic values is derived from five survey questions tapping a generalized commitment to the democratic rules of the game, such as the right of someone suspected of treason to be released on bail, equal protection under the laws, freedom of speech, and the right against self-incrimination.[4] Figure 8.3 illustrates support for democratic principles following the attacks. The question of posting bail for treason is the only factor that seems to be influenced by events surrounding the terrorist attacks. Perhaps reflecting an aspect of patriotism, relatively few people were willing to support bail for a person suspected of treason, though blacks (32 percent) were more so than whites and Latinos. How-

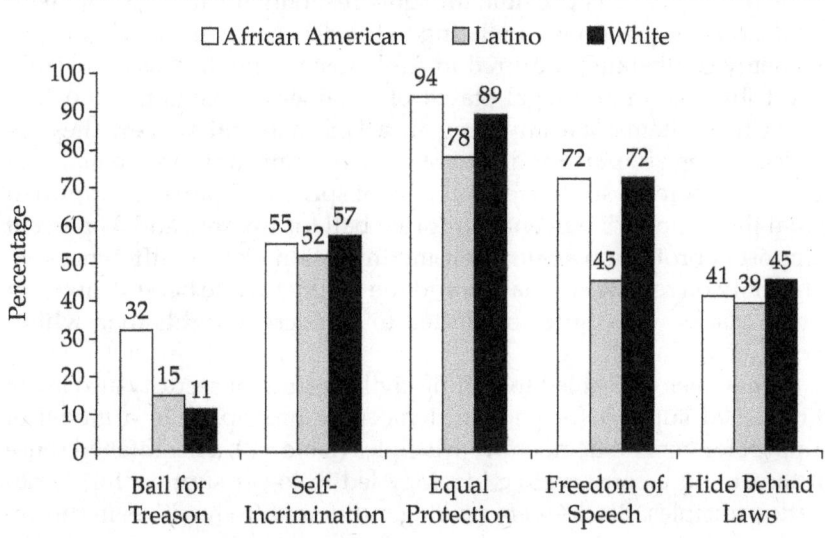

Figure 8.3 Favorable Responses to Democratic Norm Items, 2001

Source: National Civil Liberties Survey (2001).

ever, no other democratic norm received so little support. Less than a majority of respondents supported a "person being able to hide behind the laws." Whites were slightly more supportive than blacks, but the differences were small. The same can be said for the right against self-incrimination, though a majority of respondents supported it. Except among Latinos, freedom of speech received overwhelming support. Compared to the other items, freedom of speech is usually thought of as one of the more fundamental rights in a democratic society, but only 45 percent of Latino respondents supported it, compared with 72 percent of both blacks and whites. Giving individuals the same legal rights and protections received the highest level of support. Again, Latinos (78 percent) gave relatively less support for this item, but blacks (94 percent) were more supportive than whites (89 percent) were. Overall, support for general democratic principles is broad. This is a departure from the willingness to compromise civil liberties when questions are framed as choice between them and security.

An additive scale of these items is somewhat strongly correlated ($r = .48$) with the civil liberties and security trade-off decision. Some of the components are similar, though the intent was to develop a measure of democratic norms uncontaminated by the civil liberties and security framing—to the extent possible within the context of the terrorist attacks. Individuals who supported abstract democratic norms were more supportive of protecting civil liberties over security following the attacks. Despite the measures reflecting different aspects of support for democratic principles, it is possible for some respondents to view the democratic norms questions as relating to the debates over the legal rights of enemy combatants captured in Afghanistan, the discussion of military tribunals, or the legal status of detainees at Guantánamo Bay. When these items last appeared in a U.S. national survey, they revealed strong support for democracy: 96 percent supported equal protection, 83 percent supported freedom of speech, 63 percent supported equal protection, 75 percent supported bail for treason, and 39 percent supported protection against self-incrimination.[5] Racial differences existed only on self-incrimination and the ability to hide behind laws, for which blacks were more committed to democratic rights than whites were.

Several factors that led to trading civil liberties for security also led to diminished support for general democratic principles. In a model of support for general democratic principles (table 8.3), a heightened sense of threat and a conservative ideology led to lower support for democratic principles. Blacks were no longer different from whites in this regard, and Latinos still showed only a fragile commitment. Considering the groups separately, a heightened sense of threat continued to diminish support for democratic norms—even among blacks. However, as figure 8.4 shows, the effects of threat among blacks and whites were

Table 8.3 OLS Regression Coefficients of the Determinants of Democratic Norms, 2001

	All	African American	White	U.S.-Born Latino
Sociotropic threat	-.12** (.03)	-.11** (.04)	-.09** (.03)	-.40** (.08)
Personal threat	.01 (.03)	.23** (.04)	-.00 (.03)	-.29** (.08)
Conservative ideology	-.06** (.02)	-.06 (.03)	-.06** (.02)	-.07 (.06)
Female	-.04 (.03)	-.14* (.06)	-.08* (.04)	-.66** (.13)
Education	.11** (.02)	.10** (.03)	.10** (.02)	-.22** (.07)
Age	-.00 (.01)	-.02 (.02)	-.03** (.01)	.09** (.03)
African American	.06 (.05)	—	—	—
Latino	-.46** (.06)	—	—	—
Born in United States	-.12 (.07)	—	—	—
Constant	3.18** (.12)	2.65** (.18)	3.11** (.13)	4.13** (.44)
R^2/adjusted R^2	.15/.14	.18/.16	.09/.08	.55/.53
MSE	.55	.44	.54	.55
N	1100	225	689	119

Source: National Civil Liberties Survey (2001).
Note: Standard errors in parentheses.
*p < .05; **p < .01.

minimal and the predicted regression line is quite flat. Latinos, by contrast, started from a slightly higher level of commitment to democratic norms under the no-threat condition, but their predicted support for democratic norms declined substantially as the perceived level of sociotropic threat increased. Thus, only among Latinos did higher sociotropic threat produce a weaker commitment to fundamental democratic norms. Unlike questions about trust in political authorities, blacks are not significantly different from whites in their support for democratic norms.

Figure 8.4 Predicted Support for Democratic Norms, 2001

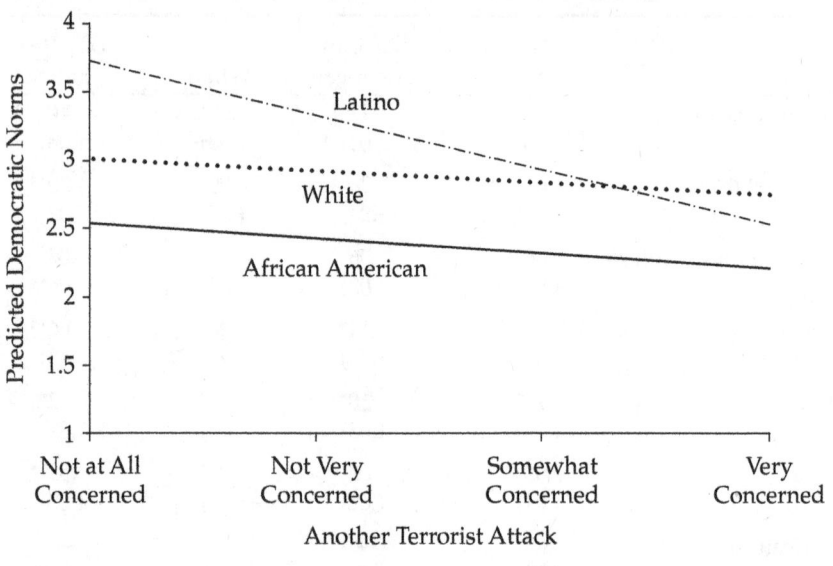

Source: National Civil Liberties Survey (2001).

Patriotism: Attachment to the Political Community

As an indicator of attachment to the political community, I use a measure of national pride, typically viewed as a component of patriotism (Hurwitz and Peffley 1990; Kosterman and Feshbach 1989). National pride captures an affective attachment to the larger political community, society, and people who share a common political identity. This form of patriotism is the last of three dimensions of system support Easton considered essential for a system to persist. The bivariate results indicate that all groups have high levels of affective attachment to the American political community. Slightly higher, though statistically insignificant, percentages of whites (95 percent) than blacks (92 percent) said that they were proud to be Americans.[6] At the same time, 85 percent of Latinos said the same thing. Based on the multivariate results reported in table 8.4, a heightened sense of sociotropic threat led to greater patriotism in the overall equation. People under a heightened sense of threat clearly supported the political community more. A conservative belief system and older individuals were associated with heightened sense of patriotism and a connection to a larger political community, whereas higher levels of education led to a weakened attachment to the political commu-

Table 8.4 OLS Regression Coefficients of the Determinants of Patriotism (National Pride), 2001

	All	African American	White	U.S.-Born Latino
Sociotropic threat	.15** (.03)	.16** (.05)	.12** (.03)	.45** (.08)
Personal threat	.01 (.03)	.01 (.05)	−.03 (.03)	.01 (.10)
Conservative ideology	.11** (.02)	.11** (.03)	.11** (.02)	−.02 (.06)
Female	.01 (.04)	.10 (.08)	.03 (.04)	.15 (.13)
Education	−.04* (.02)	.02 (.04)	−.07** (.02)	−.16* (.08)
Age	.04** (.01)	.12** (.02)	.03* (.01)	.05 (.04)
African American	−.14* (.06)	—	—	—
Latino	−.16** (.06)	—	—	—
Born in United States	.48** (.08)	—	—	—
Constant	3.32** (.13)	3.15** (.23)	4.09** (.12)	3.23** (.44)
R^2/adjusted R^2	.15/.14	.20/.18	.10/.09	.39/.36
MSE	.60	.56	.55	.62
N	1236	249	789	128

Source: National Civil Liberties Survey (2001).
Note: Standard errors in parentheses.
*p < .05; **p < .01.

nity. Disaggregating the effects by social groups revealed a similar influence of threat in increasing support for the political community across the groups. This suggests that blacks, whites, and Latinos were influenced in similar ways.

A plot of the regression estimates in figure 8.5, based on the group equations in table 8.4, shows a positive relationship between sociotropic threat and national pride for all three groups. At each level of perceived threat, whites and Latinos showed greater national pride than blacks did, but an increasing sense of threat was associated with greater na-

Figure 8.5 Predicted National Pride, 2001

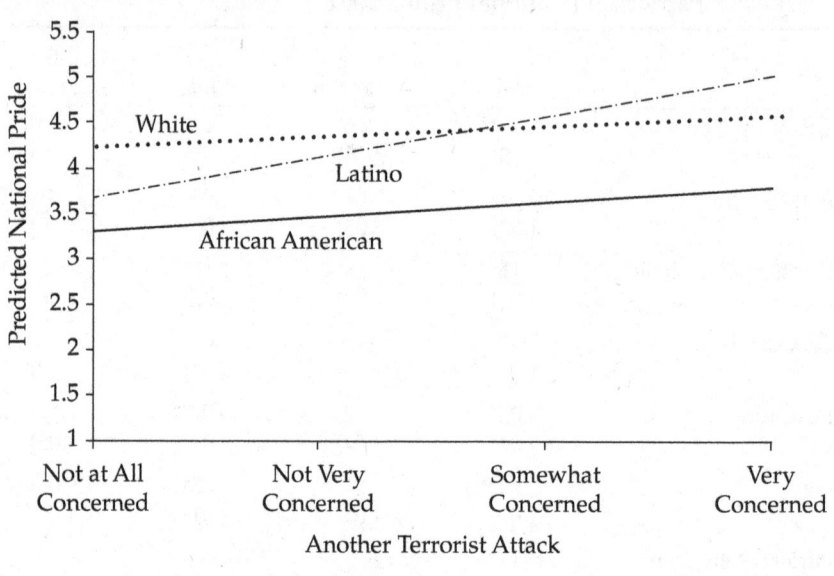

Source: National Civil Liberties Survey (2001).

tional pride among all three groups. Whites, blacks, and Latinos all gravitated toward the national community, but it is clear that they did not do so at the same level or rate. The slope of the line for Latinos is steeper than the lines for whites or blacks. A sense of sociotropic threat had a greater influence on Latinos, and at the same level of threat, whites and Latinos were always more patriotic than blacks were. Nonetheless, blacks were not out of sync with whites and Latinos. But, given the small cell frequencies and large standard errors, they are likely to be essentially the same.

Definitions of American Citizenship

Here I am interested in the extent to which definitions of American identity and citizenship became more intolerant and restrictive among individuals under a heightened sense of threat. So far, I have relied on individuals' perceptions of a liberal democracy: basically, the support for freedom, civil liberties, and political authorities. Liberal definitions of identity assume that race, ethnicity, and religious preferences are not barriers to supporting the rules of the game, whereas a nativist conceptualization of identity makes a very explicit claim about ascribed racial and ethnic characteristics. Unlike a liberal conceptualization, American identity that related to democratic support and inclusion, a normative or ethnic conceptualization involves a restrictive perception of belonging. Jack Citrin and his colleagues (Citrin, Reingold, and Green 1990; Citrin et al. 1990; Citrin et al 1994; Citrin, Wong, and Duff 2001) have argued that it is important to draw a distinction between affective and normative conceptions of American identity. Whereas affective dimensions of identity are related to the closeness and pride in one's country and its symbols, normative conceptions relate to the set of nativist or multicultural ideas about how national identity is defined. In this sense, in addition to the legal rights and norms of the political system, perceptions of the inclusiveness of those norms are critical to understanding the support for political system. It is difficult to ignore this aspect of political support when scholars such as Rogers Smith (1988) have argued that

> from the outset of the nation many Americans chiefly identified membership in their political community not with freedom for personal liberal callings or republican self-governance per se, but with a whole array of particular cultural origins and customs—with northern European, if not English, ancestry; with Christianity, especially dissenting Protestantism, and its message for the world; with the white race; with patriarchal familial leadership and female domesticity; and with all the economic and social arrangements that came to be seen as the true, traditional "American way of life." (234)

Research examining how individuals think of identity reveals an incredible sense of duality and exclusivity. In addition to espousing liberal conceptualizations of American identity, Citrin, Beth Reingold, and Donald Green (1990) found widespread acceptance of nativist ideas among whites that to be truly American one had to speak English, believe in God, and defend America when it was criticized. Additionally, the extent to which members of the dominant culture endorsed a restrictive view of identity was most significant in denying voting rights. In a different study, strong nativism was very important in that it was related to isolationism, limiting foreign imports, and wanting the United States to be the strongest world power (Citrin et al. 1994). Moreover, what it means to be a true American for blacks is very different than for whites and Latinos (Citrin, Wong, and Duff 2001). Blacks were more likely (82 percent) to endorse an ascriptive or nativist criteria of identity, that is, to think to be a true American one had to be born in America, compared to 42 percent of Latinos and 67 percent of whites. As to whether a person had to be a Christian, 77 percent of blacks agreed compared to 50 percent of whites and Latinos. However, there was overwhelming agreement that one had "to be able to speak English" to be considered a true American: 85 percent of Latinos, 91 percent of blacks, and 94 percent of whites endorsed it.

Attacking the liberal notion of identity and membership from a different angle, Thierry Devos and Mahzarin Banaji (2005) explored the qualities that people perceived as essential to being American. They found that though their study participants were committed to egalitarian principles in the treatment of ethnic groups, blacks and Asians were seen as less American than whites. People automatically associated being American with being white. Consistent with the previous research, Kelly Barlow, Donald Taylor, and Wallace Lambert (2000) found that although blacks felt a legitimate claim to being American in the sense they were not different from whites in identity, they did not feel included by whites either. Cuban Americans neither identified as American nor felt included by whites.

Following September 11, Qiong Li and Marilynn Brewer (2004) examined the extent to which patriotism and nationalism would increase beliefs about a nativist identity if respondents were primed by different meanings of American identity. Interestingly, when respondents were told to focus on "what it means to be an American" patriotism lead to a belief that a person had to be born in America to be considered a true American. Whether or not respondents were told to focus on "what it means to be an American" or "we have a common purpose to help the victims of this tragedy" patriotism led to a belief that one had to speak English to be considered a true American.

It is clear from these studies that racial and ethnic minorities can possess dual identities, but for blacks in particular there is a perception that an American identity is restrictive. In the context of the terrorist attacks, I expect how people define American identity to become more restrictive.

As another component of support for the political system, this view of American identity and citizenship probably cuts several ways. From the dominant culture perspective, whites under a heightened sense of threat may develop a restrictive or ethnocentric view in response to their concern about foreign terrorists and other threatening groups in American society. Blacks and Latinos may feel the same way because they are also citizens. But, from a minority perspective, they may agree with a restrictive view of American identity because they believe those restrictions might exist. Blacks and whites may agree on restrictive perceptions of an American identity for totally different reasons.

Respondents were asked several questions about the important qualities of a "true" American. These were linked to being born in the United States, speaking English, being a Christian, being white or Caucasian, and being willing to serve in the military. Figure 8.6 reports the distribution of responses by race and ethnicity. The most striking feature of this figure is the high level of restrictive perceptions of an American identity among blacks: 77 percent identified speaking English, 70 percent identified being born in America, and 35 percent identified being white. Whites were less supportive about being born in America or being white.

Figure 8.6 Responses to Qualities of a True American, 2001

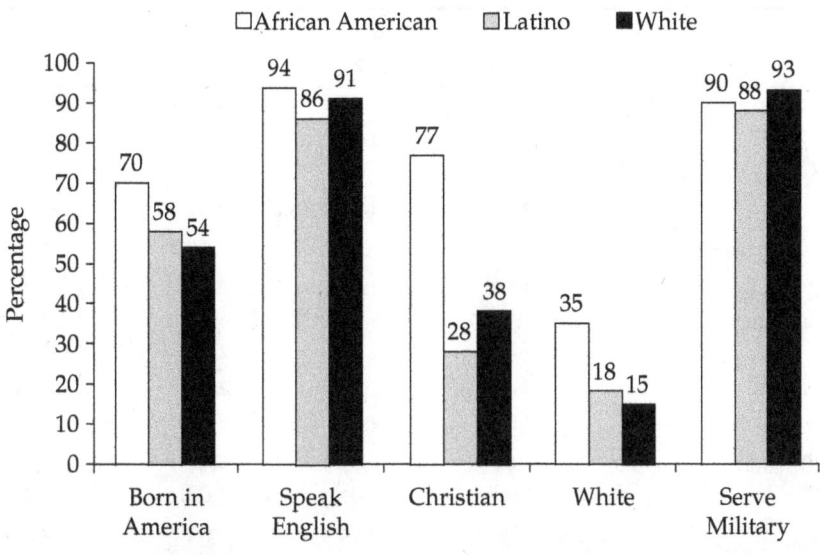

Source: National Civil Liberties Survey (2001).

The willingness to serve in the military, however, was a consensus across all three groups.

To what extent did the context of heightened threat, political trust, and patriotism after September 11 give rise to a more restrictive conception of what it means to be an American? This is the question to which I now turn. To facilitate the analysis of a restrictive American identity, an additive scale was created using the five items.[7] A high score indicates a restrictive view, and a low one indicates an egalitarian view. OLS regression results of the standard set of variables predicting support for a restrictive American identity are presented in table 8.5. Although none of the standard set of predictors are statistically significant for Latinos, the results reveal important features of the context for blacks and whites. For both, higher levels of education are related to a less restrictive view. Older African Americans and whites, however, seem to develop a more restrictive concept. In the context of the terrorist attacks, patriotism, perhaps touching more of its ethnocentric roots, leads to a restrictive American identity. A heightened sense of sociotropic threat produces a restrictive view of American identity among blacks, but among whites and Latinos is unrelated. This suggests that under a heightened sense of threat, blacks might be reminded of how different they are from what they perceive as equality. For whites, the basis of equality and an Amer-

Table 8.5 OLS Regression Coefficients of a Restrictive American Identity, 2001

	All	African American	White	U.S.-Born Latino
Sociotropic threat	.00 (.03)	.12** (.04)	−.02 (.03)	−.04 (.07)
Personal threat	.15** (.02)	.10 (.05)	.16** (.03)	.12 (.08)
Conservative ideology	.11** (.02)	.04 (.03)	.11** (.02)	.07 (.05)
Patriotism	.14** (.03)	.13* (.06)	.19** (.04)	.03 (.07)
Female	−.04 (.03)	−.01 (.07)	−.04 (.04)	−.13 (.10)
Education	−.14** (.02)	−.15** (.04)	−.14** (.02)	.01 (.06)
Age	.06** (.01)	.13** (.02)	.05** (.01)	−.03 (.03)
African American	.35** (.05)	—	—	—
Latino	−.03 (.06)	—	—	—
Born in United States	.10 (.08)	—	—	—
Constant	1.29** (.15)	1.44** (.47)	1.14** (.20)	2.21** (.41)
R^2/adjusted R^2	.27/.27	.35/.33	.24/.23	.07/.02
MSE	.55	.48	.56	.48
N	1198	240	765	126

Source: National Civil Liberties Survey (2001).
Note: Standard errors in parentheses.
*p < .05; **p < .01.

ican identity is not determined by sociotropic threat but tied instead to political conservatism, patriotism, and personal threat.

U.S. Responsibility for the Terrorist Attacks

Underlying many reactions to 9/11 was a belief that the United States and its policies were to blame for the hatred that led to the attacks. As if the attacks were justifiable, individuals with little attachment to the United States—in particular, people in other countries—often extolled the ability of international terrorists to attack the United States on its own soil. To what extent did Americans, especially aggrieved groups, display a similar reaction? Because of the symbolic attack on the American cultural worldview, increased threat should be associated with a greater likelihood of attributing blame to external enemies.

In designing questions to address responsibility for the terrorist attacks, I thought it would be counterproductive to ask directly whether the United States was to blame. Although a few people might subscribe to the conspiracy theories that became popular in some circles in the United States and Europe (in which the FBI, the CIA, or "American interests" were said to have been the culprit) or in the Middle East (in which Israel was sometimes named), few Americans would be likely to see the United States government or its agencies as directly or immediately responsible for the September 11 attacks. I thought it likely, however, that many might see links between America's foreign policy, hatred of that policy, and the terrorist attacks. I posed the question as follows: "How much responsibility do you personally believe the United States bears for the hatred that led to the terrorist attacks?" I sought to tap the idea that even though the U.S. government did not attack itself, and did nothing to justify such horrific action, an important underlying motivation for it was dislike or hatred toward America's policies or government. Because a sense of political alienation is related to perceptions of government legitimacy, I consider how race and ethnicity influence the willingness to attribute responsibility to the United States. My expectation is that though individuals may have pulled together to support the government and the political community, to African Americans, the attacks are likely to reflect duplicity and self-interest in U.S. foreign policies. To the extent that identifying with a larger distressed community creates a peripheral perspective of government, Latinos, too, can be expected to see duplicity in some U.S. policies abroad. To evaluate differences among racial and ethnic groups, it is also necessary to take into account or control for other factors that may be correlated with race and ethnicity, as well as support for aspects of the political system. As figure 8.7 shows, Latinos were much more likely (66 percent) than blacks (57 percent) and whites (49 percent) to attribute some responsibility to the United States for the hatred that led to the attacks. The proportion of whites is perhaps larger than expected, given the overall intensity of support for political authorities following the attacks.

That blacks were more likely than whites to attribute some responsibility to the United States is consistent with the idea that disaffected groups were less likely to absolve the United States of responsibility. However, Latinos may have been even more likely to attribute such re-

Figure 8.7 How Responsible Is the United States for Hatred that Led to the 9/11 Attacks?

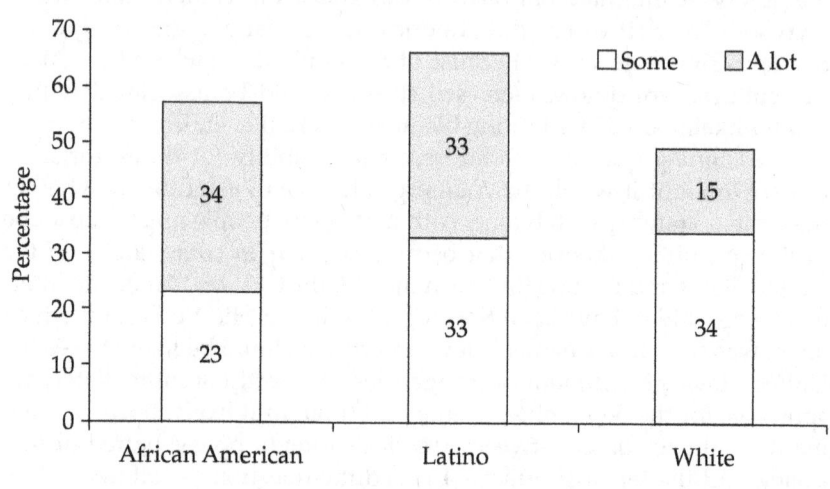

Source: National Civil Liberties Survey (2001).

sponsibility because they were very familiar with and sensitive to the effects of U.S. policies on other countries, in particular those in Latin America. In other words, Latinos were more likely to share the perceptions of many foreigners. The extent to which responses to the question of U.S. responsibility are driven by race and a sense of threat is another important dimension of people's reactions to the attacks and their perceptions of the political system. Politically alienated groups, or groups with a peripheral view of the American political system, may be more likely to attribute some responsibility to U.S. policies and behavior abroad, whereas members of the dominant culture may not see such a connection.

Using the same set of predictors, I analyze the factors that may underlie the belief that the United States was responsible for the hatred that led to the events of September 11. OLS estimates of the single item reveal (column 1 in table 8.6) that a heightened sense of sociotropic threat is not related. However, supporting the conclusions in figure 8.6, Latinos are more willing than whites to assign blame. Disaggregating the analysis by race and ethnicity reveals that the regression line for sociotropic threat for whites and blacks is virtually flat, but increases for Latinos. Although for the most part the reactions of Latinos to the threat of terrorism resembled those of whites, Latinos had distinctive views of the

Table 8.6 OLS Regression Coefficients of U.S. Responsibility, 2001

	All	African American	White	U.S.-Born Latino
Sociotropic threat	.05	–.14	.04	.87**
	(.05)	(.10)	(.06)	(.16)
Personal threat	.04	.16	.03	–.51**
	(.05)	(.11)	(.06)	(.15)
Conservative ideology	–.13**	–.06	–.13**	–.04
	(.03)	(.07)	(.03)	(.09)
Female	–.12*	–.03	–.03	–.96**
	(.06)	(.16)	(.07)	(.19)
Education	.00	.19*	–.02	.17
	(.03)	(.09)	(.03)	(.11)
Age	–.01	.04	–.01	–.06
	(.02)	(.05)	(.02)	(.06)
African American	.20*	—	—	—
	(.07)			
Latino	.44**	—	—	—
	(.10)			
Born in United States	–.09	—	—	—
	(.12)			
Constant	2.75**	2.42**	2.61**	1.85**
	(.21)	(.47)	(.21)	(.63)
R^2/adjusted R^2	.05/.04	.04/.01	.02/.01	.41/.39
MSE	1.02	1.18	.67	.89
N	1231	250	783	128

Source: National Civil Liberties Survey (2001).
Note: Standard errors in parentheses.
*p < .05; **p < .01.

American political system, perhaps reflecting their dual American and ethnic identity.

Many issues may come to mind when individuals are asked to reflect on the degree of U.S. responsibility. Following the attacks, public speculation and agonizing in the media was rife about why the terrorists hate America, but theories that highlighted teachings of Islam and hatred of American democracy were more prominent. For instance, in a speech before a joint session of Congress on September 20, 2001, President Bush suggested that they hate what the see right here in this chamber: a democratically elected government. Their leaders are self-appointed. They hate our freedoms: our freedom of religion, our freedom of speech, our freedom to vote and assemble and disagree with each other. (Office of the Press Secretary 2001a)

However, it was not until well after the attacks that speculation in the American press focused more on the U.S. image and behavior abroad, though some early polls in Europe after September 11 revealed signs of disenchantment with American foreign policy. As one example, in its *World Views 2002* survey, the Chicago Council on Foreign Relations and the German Marshall Fund revealed that majorities of citizens in France (63 percent), the Netherlands (59 percent), Great Britain (57 percent), Poland (54 percent), and Italy (51 percent) believed that U.S. foreign policy "contributed to" the terrorist attacks on America. Therefore, though some respondents may have believed, as leading American officials officially did, that the terrorists were motivated by envy of American democracy and prosperity, others may have believed that U.S. foreign policy and actions abroad contributed to the hatred that led to the terrorist attacks. Figure 8.8 shows the distribution of responses to a series of questions that might underlie beliefs about the U.S. responsibility—questions about perceived causes of the terrorist attacks (see appendix C for full question wording). The perception that U.S. support of Israel is a cause of the terrorist attacks against the United States stands out at 80 percent, with no significant racial differences in the answers. Similarly, the idea that terrorism is the only way that the terrorists can express their grievances was widely shared: 77 percent of whites, 76 percent of blacks, and 74 percent of Latinos. For most of the other potential causes of the attacks, the race and ethnicity of the respondents mattered, sometimes substantially so. In general, blacks were most likely to agree that one of the causes was an important or very important cause of the terrorism, and Latinos were the next most likely. The sharpest racial and ethnic difference is found in answer to the question about the importance of "revenge for harms done to their people," with 88 percent of blacks regarding this as an important or very important cause, 75 percent of Latinos, and 78 percent of whites. This difference suggests that blacks, because of their ethnic experience, may have a better understanding of the feelings of frustration and revenge when it comes to dealing with the U.S. government.

Americans attributed the United States' pursuing its own economic interests and feelings of revenge for harms done to its people as important causes of the terrorist attacks, but whites and Latinos also supported this idea. The two potential causes that received less support overall, but that display substantial racial and ethnic differences, are perceptions of the Islamic religion and that the United States does not provide enough

Figure 8.8 Distribution of Responses to U.S. Responsibility Items, 2001

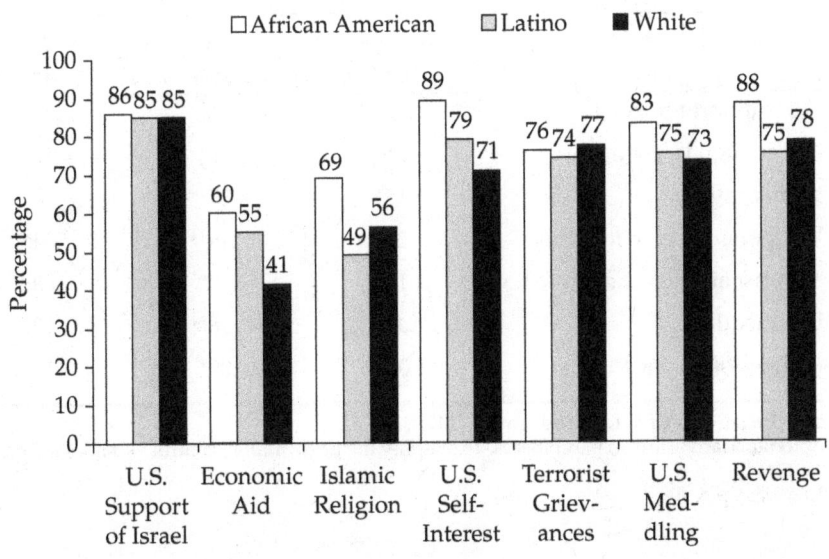

Source: National Civil Liberties Survey (2001)
Note: Responses are those who "strongly agree" and "somewhat agree" to U.S. responsibility.

economic aid: 69 percent of African Americans, 49 percent of Latinos, and 56 percent of whites. Similarly, concerning the United States not providing enough economic aid, 60 percent of blacks and 55 percent of Latinos considered this an important or very important root cause of the 9/11 terrorist attacks, versus only 41 percent of whites.

Although this graphical illustration is suggestive, it does not establish a clear link between perceptions of causes and the feelings of U.S. responsibility. To address this issue, I regressed perceptions of U.S. responsibility on each of the perceived root causes of terrorism by race and ethnicity, controlling for other factors. This allows us to understand better what people might have had in mind when assessing U.S. responsibility. Based on the standardized regression coefficients reported in table 8.7, respondents had several important issues in mind. Whites' perceptions stems from several different sources, but the most important are the United States' pursuing its own interests abroad and meddling in the affairs of the other countries. The extent to which respondents consider the Islamic religion a root cause of terrorism is not a contributing factor. Among blacks, perceived hatred is linked to its meddling in the affairs of other countries and the support for Israel. However, blacks do not see

Table 8.7 Standardized OLS Regression Coefficients of Perceived Causes of Hatred toward United States on Responsibility for Attacks, 2001

	African American	White	U.S.-Born Latino
U.S. support for Israel	.27**	.06	−.39**
Not enough U.S. aid	−.01	.10**	.10
Islamic religion	−.15*	−.17**	−.16
U.S. pursuing own interests	−.26**	.19**	.34**
Terrorist air grievances	.14*	.10*	.08
U.S. meddling	.35**	.18**	.12
Feelings of revenge	.05	.09*	.11

Source: National Civil Liberties Survey (2001).
Note: Standard errors in parentheses. To simplify the presentation, control variables are not reported.
*p < .05; **p < .01.

pursuing national interests abroad as contributing to the hatred. Latinos, on the other hand, see this as an important factor, but not the support for Israel. In sum, although there is a general perception that U.S. policies and meddling in the affairs of other countries are linked to how the United States is perceived abroad, blacks are the most likely to perceive the support for Israel as a significant factor.

Respondents who were more likely to perceive terrorists as wanting to highlight their grievances were more likely to believe the United States was liable for the hatred directed toward it. The same applies across the board for citizens who believed that the United States meddles too much in the affairs of other countries.

Conclusion

Because of greater psychological distance from the political system and political authorities, aggrieved citizens, such as African Americans, might be expected to have less sympathy for a political system when it is attacked. Political disaffection has been said to produce a level of resentment toward the political system: the government, political authorities, and the norms under which it operates. As a consequence, when the government is attacked and needs the support of its citizens, aggrieved groups would not be expected to acquiesce to government requests. Aggrieved groups would not necessarily present an internalized threat to the government. The government would simply not be able to count on their compliance and support. Such assumptions, as we have seen in this chapter, are generally false.

Most significant here is that in the context of the attacks, the influence of race extends beyond support for civil liberties to support for the political system. It appeared that whites supported the political community and authorities, and held fast to democratic principles in the abstract following the attacks. Latinos also supported the political community and political authorities, though they were more likely to see partial U.S. responsibility and more ready to abandon democratic principles in the face of a terrorist threat than whites or blacks were. Blacks supported the political community less than whites and Latinos did, did not support the political authorities, and also were more likely to see the United States as partially responsible for the hatred that led to the attacks. Comments by Vernon Jordan several months after the terrorist attacks seem, as George Curry wrote in *The Sacramento Observer*, to capture the reaction of many African Americans ("Vernon Jordan Says Blacks Are No Strangers to Terrorism," April 25, 2002):

> Black Americans hold America's values dearly. At times, it seemed as if we were the only ones who did. When this nation was in the grip of racism and segregation, it was black people who reminded America of its basic values of freedom and democracy. It was Black Americans who helped America close the gap between its beliefs and its practices. It is a role that's still being served today. We know that dangerous rhetoric can lead to acts of lunacy that kill innocents. And we know that the surest defense against terrorism is affirmation of America's basic values, the values we have learned in our churches, the values we have fought and died for in America's every war, even in segregated armies.

Chapter 9

Social Group Affect, Intolerance, and Threat

I NOW EXPLORE the extent to which the threat from the attacks of September 11 influenced affective perceptions toward various groups in American society, including Islamic fundamentalists, Arab Americans, Jews, African Americans, Latinos, whites, and Christian fundamentalists. Following the attacks, the deep political and social antagonisms that usually characterize American society did not seem to constrain citizens' need and willingness to reach out to others. As Americans attended to their newfound sense of threat and vulnerability, longstanding social conflicts and hostilities appeared trivial. Americans had been targeted without regard for race, ethnicity, gender, political viewpoint, or sexual preference, and they responded by coming together under a common national identity to fight a common enemy. People reconnected to civic life, briefly found religion, rushed to donate blood, and contributed to charities.[1] Never had American citizens appeared as indivisible as they did in what we now know was a natural response to a heightened sense of threat and vulnerability (Greenberg et al. 1997; Pyszczynski et al. 2003).

This sense of threat and vulnerability, however, also produced remarkable intolerance. Despite the insistence of tolerance by political authorities, those perceived as sympathetic to foreign terrorists, Islamic fundamentalists, or divergent from mainstream American identity were targets of violence and hate crimes. In response to reports of violence and harassment directed toward individuals perceived as Middle Eastern, President Bush remarked at the Islamic Center of Washington, D.C., on September 17, 2001 ("'Islam is Peace' Says President"), "that those who feel like they can intimidate our fellow citizens to take out their anger don't represent the best of America, they represent the worst of humankind, and they should be ashamed of that kind of behavior." Still, Middle Eastern–owned businesses and mosques were burned and desecrated. Middle Easterners were killed, physically assaulted, racially profiled, evicted and barred from housing, fired from jobs, restricted from flying on airplanes, and subjected to ethnic slurs. Because foreign terrorists were able to infiltrate American society and use its openness against it, there was an understandable concern that terrorist cells were hidden within the population, planning another attack. Such a concern did not seem too farfetched: political authorities anticipated further attacks and people were advised to be on guard.

However, other groups were also affected by the mass intolerance and uneasiness. Jews experienced a certain amount of grief because of conspiracy theories directly implicating the Israeli government in the terrorist attacks and because U.S. support for Israel was seen by many as motive for the terrorists. Latinos were deported because of stricter visa requirements and became targets of anti-immigrant sentiment. Blacks seemed to relish in, for once, not being direct targets of racial profiling and increased scrutiny, but remained guarded against the government's encroachment on civil liberties.

My main purpose in this chapter is to determine the extent to which a heightened sense of threat and vulnerability produce broad intolerance in which other minority groups in American society were at greater risk or did a heightened sense of threat produce focused intolerance where only those implicated or perceived as sympathetic to foreign terrorist were at greater risk. It is clear that when an external enemy threatens the country and people experience a heightened sense of threat, they are likely to gravitate toward members of their in-group and others who protect their cultural worldviews. That fear and threat are among the fundamental causes of intergroup hatred has been broadly endorsed. At the same time, however, it is important to consider the extent to which groups that might not conform to the traditional American identity—basically, white and Protestant—may also be perceived with some animosity. Beyond perceptions of threat, I consider other aspects of the context of the terrorist attacks, such as heightened patriotism, dogmatism, and political conservatism, that may also give rise to intolerence.

Identity, Categorization, and Threat

Marilynn Brewer's recent work (1999) on social identity and intolerance provides the theoretical foundation for understanding the tolerance of various groups following the terrorist attacks. In-group affect and out-group intolerance arise from social differentiation, a process through which individuals recognize that they are both similar and different from others (Tajfel 1981; Tajfel and Turner 1986). In-group affect does not automatically translate into out-group intolerance. According to Brewer (1999), in-group affect stems from an obligatory interdependence, whereby individuals come to rely on and cooperate with others. Such mutual dependence allows a variety of resources and information to be shared that would be rather costly for individuals to provide for themselves. Because members of a group are expected to reciprocate, social differentiation—the sorting of people into groups—facilitates and minimizes the cost of what Brewer calls "cooperative interdependence." In the end, "expectations of cooperation and security promote positive attraction toward other in-group members and motivate adherence to in-group norms of appearance and behavior that assure that one will be recognized as a good or legitimate in-group member" (1999, 433). Preference for one's own in-group results from this expectation of mutual trust and obligation.

Over time, perceptions of social groups may change or be enhanced, and new perceptions formed through interactions with members of other groups, mediated information, specific events, and their connection to other issues. For Henri Tajfel and John Turner (1986), this process of categorizing and identity formation is the foundation for many social biases, such as prejudice, discrimination, xenophobia, and group conflict. The attractive feature of this type of social differentiation is that it neither falsely requires scarcity of resources nor assumes that dissimilar individuals will be automatically rejected.

For Brewer (1999), the rejection of out-groups may result from a different set of processes, such as challenges to the beliefs of moral superiority of in-groups and political manipulation, but the process that is most relevant to the context of the terrorist attacks is threat. Brewer maintains that, "whether actual or imagined, the perception that an out-group constitutes a threat to in-group interests or survival creates a circumstance in which identification and interdependence with the in-group is directly associated with fear and hostility toward the threatening out-group and vice versa" (435–36). According to John Turner (1987), the social context, such as the terrorist attacks, prompts individuals to behave based on their national identity. As national identity is made salient, individuals can be expected to feel a greater connection to fellow citizens than they do to groups that do not fit the traditional American identity. Events like the attacks will likely have a lasting influence on feelings toward groups connected to them, such as Islamic fundamentalists and Middle Easterners.

This process is consistent with another set of explanations; realistic conflict theory (Sherif 1966) and integrated threat theory (Stephan, Ybarra, and Bachman 1999). Under each idea, out-group hostility results from real or perceived conflicting goals. Realistic conflict theory suggests that economic threat or competition increases in-group loyalty and hostility toward the out-group. However, such competition need not be strictly economic according to integrated threat theory. For instance, integrated threat theory suggests that out-group derogation may result from realistic or symbolic threats, which would include political, physical, cultural, moral, and general belief system. Therefore, in reaction to the attacks out-group derogation can be expected to be focused on those groups, namely Islamic Fundamentalists and Arabs, perceived to be either directly responsible for or sympathetic to the attacks. I argue that given that the enemy and foreign threat were clear, albeit difficult to detect, and largely foreign, other minority groups in American society were not at greater risk due to a heightened sense of threat. However, some groups might become objects of intolerance indirectly as a result of an emotionally charged context with heightened aspects of patriotism, conservatism, and dogmatism. At the same time, certain out-groups might also suffer from intolerant policies, such as tightened rules governing immigration and citizenship, that become more restrictive during social conflict. But, the threat of terrorism by itself is not going to be enough for citizens to find scapegoats in other groups in American society. Even then, we would have to question the extent to which certain values and beliefs were not already predisposed to the rejection of certain out-groups and intolerance.

Other research seems to support the role of self-categorization and threat. In an on-line survey of self-selected participants, Debra Oswald (2005) examined various psychological perspectives such self-categorization, Social Dominance Orientation (SDO), and threat on the endorsement of anti-Arab sentiment from December 2001 to February 2002. The major finding from this analysis suggests that while Social Dominance Orientation was associated with anti-Arab discrimination, prejudice, and stereotyping, self-categorization, such as "pride in America" and threat, was the most powerful predictor of Arab resentment.

The enemy was clearly identifiable following the attacks. So, there was no mistake as to the object of intolerance. But, the explicit categorization of the war and the extolling of civic values made it easy to be simultaneously tolerant and intolerant. For instance, President Bush remarked,

> As you probably figured out by now, I view this current conflict as either us versus them, and evil versus good. And there's no in between. There's no hedging. And if you want to join the war against evil, do some good.

President Bush continued:

> If you want to be part of our nation's stand against those who murder innocent people for the sake of murder, for those who believe in tyranny, for those who hijack a noble religion—if you want to take a stand, love a neighbor like you'd like to be loved yourself. If you want to be part of the war, walk across the street and say to a shut-in elderly person, what can I do to help you? Or mentor a child. Or get into your public schools here in

Anchorage. Or provide support for people. Or go to your church or synagogue or mosque and walk out with a program that says, I want to help somebody in need. Feed the hungry. If you want to be part of the war against terror, remember that it's the gathering momentum and millions of acts of kindness that take place in America that stands squarely in the face of evil. (President Rallies the Troops in Alaska, February 16, 2002)

This statement clearly frames the issue of tolerance as one in which citizens should reach out to others but that the war on terrorism is directed toward those sympathetic to the terrorists. If individual citizens followed such a directive, intolerance should be focused, as opposed to diffuse. It is also reasonable to expect individuals to express greater affection toward the groups to which they belong. Blacks should rate blacks more warmly than others, as should whites and Latinos rate whites and Latinos. Such expectations for in-group affect are straightforward and reflect a fundamental tenet of social identity theory and an evolutionary perspective on identity.

Importance of Group Related Cues

Because individuals rely on cues and shortcuts when making choices, perceptions of social groups become very useful in understanding politics. Henry Brady and Paul Sniderman (1985) suggest that out-group perceptions help people make sense of politics. People were observed to rely basically on their feelings and emotions, and were said to organize their feelings around a likability heuristic, simplifying potentially complex information into readily interpretable information that does not require one to know a lot about politics. Out-group affect, such as likes and dislikes of social groups, is seen as an efficient way to encode and store what is, after all, the most vital political information: who and what one is for or against (1075). The more people like a group, the more they support the group's positions on national issues; the more people dislike a group, the less they support it.

In the end, perceptions and feelings toward social groups become important frames of reference for people organizing and evaluating political phenomena (Campbell et al. 1960; Hagner and Pierce 1984; Kinder and Sanders 1996; Kluegel and Smith 1986; Knight 1984; Nie, Verba, and Petrocik 1976; Nelson 1999; Nelson and Kinder 1996). This role of social group perceptions has been extremely important when it comes to political tolerance (Gibson 2004; Gibson and Gouws 2003). Perceptions of social groups since Stouffer (1955) have anchored political tolerance judgments. In the clash of political values and civil liberties, individuals weigh their personal needs to the benefits of their group and the costs of other groups. Zero-sum politics presupposes that groups benefit at the expense of others. Stouffer (1955), and many scholars to follow, asked about the tolerance of specific groups to attach support for civil liberties to substantive issues rather than abstract norms. It seemed logical during the 1950s, given the perils of the Cold War and the communist threat. Outside contentious periods, social groups compete across a variety of issues. Political issues are not contested in abstract environments, and most become attached to groups. Not only are politics organized along competing group interests, but individuals also structure their thinking and positions around what groups benefit. In a content analysis of open-ended discussion of support for civil liberties, Dennis Chong (1993) reports that social group-related cues were a major factor in how people understand tolerance decisions. He argued that group-related cues were probably more accessible and easier than a response based on principle, but that "respondents can often get a handle on a difficult issue by relating to how it directly affects them or the groups to which they belong. This transforms a relatively abstract matter into a subject that they can more readily identify with" (887).

These studies underscore a larger body of literature suggesting that under normal quiescent conditions, though social categorization and in-group favorability are natural and help people understand politics, out-groups may already be viewed unfavorably. Social identity and categorization may be enough to account for the level of antipathy expressed toward out-groups after the 9/11 attacks (Gibson and Gouws 2003). But terror management theory (TMT) provides another direct theoretical connection between a heightened sense of threat and disdain for out-groups. TMT suggests that threat, at least in laboratory experiments, leads to intolerance and tolerance simultaneously (see chapter 4). The awareness of threat intensifies the desire for faith in one's cultural worldview because it offers stability and protection from existential fear. Individuals under a heightened sense of threat will defend their worldview, reacting positively to those who uphold their cultural values and negatively to those who violate or otherwise threaten them, as shown in numerous studies, conducted across several societies and under various conditions (Pyszczynski, Greenberg, and Solomon 1997).

The conclusion I draw from this body of literature is that a heightened sense of threat and vulnerability from the attacks would predict a great deal of intolerance for groups that challenged one's cultural worldview, at the same time making certain racist, xenophobic, and ethnocentric statements more appealing. Islamic fundamentalists and Arab Americans can be expected to be direct targets of intolerance because of a perceived connection to foreign terrorists. But intolerance may also be pluralistic, generalized to intolerance toward immigrants, anti-American groups, and those who might not fit in the dominant culture.

Measuring Group Affect: Feeling Thermometers

This analysis uses feeling thermometer ratings, which were first introduced in the 1964 National Election Study and used extensively in public opinion research to measure attachment to social and political groups as well as political candidates. Respondents are asked to rate either social groups or individuals on an imaginary scale, ranging from 0 (very cold) to 100 (very warm). Lower ratings are intended to measure enmity or hate, and warmer ratings are intended to measure amity and reverence. Ratings at the midpoint are intended to reflect indifference or ambivalence. Objects of affection in the ratings include Middle Easterners and people with Arabic backgrounds, whites, Islamic fundamentalists, Latinos, Jews, Christian fundamentalists, and blacks.

Although feeling thermometers have been shown to produce a bias in which respondents evaluate a range of groups favorably (Knight 1984) and another in which respondents apply different standards to judge groups (Green 1988). Although respondents tend to be warmer to certain groups (Wilcox, Sigelman, and Cook 1989), traits measured using more response categories are more highly correlated with the underlying trait than is the case with other measures (Alwin 1997). It is probably impossible to overcome survey respondents' idiosyncrasies using feeling thermometers; I attempt to minimize these in scaling by using a more reliable range of 0 to 10 (Gibson and Gouws 2003). Not that it makes a huge difference, but I found it easier in a telephone survey to ask about a scale with a smaller range. I also expected that, because survey respondents might be more accustomed to using a 0 to 10 range in daily affairs, it might reduce unreliability in the scale.[2] To further minimize idiosyncrasies in the feeling thermometers, Clyde Wilcox and his colleagues (1989) and Kathleen Knight (1984) recommend some form of adjustment, such as subtracting the mean score for all thermometers from the score for the group in question, to account for individual variation in the items. This adjustment revealed a more valid measure of group affection than the unadjusted items did. Relative mean differences in the thermometers, derived by subtracting the difference in each scale from the grand mean of all groups, standardize the measures. The scale ranges from 8.57 positive group affect to –8.57 negative group affect. All scales are highly correlated to the original ratings, but it is clear that there were some idiosyncratic effects.[3]

Selection of Groups

Survey respondents were asked about their feelings toward Islamic fundamentalists, identified as the group and underlying ideology responsible for the September 11 attacks, as well as the driving force behind the hatred toward the United States. Islamic fundamentalism was distinguished from Islam, Muslims, and individuals with Middle Eastern or Arabic backgrounds.[4] By identifying groups directly, President Bush framed the target of retribution and anger. In a speech given at the Islamic Center of Washington, D.C., a week after the attacks, he declared, "these acts of violence against innocents violate the fundamental tenets of the Islamic faith. And it's important for my fellow Americans to understand that. . . . The face of terror is not the true faith of Islam. That's not what Islam is all about. Islam is peace. These terrorists don't represent peace. They represent evil and war" ("'Islam is Peace,' Says President," September 17, 2001). The question about Islamic fundamentalists was intended to capture images of al Qaeda, members of the Taliban, terrorists, and insurgents in Afghanistan.

Feeling thermometer ratings for Arabs and Middle Easterners were asked because that group is more easily identified than Islamic fundamentalists, and because the rating captures the extent of racism, or the degree to which citizens are willing to attribute responsibility for the attacks to an uninvolved group. As mentioned, many people attributed fundamentalist beliefs and sympathy for the terrorist attacks to people they perceived as Middle Eastern and Arab. As a result, people perceived as Middle Easterners were targets of violence, harassment, and discrimination. Reminiscent of the scapegoating following the 1995 attack on the Alfred P. Murrah Federal Building in Oklahoma City, they were immediately assumed to be responsible. American citizens are likely to show a deep-seated hatred toward Middle Easterners generally, comparable to their disdain for Islamic fundamentalists.

Christian fundamentalists were initially included in the list of groups as a control and to explore the extent to which the context would lead to intolerance of other fundamentalist groups following the attacks. The idea was that if people under a heightened sense of threat showed similar disdain for Christian fundamentalists, this would mean that extremism, not just Islamic extremism, might be the perceived problem. Christian fundamentalist beliefs were interjected in the political discourse following the attacks because of comments made by the Reverend Jerry Falwell, televangelist and fundamentalist Baptist minister. Two days after the attacks, Falwell surprised many individuals with these intolerant statements on national television:

> And, I know that I'll hear from them for this. But, throwing God out successfully with the help of the federal court system, throwing God out of the public square, out of the schools. The abortionists have got to bear some burden for this because God will not be mocked. And when we destroy 40 million little innocent babies, we make God mad. I really believe that the

pagans, and the abortionists, and the feminists, and the gays and the lesbians who are actively trying to make that an alternative lifestyle, the ACLU, People for the American Way—all of them who have tried to secularize America—I point the finger in their face and say, "you helped this happen." ("Jerry-Maid; Falwell Blames Liberals, Gays, Judges for Terror," *Pittsburgh Post-Gazette*, September 17, 2001, A14)

With such broad accusations and attributions of blame, Christian fundamentalists might be likely to be perceived as sympathetic to certain intolerant viewpoints, which would resonate with some citizens, but perhaps make people less supportive of them.

Respondents were also asked about their feelings toward Jews, another group that could have been scapegoated following the attacks. Jews were immediately implicated in conspiracy theories suggesting that the Israeli government had been involved in the attacks to incriminate Islamist groups. Israeli intelligence was also alleged to have had prior knowledge of the attacks, and warned Jews who worked in the World Trade Center to stay home. Although there was no evidence to suggest that American citizens endorsed these theories, people did see a connection between U.S. support for Israel and growing hatred in the Middle East. In the fall of 2001, U.S. policy toward Israel came under greater scrutiny. In my data, 85 percent of American citizens believed that U.S. support for Israel was an important factor in the attacks. Thus, perceptions and feelings toward Jews may have become linked to the level of threat. Asking about Jews also balanced the questions about Middle Easterners.

The last groups included in feeling thermometers were blacks, Latinos, and whites. Although these groups have no particular connection to the attacks of September 11, they are useful in testing an aspect of social identity theory and a core component of TMT. That is, under a heightened sense of threat and vulnerability, people should develop greater affection toward members of their own social group.

Contextualizing Social Group Perceptions

Social group perceptions from before 9/11 are important in understanding how they changed in context. If certain groups were already negatively perceived before the attacks, a heightened sense of threat could not be considered to change perceptions, only to exacerbate negative perceptions. It is tempting to assert that perceptions were caused by the attacks, but without previous measures, such a statement would be untenable.

What is needed is an indication from before September 11 of how Americans perceived Islamic, Muslim, and Middle Eastern groups. The problem is that such perceptions escaped the attention of survey researchers. Despite being implicated in other terrorist activities, such as the 1993 World Trade Center, the 2000 attack on the USS Cole in Yemen, and the 1998 bombings of the U.S. embassies in Kenya and Tanzania, the extent to which citizens' perceptions were affected by and influenced reactions to the events was not considered very meaningful. However, some survey evidence from before September 11 conveys an image of Muslims, Middle Easterners, and Islamic fundamentalists in the minds of Americans. Most Americans citizens are not likely to differentiate among the various nationalities of the Middle East, just as they do not distinguish among those of South and Central America, Africa, and Asia. Thus, underlying the media portrayals, stereotypes, and other heuristics that influence how citizens perceive Middle Easterners, individuals were likely grouped together based on ascribed features that had little to do with knowledge of the region or the cultural and historical differences among the countries there. Sikhs—individuals from India who, because of their religion, are required to wear turbans—became likely targets of violence and intimidation because of stereotypes about terrorists and Muslims.

Before the attacks, there was surprisingly little interest in American perceptions of Islam and the Middle East. Fortunately, the *Los Angeles Times* asked a series of questions in 1993 that capture a sense of this, though many questions involved perceptions of the Nation of Islam and Reverend Louis Farrakhan. Based on the question marginals reported in table 9.1, the disagreement was considerable, but overall the perception seemed negative. Fifty-six percent reported that they had not heard anything about Islam, and 22 percent had an unfavorable opinion. When asked what came to mind when one thought about Islam in an open-ended format, 27 percent said nothing and 13 percent said the Middle East. But the range of responses varied from thoughts about black Muslims to fanatics and zealots. Asked about Islam's compatibility with democracy, 41 percent thought Islam was antidemocratic and 28 percent thought it a threat to the United States.

Feeling thermometer ratings in the 2000 National Election Study provide useful pre–September 11 data to contextualize the relative standing of blacks, whites, Latinos, Christian fundamentalists, and Jews. It should not be surprising that no questions were asked about perceptions of Islamic fundamentalists, Middle Easterners, or Arabs. I also included a variety of different groups not addressed in this analysis (that is, homosexuals, welfare recipients, feminists, environmentalists, Asian Americans, the poor, Catholics, and the elderly) to contextualize the relative standing of groups I do analyze. The relative feeling thermometer ratings using NES data, reported in figure 9.1, yield several findings. Among the groups that American citizens viewed more negatively than average, Christian fundamentalists were perceived almost as negatively as homosexuals. This view has been somewhat consistent over time—at least

Table 9.1   Perceptions of Islam before September 11, 2001 (Percentages)

"What is your impression of the religion called Islam?"
Haven't heard enough to say	56
Very favorable	2
Somewhat favorable	12
Somewhat unfavorable	11
Very unfavorable	11

"When you think of the religion called Islam, what comes to your mind?"
Nothing (27)	Fanatics-Zealots
The Middle East (13)	Great Religion
The Arab countries (8)	Anti-Israel
Black Muslims (3)	Violence-Terrorism
Iran (2)	Foreign religion
Ayatollah Khomeini	Mohammed
Saddem Hussein	Mecca
Rev. Louis Farrakhan	War
Malcolm X	Israel
Fundamentalism	Other
Anti-American	Not Sure
Women subservient	Refused

"Do you think the religion called Islam is compatible with western style political democracy or is Islam basically an anti-democratic religion?"
Democrat	10
Antidemocratic	41
Not sure	45

"Do you think the religion called Islam poses a threat to the security to the United States and its western allies or not?"
Not threat	38
Major	13
Minor	15
Not sure	30

Source: Los Angeles Times (February 18–19, 1993).
Note: This survey was a national survey with a sample of 1,273.

since 1988, when the NES first asked about them in a feeling thermometer. With a raw feeling thermometer score of 51 degrees, Christian fundamentalists were also perceived somewhat negatively in the late 1980s as the religious right began to exert greater political influence and take positions on abortion, school prayer, and homosexuality. According to Louis Bolce and Gerald de Maio (1999), citizens developed more antago-

Figure 9.1 Relative Feeling Thermometer Ratings (2000 National Election Study)

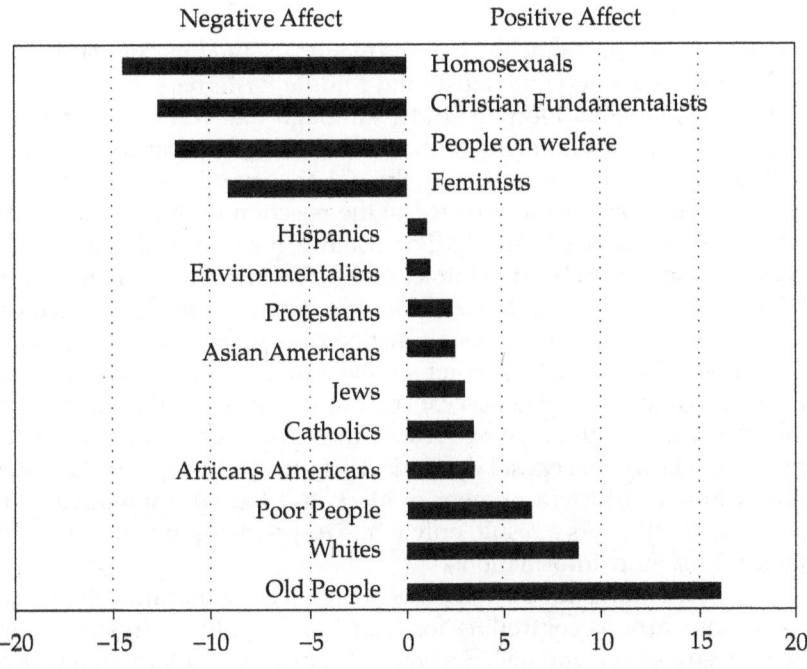

Source: Author's compilations.

nistic feelings toward evangelical, fundamentalist, and born-again Christians than toward more mainline Protestant groups. Furthermore, Christian fundamentalists were considered a negative political reference group, diminishing support for groups closely associated with them, such as the Republican Party and GOP presidential candidates (Bolce and de Maio 1999).

Americans' affection for Latinos is lower than it is for blacks and whites. In 2000, Latinos were ranked just below environmentalists and Protestants, though affective evaluations of Latinos have improved over time. In 1976, Latinos received a 55 degree feeling thermometer rating, 6 degrees lower than blacks. Before the attacks, affection for Latinos increased steadily to 64 degrees. Latinos continue to be associated, however, with negative issues, such as immigration and making illegitimate demands on the political system. Blacks as a social group were viewed relatively positively in 1964, with a 63 degree rating. Before the terrorist attacks, in 2000, positive affect toward African Americans had increased to 67 degrees. Americans were also relatively supportive of Jews, which has been generally the case since 1964. Whites have been consistently ranked among the highest social groups. But, since 1964, positive affect toward whites has steadily declined, from 83 to 73 degrees in 2000.

Most of the groups included in the National Civil Liberties Survey, except for Islamic Fundamentalists and Middle Easterners, were included in the 2000 National Election Study. Although the NES survey is not directly comparable and many of the measures, such as patriotism, threat, and dogmatism are not included, these data, nevertheless, are useful in determining if the factors that led to the rejection of out-groups existed before the September 11 attacks. For instance, if we know that the level of conservatism was related to intolerance before the attacks then it would be somewhat erroneous to conclude that broad intolerance linked to a heightened conservatism was a function of context. It is quite possible for context of the attacks to heighten the intolerant beliefs such as patriotism, dogmatism, and conservatism, but it is an entirely different matter to assert that the context created those feelings. NES data are expected to clarify this causal dynamic. Unfortunately, the 2000 NES does not include a sufficient number of black and Latino respondents for a separate analysis. As a result, only white respondents are analyzed. (See table 9.2 for more information.)

Table 9.2 reports the OLS analysis of NES feeling thermometer ratings for various groups controlling for white affect, political trust, ideology, gender, education, and age. Several results are particularly noteworthy. First, before September 11, a heightened conservative ideology was significantly related to the derogation of African Americans, Latinos, and Jews, but positively related to Christian Fundamentalists. What this result says about conservatism is that apart from an emotionally charged and threatening environment people who label themselves as conservative show greater antipathy for racial and ethnic minorities. Numerous studies have linked a conservative ideology to heightened prejudice. Sidanius, Pratto, and Bobo (1996) argue that link between conservatism and prejudice is likely grounded in a social dominance orientation that is driven by beliefs in nonegalitarian and hierarchically structured group relations. An emotionally charged environment like the terrorist attacks can exacerbate conservative beliefs, but it would be clearly erroneous to suggest that the context creates such propensities, though it certainly has that potential.

Second, higher levels of education are positively related to the endorsement of Jews, Latinos, and African Americans before the attacks, but negatively related to the endorsement of Christian Fundamentalists and whites. Third, the stronger attachment whites feel toward their in-group the more negatively they perceive Latinos, African Americans, and Christian Fundamentalists. The implication is that while education may potentially offset the consequences of a conservative ideology, cer-

Table 9.2 OLS Regression of Relative Feeling Thermometer Ratings (2000 National Election Study)

	Christian Fundamentalists	Jews	Latinos	African Americans	Whites
White affect	−.29**	−.05	−.17**	−.12**	—
	(.05)	(.03)	(.03)	(.03)	
Political trust	−.30	−.17	.08	.53*	−.44
	(.47)	(.28)	(.28)	(.27)	(.35)
Conservative ideology	4.44**	−1.23**	−.77**	−.99**	.40
	(.37)	(.22)	(.22)	(.22)	(.28)
Education	−2.50**	.81**	.53**	.88**	−.94**
	(.28)	(.17)	(.17)	(.16)	(.21)
Sex (1 = female)	.54	−.22	−1.37	.39	.28
	(1.23)	(.75)	(.74)	(.72)	(.92)
Age	−.15**	.09**	−.06	.02	.03
	(.04)	(.02)	(.02)	(.02)	(.03)
Constant	14.72	−3.33	4.70	−6.17	22.30**
	(5.44)	(3.30)	(3.28)	(3.16)	(3.99)
R^2/adjusted R^2	.23/.23	.08/.09	.10/.09	.10/.09	.03/.03
Root MSE	17.99	10.92	10.85	10.45	13.46
N	865	865	865	865	865

Source: 2000 National Election Study.
Note: Standard errors in parentheses.
*p < .05; **p < .01.

tain minorities might be at greater risk if whites' sense of identity becomes activated in context.

Social Group Affect and Threat

The relative feeling thermometer ratings for the seven groups following the terrorist attacks of September 11 are illustrated in figure 9.2. As expected, Islamic fundamentalists were looked on least favorably. Although all groups evaluated Islamic fundamentalists and Middle Easterners negatively, blacks had the least negative opinion, and the difference is notable. However, it is this sort of consensus on maligned groups that can lead to political repression. Sullivan and his colleagues (1982) observed that when there is no general consensus on threatening groups (pluralistic intolerance), it is difficult to get majority support for policies constraining their behavior. Repression is facilitated when citizens agree generally, and are able to zero in on a group. The context of the terrorist

Figure 9.2 Relative Feeling Thermometer Ratings, 2001

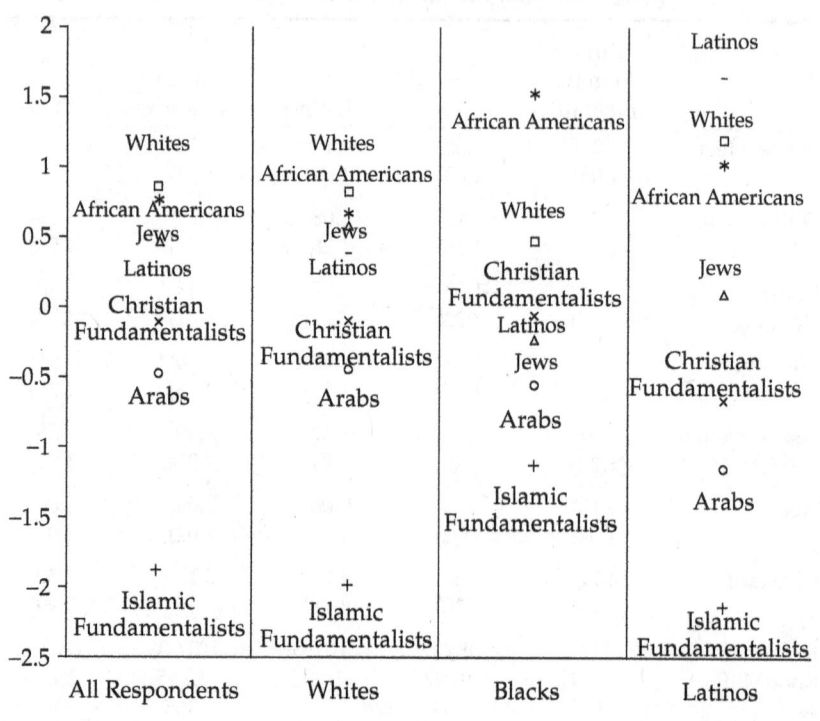

Source: National Civil Liberties Survey (2001).

attacks exacerbated negative perceptions, making policies that limit the behavior and civil liberties of Islamic fundamentalists—such as racial profiling, strict immigration rules, and violations of habeas corpus—more tolerable. Such policies would probably receive majority support.

Arabs, though also seen in a negative light, are not considered as extreme as Islamic fundamentalists. Respondents looked on Arabs with suspicion and perceived them as possibly sympathetic to foreign terrorists. The level of antipathy for Arabs is probably not enough to produce consensus on measures to curtail their freedom, but as seen following the attacks, Arabs and those perceived as Arab were targets of violence, intimidation, and discrimination by political authorities and citizens. Because of a perceived connection to terrorists, citizens attributed certain motives and behavior to Arabs.

Because the country fixated on Islamic fundamentalists and Middle Easterners as inspiring the greatest threat and anxiety, an important question I might ask is how were other social groups in American society perceived? I am able to address this question directly with the National Civil Liberties Survey. Based on these data, whites were the most positively evaluated group, followed by blacks, Jews, Latinos, and (relative to Arabs and Islamic fundamentalists) Christian fundamentalists. When social group perceptions are considered by race and ethnicity, affections become slightly reordered, but objects of negative affection do not change. Race and ethnicity continued to make a big difference in perceptions after September 11. As predicted from social identity theory, respondents rated their own groups more positively than others. Whites saw Christian fundamentalists more negatively. Blacks were less receptive to whites, Latinos, and Jews, but these perceptions likely predated the attacks. Blacks have traditionally viewed Latinos with some distrust because of greater competitiveness and perceived illegitimate claims on the political system. Jews and blacks have had a somewhat contentious recent history, but the negative evaluation of Jews following the attacks was probably linked to U.S. policies toward Israel and its perceived connection to the attacks. Before September 11, Latinos were positively disposed toward whites, more so than whites were to Latinos. I interpret this as a concern for acculturation, in that the dominant culture in American society was evaluated more favorably. Latinos also evaluated blacks positively.

Threat and Social Group Perceptions

Caution is warranted in attributing social group perceptions to the terrorist attacks of September 11. Up to now at least, given the lack of previous measures of such perceptions, variations in threat are used to explore how social groups were affected by the event. Although many factors influence these perceptions, I begin with a naïve approach, using only a bivariate relation between threat and group affect. To simplify the analysis, I dichotomized sociotropic threat into high threat (combining "very concerned" and "somewhat concerned") and low threat (combining "not very concerned" or "not concerned at all"). The adjusted feeling thermometer ratings by threat are illustrated in figures 9.3, 9.4, and 9.5. Ratings greater than zero represent groups rated more positively than average; ratings less than zero represent those rated more negatively than average. Interestingly, in the bivariate relationships, threat seems to be unrelated to perceptions of Islamic fundamentalists. Although other factors, such as conservatism and patriotism, may be masking threat's effects, it is clear that whites were fairly uniform in their negative feelings toward Islamic fundamentalists and Arabs, regardless of threat. A heightened sense of threat among blacks (figure 9.4), on the other hand, resulted in higher negative evaluations of Islamic fundamentalists and Arabs. Latinos were also uniformly negative toward Islamic fundamen-

Figure 9.3 Mean Relative Feeling Thermometer Ratings by Sociotropic Threat (White Respondents)

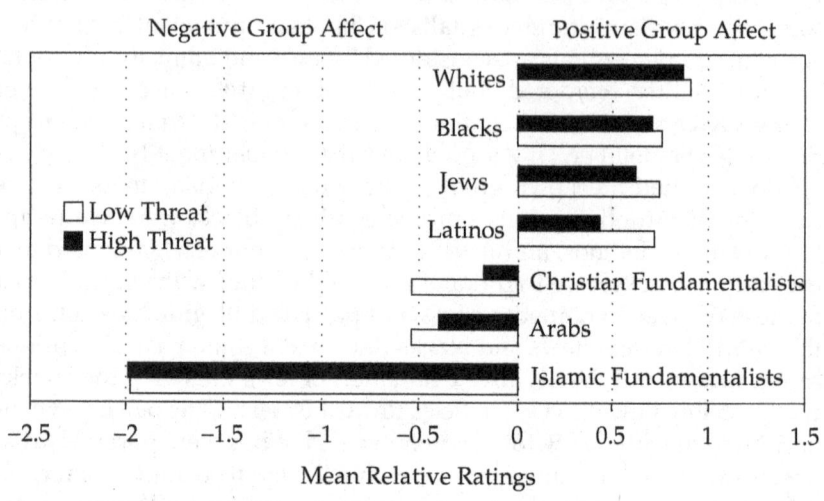

Source: National Civil Liberties Survey (2001).

talists (figure 9.5), but under a heightened sense of threat, they developed more negative perceptions of Arabs. In short, Latinos and whites perceived Islamic fundamentalists more negatively than blacks did, but the level of threat did not seem to matter much. This suggests a more complex process that is not being captured in the bivariate relation. Also, although whites, blacks, and Latinos evaluated their own social groups more positively than other groups, only among Latinos did a high level of threat result in positive in-group affect. However, a high level of threat also made Latinos turn away from Jews.

The perceptions of blacks, Latinos, and whites of each other underscore the results from previous chapters. Although whites had positive affect toward blacks and Latinos, a heightened sense of threat among whites led to more negative perceptions of Latinos. Concerns about immigration likely drive this reaction. Latinos might not pose a direct threat in the context of terrorism, but the issue of their immigration status may resonate with whites concerned about future terrorist attacks. Among blacks, a heightened sense of threat led to positive evaluations of whites. This is a big turnaround, considering that blacks under low threat perceive whites more negatively. It is perhaps a sign of terror management theory that blacks may gravitate very slightly toward whites when the country is attacked, but certainly not to the extent that they do toward Latinos. Latinos were perceived positively by blacks, but the

Social Group Affect, Intolerance, and Threat   209

Figure 9.4   Mean Relative Feeling Thermometer Ratings by Sociotropic Threat (Black Respondents)

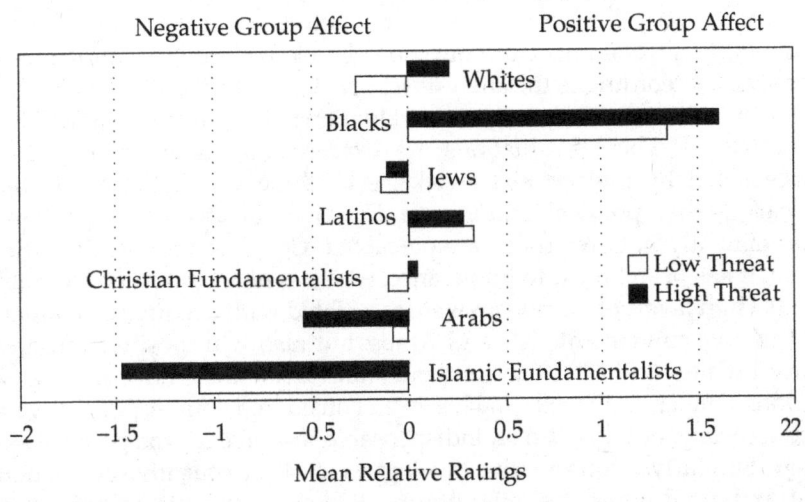

Source: National Civil Liberties Survey (2001).

Figure 9.5   Mean Relative Feeling Thermometer Ratings by Sociotropic Threat (Latino Respondents)

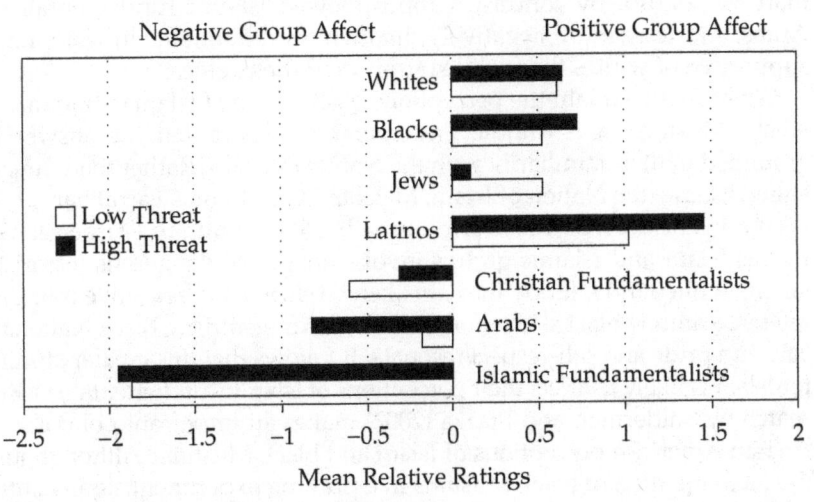

Source: National Civil Liberties Survey (2001).

level of threat did not seem to matter much. Latinos were positively disposed to both blacks and whites, but Latinos under greater threat seemed to gravitate toward blacks.

This cursory view of the relationship between threat and group affection raises several important questions I seek to clarify in a multivariate analysis. According to the analysis reported in table 9.3, high levels of sociotropic threat leads to negative evaluations of Islamic fundamentalists and Arabs. These evaluations are exacerbated among people most threatened by the terrorist attacks, everything else being equal. But, clearly, other political attitudes and individual characteristics figure prominently in how groups are perceived. Consider the role of patriotism. It has been linked to intolerance, which is now confirmed (see table 9.3). High levels of patriotism were associated with negative evaluations of Islamic fundamentalists and Arabs, but also with positive affect toward whites and Christian fundamentalists. As others have shown, patriotism taken to the extreme has been considered counterproductive to civil society, but it is also an indispensable resource for the political system. Similarly, a conservative ideology is related to negative evaluations of Arabs and other dissimilar groups. Following the attacks of September 11, conservatives not only viewed Arabs with a sense of hatred, but Jews, Latinos, and blacks with a certain amount of loathing as well. Extreme conservatism has also been recognized as intolerant. A conservative ideology was also related to positive affect toward Christian fundamentalists. Replicating previous bivariate results, blacks were more positively disposed to Islamic fundamentalists than whites were, but at the same time, they perceived Jews, Latinos, and whites more negatively than whites did. By contrast, Latinos viewed Islamic fundamentalists, Arabs, and Jews more negatively than whites did, but again were more supportive of whites than whites supported themselves.

What might explain the perceptions blacks have of Islamic fundamentalists, Muslims, and Middle Easterners? I suspect that the answer is grounded in their familiarity with the Nation of Islam. Rather than threatening, Islam—the Nation of Islam, Malcolm X, and Louis Farrakhan—has been a historically positive force in the black community (Turner 2003). Just as Islam and Islamic groups invoke images of dangerous terrorists among whites and Latinos, they are likely to elicit a more positive frame of reference among blacks, in whom themes of Afrocentrism, Black Nationalism, and pride and self-respect resonate. It follows that this greater affinity for Islam is likely to affect their perceptions of Islamic fundamentalists. Research by Sniderman and Piazza (2002) makes an important point about African American perceptions of Islam and black Muslims. Although just the mere mention of black Muslims in a priming experiment significantly increased the popularity rating of Louis Farrakhan, the black Muslim prime also led to the endorsement of negative stereotypes of Jews. This goes directly to the point that the reactions of African Americans may be

Table 9.3 OLS Regression of Relative Feeling Thermometer Ratings, 2001

	Islamic Fundamentalists	Christian Fundamentalists	Arabs	Jews	Latinos	Blacks	Whites
Sociotropic threat	−.18* (.08)	.01 (.07)	−.14* (.06)	.04 (.05)	.13** (.05)	.12* (.05)	−.02 (.05)
Political trust	.23** (.09)	−.01 (.08)	−.03 (.07)	−.01 (.05)	−.04 (.05)	−.13* (.05)	−.01 (.05)
Patriotism	−.27** (.10)	.15 (.09)	−.29** (.08)	.11 (.06)	.13* (.06)	.04 (.06)	.13 (.06)
Conservative ideology	−.05 (.06)	.42** (.05)	−.09 (.05)	−.02 (.04)	−.11** (.03)	−.11** (.03)	−.03 (.03)
Dogmatism	−.06 (.07)	.39** (.06)	−.30** (.06)	.04 −(.04)	.08* −(.04)	−.04 (.04)	.13** (.04)
African American	.82** (.19)	−.08 (.17)	.04 (.15)	−.66** (.12)	−.40** (.11)	.67** (.11)	−.54** (.12)
Latino	−.61* (.22)	−.50* (.19)	−.75** (.17)	−.31* (.13)	1.45** (.12)	.27 (.13)	.45** (.13)
Education	−.12** (.06)	−.10 (.05)	.06 (.05)	.11** (.04)	.15** (.04)	−.07* (.03)	−.04 (.04)
Sex (1 = female)	.18 (.12)	−.10 (.10)	−.01 (.09)	−.04 (.07)	−.02 (.07)	−.04 (.07)	.04 (.07)
Age	.04 (.03)	−.09** (.03)	.01 (.03)	.10** (.02)	−.07** (.02)	−.02 (.02)	.02 (.02)
Constant	−.50 (.57)	−2.81** (.48)	2.43** (.44)	−.42 (.34)	.11 (.32)	1.22** (.32)	−.02 (.34)
R^2/adjusted R^2	.06/.05	.15/.14	.16/.15	.08/.08	.19/.18	.07/.06	.05/.05
Root MSE	1.96	1.68	1.51	1.17	1.11	1.13	1.19
N	1055	1055	1055	1055	1055	1055	1055

Source: National Civil Liberties Survey (2001).
Note: Standard errors in parentheses.
*p < .05; **p < .01.

conditioned by their perceptions of the Nation of Islam, regardless of whether there is no direct link to Islam and Islamic fundamentalism.

Did Americans Gravitate Toward Others After the Attacks?

This chapter began with a very big assumption, that Americans reached out or gravitated toward each other in response to the horror of the September 11 attacks. Americans had very heavy hearts afterward. Like people do after most terrible experiences, they paused, realized the fragility of life, and found a new appreciation in things that were most precious and irreplaceable, such as family, friends, community, helping others, and supporting one's country. The terrorist attacks were frequently observed as an event around which citizens could reconnect to each other and to a larger political community. Emotional reactions that cut across American society, such as the heightened sense of threat and patriotism, were seen as catalysts to bringing people together. Beyond increased volunteerism, donating blood and money, and briefly finding religion, however, the willingness to reach out to others was only anecdotal. Did in fact the context of the terrorist attacks with its heightened sense of threat, political trust, and patriotic sentiment make individuals, at least, think of others in less affectionate terms?

For this part of the analysis, I refer to the regressions in tables 9.4 (whites), 9.5 (blacks), and 9.6 (Latinos). The dependent variable is the relative feeling thermometer ratings for various groups in American society with the normal set of explanatory variables. One of the most important hypotheses, about the extent to which threat led to the rejection of outgroups, finds limited support. For instance, a heightened sense of threat among whites (table 9.4) led to greater antipathy toward Islamic fundamentalists but did not transfer to Arabs, or any groups, for that matter. In this case, the intolerance of sociotropic threat was more narrowly focused on the group most directly connected to the terrorist attacks, as there are no other significant sociotropic threat coefficients among whites. At that same time, however, sociotropic threat did not endear other groups to whites either.

A heightened sense of threat among blacks (table 9.5) did not lead to them to reject Islamic fundamentalists. Instead, it appears to have focused their intolerance of Arabs, though they were less antagonistic toward them than whites and Latinos were. Sociotropic threat nonetheless has a negative and significant effect. Even though heightened threat among blacks neither draws them toward nor pushes them to reject other groups, with the exception of Latinos, those who perceived greater threat rated Latinos more favorably than other blacks who perceived less threat.

For Latinos (table 9.6), the findings are similar. Under a heightened sense of threat, they are less tolerant of Arabs and increase their affect toward Christian fundamentalists and blacks. This effect for African Americans is understandable, given their minority status and similar experiences. The only explanation for Christian fundamentalists, whom they rank fairly low (see figure 9.2), is that the possibly more attractive religious (but not necessarily fundamentalist) component.

A fundamental tenet of social identity and terror management theory

(text continues on p. 216)

Table 9.4 OLS Regression of Relative Feeling Thermometer Ratings, 2001 (White Respondents)

	Islamic Fundamentalists	Christian Fundamentalists	Arabs	Jews	Latinos	Blacks	Whites
White affect	-.91** (.05)	-.12** (.05)	-.53** (.04)	.16** (.04)	.12** (.03)	.28** (.03)	—
Sociotropic threat	-.23* (.10)	-.02 (.09)	-.06 (.07)	.09 (.06)	.08 (.06)	.02 (.05)	-.01 (.06)
Political trust	.04 (.10)	.03 (.09)	-.10 (.08)	.08 (.07)	-.06 (.06)	.01 (.05)	.03 (.07)
Patriotism	-.08 (.12)	.20 (.11)	-.11 (.09)	.07 (.08)	-.08 (.07)	.01 (.06)	.09 (.08)
Conservative ideology	-.07 (.06)	.46** (.06)	-.14** (.05)	-.05 (.04)	-.09* (.04)	-.11** (.03)	-.01 (.04)
Dogmatism	-.03 (.09)	.43** (.07)	-.20** (.06)	-.09 (.05)	-.14** (.04)	-.04 (.04)	.08 (.05)
Education	-.18* (.07)	-.12 (.06)	.09 (.05)	.08** (.04)	.15** (.04)	.01 (.04)	-.01 (.04)
Sex (1 = female)	.16 (.13)	.04 (.13)	-.02 (.10)	-.11 (.09)	-.06 (.08)	-.01 (.07)	-.02 (.09)
Age	.06 (.04)	-.08** (.03)	-.01 (.03)	.08** (.02)	-.05* (.02)	-.00 (.02)	.03 (.02)
Constant	-.14 (.67)	-3.32** (.63)	1.54** (.52)	-.33 (.44)	1.36** (.41)	.89** (.35)	-.07 (.44)
R²/adjusted R²	.28/.27	.19/.18	.21/.21	.07/.06	.09/.07	.13/.12	.01/.01
Root MSE	1.77	1.65	1.39	1.15	1.09	.94	1.15
N	727	727	727	727	727	727	727

Source: National Civil Liberties Survey (2001).
Note: Standard errors in parentheses.
*p < .05; **p < .01.

Table 9.5 OLS Regression of Relative Feeling Thermometer Ratings (Black Respondents)

	Islamic Fundamentalists	Christian Fundamentalists	Arabs	Jews	Latinos	Whites	Blacks
Black affect	-.39** (.05)	-.17** (.07)	-.03 (.06)	-.31** (.05)	-.18** (.05)	.08 (.05)	—
Sociotropic threat	.06 (.09)	-.01 (.12)	-.47** (.10)	.14 (.09)	.30** (.09)	-.03 (.08)	.19 (.12)
Political trust	.29** (.10)	-.06 (.13)	.16 (.12)	-.45** (.09)	-.19 (.09)	.23** (.09)	.01 (.13)
Patriotism	-.49** (.14)	-.62** (.18)	.07 (.16)	.37** (.13)	.16 (.13)	.52** (.13)	.13 (.18)
Conservative ideology	.18** (.07)	.24** (.09)	-.09 (.08)	-.00 (.06)	-.25** (.06)	-.08 (.06)	.17 (.09)
Dogmatism	-.21* (.09)	-.18 (.12)	.01 (.10)	.46** (.08)	-.13** (.08)	.06 (.08)	-.19 (.11)
Education	-.01 (.08)	-.15 (.11)	.22* (.10)	.18* (.08)	-.04 (.08)	-.21** (.08)	-.17 (.11)
Sex (1 = female)	-.28 (.16)	-.16 (.22)	-.32 (.19)	-.06 (.15)	-.04 (.15)	.78** (.15)	.74** (.21)
Age	-.09 (.05)	-.00 (.06)	-.06 (.05)	.18** (.05)	-.02 (.04)	-.02 (.04)	.15 (.06)
Constant	1.33* (.64)	3.38** (.86)	.62 (.75)	-3.13** (.61)	.33 (.60)	-2.54** (.59)	-.43 (.84)
R^2/adjusted R^2	.36/.34	.14/.10	.17/.13	.37/.34	.21/.17	.29/.26	.13/.10
Root MSE	1.06	1.43	1.24	1.01	1.00	.98	1.40
N	224	224	224	224	224	224	224

Source: National Civil Liberties Survey (2001).
Note: Standard errors in parentheses.
*$p < .05$; **$p < .01$.

Table 9.6 OLS Regression of Relative Feeling Thermometer Ratings (Latino Respondents)

	Islamic Fundamentalists	Christian Fundamentalists	Arabs	Jews	Blacks	Whites	Latinos
Latino affect	-.68** (.14)	-.24 (.15)	-.37** (.10)	-.21* (.10)	.10 (.09)	.40** (.10)	—
Sociotropic threat	-.22 (.23)	.80** (.23)	-1.17** (.17)	-.05 (.17)	.35* (.15)	.30 (.16)	.07 (.13)
Political trust	.88** (.26)	-.66** (.26)	.51** (.19)	-.41* (.19)	-.51** (.17)	.18 (.18)	.02 (.15)
Patriotism	-.28 (.24)	.01 (.25)	-.34 (.18)	.10 (.18)	.36* (.16)	.14 (.17)	.16 (.11)
Conservative ideology	-.31 (.17)	.05 (.17)	.23 (.12)	.08 (.12)	-.05 (.11)	-.01 (.12)	-.14 (.09)
Dogmatism	.09 (.23)	.30 (.24)	-.65** (.17)	-.24 (.17)	.21 (.15)	.29 (.16)	.37** (.13)
Education	-.47* (.23)	.21 (.23)	-.79** (.16)	.21 (.16)	.52 (.14)	.31 (.16)	-.04 (.11)
Sex (1 = female)	.87* (.39)	.56 (.39)	-.35 (.28)	.24 (.27)	-.75** (.25)	-.58* (.27)	.14 (.21)
Age	.01 (.10)	-.31** (.10)	.25** (.07)	.11 (.07)	-.14** (.06)	.10 (.07)	-.32** (.05)
Constant	-.59 (1.55)	-1.88** (1.57)	5.46** (1.12)	.99 (1.12)	1.20 (.98)	-2.78** (1.07)	1.01 (.88)
R²/adjusted R²	.37/.32	.23/.16	.67/.64	.24/.18	.41/.36	.33/.27	.30/.26
Root MSE	1.60	1.62	1.15	1.15	1.02	1.10	1.05
N	122	122	122	122	122	122	122

Source: National Civil Liberties Survey (2001).
Note: Standard errors in parentheses.
*p < .05; **p < .01.

concerning the role of threat and gravitation toward one's own in-group is not supported in this analysis. As shown in figures 9.3, 9.4, and 9.5, blacks, Latinos, and whites supported their own group more than any other regardless of their sense of sociotropic threat. At all levels of threat, then, there are no significant differences across groups in the affinity for one's own.

Another important question pertains to the role of identity and rejection of out-groups. Independent of threat perceptions, did the support for one's in-group translate into the rejection of out-groups in the context of the September 11 attacks? Among whites the answer is no, with the exception of Christian fundamentalists and groups perceived to be implicated in the attacks. That is, whites for the most part did not view other groups in American society as threatening. Among blacks, greater affinity for other blacks did indeed lead to their rejecting other groups, such as Christian fundamentalists, Jews, and Latinos, but not whites. For Latinos, greater affinity for other Latinos led to a rejection of Jews, but a greater affinity for whites.

In the end, negative aspects of threat were directed toward groups perceived to be implicated in the attacks and did not translate into the intolerance toward other groups. Intolerance, especially among blacks, probably had little to do with the attacks. However, I do not want to minimize the intolerant atmosphere that followed September 11 because sociotropic threat is not the sole motivation for intolerance. Although the effects of political trust, patriotism, and dogmatism on out-group perceptions are inconclusive, the influence of a conservative ideology is somewhat consistent among whites. As one might expect, self-identified conservatives are more supportive of Christian fundamentalists than self-identified liberals are. Some might find it surprising that a conservative ideology was also related to a heightened antipathy for blacks and Latinos. Others will note, however, that scholars like McClosky (1958) and Rokeach (1960) identified the connection between conservatism and intolerance decades ago. But, the context of 9/11 did not create the level of conservatism that led to the derogation of others. This existed before the terrorist attacks, though a conservative ideology is connected to heightened patriotism and dogmatism. It is easy to see how the context could indirectly create mass intolerance by exacerbating other intolerant beliefs.

Conclusion

This chapter began with two simple and important questions. To what extent did the sense of threat experienced in the context of the 9/11 attacks lead to disaffection toward out-groups? To what extent were dissimilar social groups, particularly those perceived to be sympathetic to the terrorists' position, placed at risk when the country was threatened? In addressing these questions, I had to confront theoretically the possibility that certain groups would naturally fall out of favor as people began to understand their political world and make sense of group differences. Although this type of sorting is functional for the individual, because it permits evaluating groups and political issues with little or no information, it also leads to stereotyping and reactions such as racism, ethnocentrism, homophobia, and xenophobia. The attacks cannot be said to have fundamentally changed individual perceptions of social groups in this sense. That is, the disposition toward liking or hating particular groups was already ingrained in the American psyche. A heightened sense of threat, however, likely intensified ethnocentric views as individuals come to rely more on such stereotypes, become resistant to new information, and seek to defend their cultural worldviews.

Islamic fundamentalists and Middle Easterners were viewed with hostility following the attacks of September 11. A heightened sense of threat was understandably more likely to produce highly negative evaluations of Islamic fundamentalists, because this group was linked directly to the terrorist attacks. Middle Easterners in general, however, were also targets of hatred and mistrust. An intriguing problem for American citizens and political authorities is that there are no social markers to distinguish terrorists, and that social markers change. On paper, people might have been willing to distinguish between Islamic fundamentalists and Arabs, but the reality of the situation was more vague. People perceived as sympathetic to fundamentalist views became suspect.

American minority groups were not threatened in the same way. Mass threat did not put other groups at risk, but the level of threat tended to heighten the effects of other political views leading to intolerance, such as patriotism and political conservatism. Before 9/11, political conservatives were already suspicious of minority groups, such as African Americans, Jews, and Latinos.

Chapter 10

Conclusion

Tolerance is not absolute. It may be presumed that almost nobody would support the right to cry "Fire!" in a crowded theater; to engage, if a teacher, in sexual relations with students; to conspire, if a government official, with agents of the Soviet Union. The issues before America are not and never have been the preservation of absolute rights of freedom, but rather how and where to set the limits. If the limits are set too high, orderly activity and even the life of the nation might become impossible. If the limits are set too low, the Anglo-Saxon heritage of relative freedom may be endangered.
—Samuel Andrew Stouffer (1955, 27–28)

MY INTENT in this final chapter is to step back from the data to offer a broader picture of the findings and how they inform both the theoretical literature and individual reactions to the terrorist attacks of September 11. As tragic and horrifying as the attacks were, they created a unique context to study the compromise between liberty and security. Because support for democracy and freedom is situational, it is only when they clash with real events that we can understand the nature of democratic support. At no other time in American history have citizens believed that they would have to sacrifice a certain measure of freedom and liberty to be safe and secure. Cherished values of liberty and security, usually unnoticed, taken for granted, now had tangible consequences. The overall theme of this analysis is that support for democracy is neither absolute nor unequivocal: the most ardent supporters of civil liberties can became reluctant antagonists, and vice versa. As Stouffer recognized, any other way is untenable. Democracy requires some give and take, some flexibility, among its citizens. Unconditional support on either side leads to societies in which there is either no freedom or complete chaos.

This analysis does not ask what is the proper balance between liberty and security in national crisis. I am not sure if such a question can be answered. Rather, my purpose has been to understand the processes that govern the trade-off between liberty and security among individual citizens. Although this analysis sheds light on how individuals respond to crisis, it also informs the theoretical literature.

A "New Normal": Has America Changed?

In the aftermath of the 9/11 attacks, America citizens were expected to adjust to a new sense of vulnerability and restrictions on their civil liberties and freedom. Both expectations have meaningful theoretical implications. Concerning the new sense of vulnerability, this analysis reveals that over a three-year period following the attacks, perceptions of threat among individual citizens remained quite high and stable. Such sustained perceptions were not so much a response to the attacks as to the events and policies intended to make people feel safe afterward. The invasion of Afghanistan, the protracted war in Iraq, failure to find weapons of mass destruction in Iraq—the justification for going to war—and the release of the 9/11 Commission's report so critical of the administration for its intelligence failures were all intended to make people feel more secure in the long term. However, they had the short-term consequence of making people less secure and questioning trust in political authorities. No matter how well intentioned policies to combat terrorism were, citizens remained vigilant.

Despite the sustained perceptions of threat, Americans have not shown a penchant for tolerating restrictions on their freedom and civil liberties. In fact, the opposite is true. Over time, citizens became more protective of civil liberties than concerned about their security. This was a major reversal of the position held immediately after the attacks, when Americans were willing to sacrifice a great deal in their concern for security. Under a heightened sense of threat, many respondents were justifiably concerned, but nevertheless understood the antidemocratic consequences of their security preferences. When presented with these consequences, respondents favored restricting civil liberties even more than moderating their views. However, the willingness to compromise rights for security proved only temporary and was tied to trust in political authorities.

Commitment to Liberty and Freedom

Despite initial willingness to compromise rights, American society was far from complete agreement on the need to concede civil liberties for security. Most people did not think in terms of absolutes nor hold unequivocal preferences following the attacks. Few wanted to give the government complete authority, and few wanted to give it none. American citizens seemed to understand that the situation required some flexibility and compromise. Removing the ability to adjust the balance between civil liberties and security would inevitably lead to constitutional suicide, in which democracy is defended for the sake of democracy or becomes so restrictive that there is no freedom. Individuals were probably not thinking in these terms when they responded to my survey, but it is relatively clear that they found both extremes undesirable. Thus, consistent with the larger literature, support for civil liberties should be seen as situational, with people picking and choosing which values they are willing to concede and the type of security it might provide. But democracy endures not only because individuals remain committed to the democratic ideal, but also because there is never a time when all aspects of democracy simultaneously fall into disrepute. Overall, Americans were willing to temporarily acquiesce in the immediate aftermath of the attacks, but not willing to concede all of their rights.

Based on the theoretical model, I showed that the extent to which citizens were willing to concede civil liberties for greater security was tied significantly to their sense of threat in the immediate aftermath of the attacks, but as mentioned above, this decision could not be sustained without the requisite trust in the government and political authorities. Initially, trust in the political authorities, a sense of vulnerability, and patriotism moved in the same direction as the willingness to concede civil liberties for security. Over time, however, as protection for civil liberties increased and threat and patriotism remained the same, trust declined. That is, American citizens need to trust political authorities before they sacrifice their freedom and liberty to them.

Underlying the general stability of support for civil liberties was considerable individual-level movement. Support for civil liberties is neither immutable nor unequivocal: expose individuals to the appropriate stimuli and they will either support policies they would not ordinarily support or fall silent. The incredible sense of threat and vulnerability following the 9/11 attacks led political liberals, who are traditionally protective of civil liberties, to behave remarkably like political conservatives. Similarly, individuals typically the least trustful of political authorities responded much like those most trustful. However, as the political climate changed, so did these relations.

Perceptions of Threat

Sociotropic threat was the most important determinant of the willingness to concede civil liberties for security in the immediate aftermath of the attacks and outweighed several other factors, such as political trust, patriotism, dogmatism, political ideology, and racial-ethnic characteristics. Reports following the attacks noted widespread signs of post-traumatic stress disorder (PTSD), in which people, especially victims and those closest to ground zero, developed problems with sleeping and concentrating and were plagued by thoughts of guilt. For many Americans, the risk of personalizing their own sense of threat and vulnerability by becoming concerned about flying on airplanes, going into tall buildings, eating food and drinking water that were possibly contaminated, opening the mail, and being in large crowds and stadiums was real. All these behaviors were perceived as major personal threats following the attacks. However, I found that individuals were more threatened by the idea of the country coming under another attack than by being attacked personally. This sense of vulnerability was perfectly rational, because political authorities and the media were telling people that attacks were imminent and that they needed to be vigilant. Whether this was an aspect of political manipulation is beyond the scope of this book, but Americans responded in important ways to the hyped-up fear assessments.

However, as the climate changed from high trust to lower trust in political authorities, support for civil liberties increased, despite near-constant levels of threat. Clearly, without firm faith and trust in authorities, people are not willing to concede freedoms and liberties. I believe this finding is consistent with the theoretical expectations of terror management theory, which would predict that individuals under a heightened sense of threat gravitate toward groups that bolster their worldview. In the context of the attacks, individuals acquiesced in and supported government policies because of their identification with the country—in other words, because of their national identity. But this observation should be qualified: People may be willing to gravitate to those who bolster their worldview as long as high levels of trust are involved. Under a heightened sense of threat and lower levels of political trust, individuals can be expected to reaffirm their civil liberties. The data showed that over time, sociotropic threat lost its potency in determining support for civil liberties and political trust became more important. Without trust, political authorities would have to resort to coercion and force to achieve their goals.

Racial Perceptions Are Extremely Powerful

One would be hard-pressed to find a political concept in which race was not significant or relevant, and the terrorist attacks are no exception. Race was just as important as threat, political trust, patriotism, and political ideology to understanding the trade-off of civil liberties and security. As other groups—whites and Latinos—caved in to their sense of threat and vulnerability, African Americans became more protective of civil liberties. Put another way, one of the most aggrieved groups in American society most strongly supported its civil liberties. As to more abstract democratic principles, intended to decontextualize the support for constitutional norms, blacks remained strong in their support, similar to whites.

I did not seek to tell a story about race, but the reactions of African Americans to the attacks and to the government response stood out. They reflect deep-seated cultural and historical experiences with both civil rights and blacks' own brand of terror. Many will not find their response to terror surprising, because blacks have always supported democratic and constitutional principles, using them to assert claims of equality and freedom. They have certainly wished that American society in general were equally committed to those ideals. It is neither unusual nor strange for African Americans, more than any other groups, to want to preserve their civil rights in the face of threats by an external enemy and from a government asking for greater surveillance authority. Hard-fought rights are not easily relinquished to political authorities not perceived as trustworthy. I have argued that this racial difference also implies, more broadly, a belief among American blacks that America got what it deserved.

Political Silence and Acquiescence

Political acquiescence and willingness to support restrictions on civil liberties for security should not be interpreted as direct support. After the attacks, the usual partisan and ideological polarizations were simply absent. Whether the lack of debate reflected acquiescence or just silence, there was a perception of agreement. Conceding civil liberties required many people—Democrats in particular—to support policies they would not ordinarily support. What led to this dynamic, and why were people willing to acquiesce or remain silent as civil liberties were restricted? I explored this question in great detail using the most ideologically polarized groups in American politics: strong Democratic and Republican identifiers. The political parties together have been the most polarized groups in American society, and examining their movement on civil liberties issues following the attacks reveals another important aspect of the event and of support for civil liberties.

In the context of the attacks, the usual divergence of political and ideological preferences of the two political parties was somewhat reversed, though also one-sided. Democrats made a much larger move than Republicans to support the security proposals of the Bush administration. Beyond the security policies, Democrats also overwhelmingly approved of President Bush. But this support did not last, began in fact to diminish almost immediately. Political partisans did not feel the need to shift their political orientations or affiliations, though many political observers expected them to do so. I always thought that such expectations were bizarre, because they did not consider that the psychological attachment to political parties was comparable to a social group identity. Such a position also did not consider what people would have to accept, or how much they would have to change. Given Democratic positions on civil liberties and civil rights, this was not the issue to make them reconsider their partisan orientations, regardless of their sense of vulnerability.

It is clear that Democratic identifiers were moved by their sense of patriotism and trust in political authorities after September 11. This translated into greater support for security over protecting civil liberties. However, as trust declined, so did the level of support among Democratic identifiers, and politics returned to its usual polarized state.

Group Affect and Tolerance

Underlying the renewed sense of identity and weakening social antagonisms following the attacks, a heightened sense of threat led to intolerance toward anyone perceived as sympathetic to or supportive of the foreign terrorists. In the immediate aftermath, both citizens and noncitizens perceived as Muslim, Middle Eastern, or sympathetic to the terrorist attacks, based on clothing, name, or even accent, were singled out for violence, harassment, and discrimination. I initially suspected that a sense of threat would lead to greater intolerance for social groups perceived as nonconformist or "un-American." Examining group affect toward a host of social groups in American society, among them Islamic fundamentalists, Arabs, Christian fundamentalists, blacks, whites, Latinos, and Jews, I took a different stab at trying to understand the role of threat and outgroup antipathy.

My suspicions were clearly wrong on this account. Although a sense of vulnerability and threat led to rejecting social groups that appeared sympathetic to foreign terrorists, threat did not lead to mass disaffection or intolerance of other groups. Also, Americans already were highly mistrustful of Islamic and Middle Eastern groups and had been since the first bombing of the World Trade Center, in 1993. A heightened sense of threat and vulnerability in context exacerbated negative affect toward Islamic fundamentalists and Arabs but did not influence the perceptions of other groups.

However, other minority groups were not completely off the hook with respect to a sense of threat, because other motivations in context placed them at further risk. A sense of intolerance and conformity is imbedded in the core of political conservatism. In the immediate aftermath of the attacks, both intensified. Whites and Christian fundamentalists were spared, but the rejection of Jews, African Americans, and Latinos by political conservatives resembled that of Islamic fundamentalists and Middle Easterners.

As extensive as these findings may appear, many questions are unanswered. The ultimate uncertainty is how people will react to future terrorist attacks. The original intent of conducting subsequent panel waves was to examine how people reacted under different aspects of threat and vulnerability. Although I initially anticipated a similar reaction to September 11 had another attack occurred, based on the data I changed my opinion. I now expect that Americans, because they now have the experience of anxiety and what might be expected when the government needs to provide for their safety and security, will be more reluctant to concede civil liberties in the future. Thus, conducting the subsequent panel waves after a seeming return to normalcy has proven extremely useful.

Many of the federal government's new powers of surveillance are not readily discernable to most Americans. We know about other government actions, such as long detentions of suspected al Qaeda operatives, but people are for the most part unaware of when their financial records, reading habits, and Internet searches might be monitored. I believe that most citizens, who almost invariably say that they are doing nothing wrong and have nothing to hide, would not have a problem with continued surveillance and encroachment on civil liberties. But trust in government and political authorities is still extremely important. Given a general lack of it, American citizens might not be as willing to concede their civil liberties on principle, even if the personal costs are not immediately obvious. Just as the threat to the country seemed more important than the threat to one's person after the attacks, so regard for civil liberties may also be tied to broader considerations than one's personal circumstances.

Appendix A

Terror Event Timeline

Table A.1 Timeline

2001	11-Sep	World Trade Center and Pentagon struck by airplanes
	14-Sep	President at Ground Zero: "The people who knocked these buildings down will hear all of us soon."
	20-Sep	President speaks to the nation in Joint Session of Congress
	5-Oct	Anthrax death: Robert Stevens first of five to die, awakens national concern about bioterrorism
	7-Oct	Invasion of Afghanistan ("Operation Enduring Freedom")
	8-Oct	Office of Homeland Security set up in White House, headed by Tom Ridge
	26-Oct	President signs USA Patriot Act after overwhelming support in Congress
	12-Nov	Taliban flee Kabul, Northern Alliance enters on 13-November
	12-Nov	AA Flight 587 crashes shortly after takeoff from LaGuardia, initial concern it is caused by terrorists
	22-Dec	"Shoe bomber" Richard Reid attempts to blow up Paris to Miami flight, subdued by crew
2002	17-Jan	Ashcroft, Mueller news conf.—release tapes recovered from rubble of Afghanistan, name suspects
	25-Jan	Ashcroft, Mueller news conf—release photos of five suspected terrorists
	29-Jan	Ashcroft press release announces heightened security at Winter Olympics
	29-Jan	Bush State of Union: "states in the…axis of evil…pose a grave and growing danger."
	3-Feb	Terrorism alert (before the color-coded scheme introduced)
	8-Feb	Winter Olympic Games open in Salt Lake City
	24-Feb	Winter Olympic Games end
	27-Feb	Terrorism alert ends
	12-Mar	Color-coded "Homeland Security Advisory System" created by presidential order

	26-Aug	Cheney to VFW in Nashville: "The risks of inaction are far greater than the risks of action" in Iraq.
	10-Sep	Orange alert – anniversary of 9/11 (first actual use of color-coded system)
	12-Sep	Bush to UN General Assembly: Iraqi regime a threat to the UN and to peace
	24-Sep	Alert back to yellow
	4-Oct	"Shoe bomber" pleads guilty, sentenced to 20 years
	11-Oct	Congress authorizes the use of U.S. military force against Iraq
	12-Oct	Jemaah Islamiyah terrorist bomb in Bali nightclub kills 202 people
	25-Nov	Homeland Security Act signed by President, authorizes Dept. of Homeland Security
2003	24-Jan	Dept. of Homeland Security (DHS) opens, ending WH Office of Homeland Security
	29-Jan	Bush State of Union: "If Saddam Hussein does not fully disarm we will lead a coalition to disarm him."
	5-Feb	Colin Powell addresses UN Security Council on Iraq denial and deception on WMD
	7-Feb	Orange alert (run on sales of duct tape and plastic sheeting)
	13-Feb	Law enforcement, Americans brace for imminent attack on NY, DC, or FL: "dirty bomb scare"
	27-Feb	Alert back to yellow
	1-Mar	DHS absorbs 180,000 employees from other agencies and offices
	1-Mar	Announcement of arrest of Khalid Sheikh Mohammed in Pakistan
	17-Mar	Bush 48-hour ultimatum to Saddam Hussein
	17-Mar	Orange alert (DHS announces "Operation Liberty Shield")
	19-Mar	Bush speech from Oval Office (bombs over Baghdad 20 Mar) ("Operation Iraqi Freedom")
	25-Mar	Texas oil plants on terror alert
	9-Apr	Saddam Hussein statue pulled down in Firdos Square in Baghdad
	11-Apr	101st Airborne enters Baghdad
	16-Apr	Alert back to yellow
	1-May	Bush on deck of USS Abraham Lincoln, declares "major combat operations in Iraq have ended"
	12-May	Bombings in Saudi Arabia (May 12), Morocco (May 16)
	20-May	Orange alert—Boston, NY, in wake of Saudi Arabia and Morocco bombings
	30-May	Alert back to yellow
	22-Jul	Saddam Hussein's sons killed in shoot-out with American troops in Mosul
	4-Sep	DHS warning of al Qaeda plans to hijack airliners between international points and U.S.
	21-Nov	DHS urges vigilance in holiday season, refers to aircraft and chemical/hazmat facilities
	13-Dec	Saddam Hussein rooted out of spider hole
	21-Dec	Orange alert—"chatter" suggests could be holiday attack

2004	9-Jan	Alert back to yellow, but stays orange for NYC, LA, DC, and Las Vegas
	11-Mar	Madrid train bombings kill 191, injure 2,000 (no Orange Alert)
	24-Mar	Richard Clarke testimony before 9/11 Commission
	8-Apr	Condoleezza Rice testimony before 9/11 Commission
	29-Apr	Bush and Cheney testimony before 9/11 Commission in closed-door session
	26-May	Ashcroft warning of terrorist plans related to coming major political events
	28-May	Ashcroft-Ridge joint press release strikes calmer tone
	25-Jun	AP story about Fed. Election Assistance Comm. researching how to "cancel the election"
	25-Jun	"Fahrenheit 9/11" released in movie theaters
	1-Jul	Ashcroft in Miami: plot to attack U.S. this year is "between 75 and 90 percent complete"
	2-Jul	FBI urges increased vigilance for July 4th weekend
	8-Jul	Ridge reports al Qaeda plans major attack on U.S. to "disrupt our democratic process"
	22-Jul	9/11 Commission issues report: "We are not safe"
	26-29 Jul	Democratic National Convention
	1-Aug	Orange alert – DC, NY, northern New Jersey "iconic economic targets"
	4-Aug	Swift Boat Vets for Truth political ads begin (first of nine new ads released through 13-Oct)
	30-Aug-2-Sep	Republican National Convention
	7-Sep	Cheney "wrong choice" comment concerning terror and 2004 Presidential election
	30-Sep	First Presidential debate (focusing on foreign policy and homeland security)
	5-Oct	Vice Presidential debate
	8-Oct	Second Presidential debate (town-hall debate on foreign and domestic policy)
	19-Oct	Progress for America Voter Fund releases "Ashley's Story" political advertisement
	22-Oct	Bush-Cheney campaign begins using "Wolves" political advertisement
	2-Nov	Election Day
	10-Nov	Alert back to yellow

Source: Adapted from Davis, Silver, and Raile (2005).

Appendix B

Data and Research Design

THE DATA on which this analysis is based come from a national survey of noninstitutionalized adults in United States. All interviews were conducted by telephone using computer assisted telephone interviewing (CATI) technology by the Office of Survey Research (OSR) in the Institute for Public Policy and Social Research (IPPSR) at Michigan State University. The overall sampling design involved a truncated disproportionate stratified, list-assisted random-digit sample, which included African American and Latino oversamples. The primary goal of the first wave survey, which was conducted eight weeks after the attacks (November 15, 2001, to December 12, 2001), was to understand how the attacks would influence American public opinion on civil liberties, social group affect, perceptions of threat, political trust, ideology, partisanship, presidential approval, and a host of other attitudes. I will use most of the items covered in the survey, except for a battery of items that explored perceptions of the root causes of terrorism and the qualities of a true American. The initial interest in conducting the second wave panel involved the need to assess change in the event of another terrorist attack on America. There was an expectation that terrorists would strike again and it was important to have before and after measures. Because no attacks occurred, the decision was made to wait no longer than a year to do follow-up interviews. The first of these were conducted from January 21, 2003, to May 28, 2003. Most of the initial items were repeated in this survey, but new items were included to reflect the changing preferences and climate of the attacks. The third-wave interviews were intended to capture aspects of the 2004 presidential elections.

Table B.1 Data Description

	Field Dates	N	Samples	Completion Rate	Language
Wave-1	November 15, 2001 to January 14, 2002	1,448	National, random digit dialing, oversamples of African Americans and Latinos	52.4 percent	English
Wave-2 panel	January 31, 2003 to May 28, 2003	679	Re-interview of wave-1 respondents[a]	46.9 percent	English and Spanish
Wave-2 new cross-section	January 31, 2003 to May 28, 2003	1,284	National random digit dialing, oversamples of African Americans and Latinos	41.1 percent	English and Spanish
Wave-3 all panel (W1+W2+W3)	July 20, 2004 to November 5, 2004	342	Re-interview of wave-1 and wave-2 respondents		English and Spanish
Wave-3 W2+W3 panel	July 20, 2004 to November 5, 2004	811	Re-interview of wave-1 and wave-2 respondents	41.3 percent	English and Spanish
Wave-3 new cross-section	July 20, 2004 to November 5, 2004	960	National random digit dialing, oversamples of African Americans and Latinos[b]	49.4 percent	English and Spanish

Source: Author's compilation.

The data from each wave are weighted to account for the oversampling of African Americans and Latinos, as well as to adjust for differences by education, age, and sex between the respondents and the U.S. population for the year 2002.

[a] In Wave-2, interviews were attempted only with respondents from the first wave who agreed to be recontacted (93 percent). Of the 1,298 who agreed, interviews were completed with 679 (53.2 percent). Most of the attrition was due to not being able to locate some respondents.

[b] Follow-up interviews were attempted only with respondents from the second wave who agreed to be recontacted (95 percent). Of the 1,832 who agreed, interviews were completed with 811 (44.3 percent). Again, most of the attrition was due to not being able to locate respondents.

Table B.2 Assessment of Panel Differences (Differences in Means)

	Wave 1 Measures			Wave 2 Measures		
	Refused	Panel	t	Refused	Panel	t
Attitudinal						
Civil liberties	61.38	59.50	−1.52	56.10	58.52	1.66
Sociotropic threat	3.16	3.23	1.77	3.20	3.06	−2.94**
Personal threat	2.43	2.35	3.63**	2.43	2.19	−4.77**
Political trust	2.56	2.52	−1.19	2.54	2.50	−.94
Patriotism	4.68	4.65	.32	4.56	4.57	.33
Ideology	3.28	3.26	.78	3.33	3.11	−2.99**
Demographic						
Female	.55	.59	1.60	.61	.61	.06
Education	2.17	1.89	−4.67**	1.69	2.17	6.98**
Age	49.14	45.24	−4.32**	45.84	53.45	7.44**
African American	.17	.27	4.59**	.24	.16	−3.42**
Latino	.10	.18	4.42**	.30	.22	−3.42**
White	.71	.52	−7.47**	.42	.60	.06

Source: Author's compilation.
**$p < .01$.

Appendix C

Survey Questions

Sociotropic Threat

I'd like to start by asking you some questions about your feelings since the terrorist attacks of September 11. All in all, how concerned are you that the United States might suffer another terrorist attack in the next three months?

1. Not concerned at all
2. Not very concerned
3. Somewhat concerned
4. Very concerned

Personal Threat

1. How concerned are you about flying on airplane?
    1. Not concerned at all
    2. Not very concerned
    3. Somewhat concerned
    4. Very concerned

2. How concerned are you about opening your mail?
    1. Not concerned at all
    2. Not very concerned
    3. Somewhat concerned
    4. Very concerned

3. How concerned are you about the safety of food and drinking water?
    1. Not concerned at all
    2. Not very concerned

3. Somewhat concerned
4. Very concerned

4. How concerned are you about going into tall buildings?
    1. Not concerned at all
    2. Not very concerned
    3. Somewhat concerned
    4. Very concerned

5. How concerned are you about being in large crowds or stadiums?
    1. Not concerned at all
    2. Not very concerned
    3. Somewhat concerned
    4. Very concerned

Dogmatism

Next, I would like to read you a series of statements and have you tell me to what extent you agree or disagree with each.

1. There are two kinds of people in this world: those who are for the truth and those who are against it. Would you say you strongly agree, somewhat agree, somewhat disagree, or strongly disagree with the statement?
    1. Strongly disagree
    2. Somewhat disagree
    3. Somewhat agree
    4. Strongly agree

2. A group that tolerates too many differences of opinions among its members cannot exist for long. Would you say you strongly agree, somewhat agree, somewhat disagree, or strongly disagree with the statement?
    1. Strongly disagree
    2. Somewhat disagree
    3. Somewhat agree
    4. Strongly agree

3. To compromise with our political opponents is dangerous because it usually leads to the betrayal of our own side. Would you say you

strongly agree, somewhat agree, somewhat disagree, or strongly disagree with the statement?

   1. Strongly disagree
   2. Somewhat disagree
   3. Somewhat agree
   4. Strongly agree

4. Of all the philosophies that exist in the world there is probably only one that is correct. Would you say you strongly agree, somewhat agree, somewhat disagree, or strongly disagree with the statement?

   1. Strongly disagree
   2. Somewhat disagree
   3. Somewhat agree
   4. Strongly agree

5. In the long run, the best way to live is to pick friends and associates whose tastes and beliefs are the same as one's own. Would you say you strongly agree, somewhat agree, somewhat disagree, or strongly disagree with the statement?

   1. Strongly disagree
   2. Somewhat disagree
   3. Somewhat agree
   4. Strongly agree

6. Most of the ideas that get printed nowadays aren't worth the paper they are printed on. Would you say you strongly agree, somewhat agree, somewhat disagree, or strongly disagree with the statement?

   1. Strongly disagree
   2. Somewhat disagree
   3. Somewhat agree
   4. Strongly agree

Democratic Norms

1. If someone is suspected of treason or other serious crimes, he or she should be entitled to be released on bail. Would you say you strongly agree, somewhat agree, somewhat disagree, or strongly disagree with the statement?

234   Negative Liberty

   1. Strongly disagree
   2. Somewhat disagree
   3. Somewhat agree
   4. Strongly agree

2. When the country is in great danger we may have to force people to testify against themselves in court even if it violates their rights. Would you say you strongly agree, somewhat agree, somewhat disagree, or strongly disagree with the statement?

   1. Strongly agree
   2. Somewhat agree
   3. Somewhat disagree
   4. Strongly disagree

3. No matter what a person's political beliefs are, he or she is entitled to the same legal rights and protections as anyone else. Would you say you strongly agree, somewhat agree, somewhat disagree, or strongly disagree with the statement?

   1. Strongly disagree
   2. Somewhat disagree
   3. Somewhat agree
   4. Strongly agree

4. Free speech ought to be allowed for all political groups even if some of the things they say are highly insulting and threatening to some segments of society. Would you say you strongly agree, somewhat agree, somewhat disagree, or strongly disagree with the statement?

   1. Strongly disagree
   2. Somewhat disagree
   3. Somewhat agree
   4. Strongly agree

5. Any person who hides behind the laws when he or she is questioned about his or her activities doesn't deserve much consideration. Would you say you strongly agree, somewhat agree, somewhat disagree, or strongly disagree with the statement?

   1. Strongly agree

2. Somewhat agree
3. Somewhat disagree
4. Strongly disagree

Political Trust

The next set of questions is about trust. How much of the time do you think you can trust the government in Washington to do what is right?

1. None of the time
2. Some of the time
3. Most of the time
4. Just about always

Feeling Thermometer Ratings

The next questions are about some groups of people. I'll name some groups of people and ask you to rate how you feel toward that group on a thermometer that runs from zero (0) to ten (10). The higher the number, the warmer or more favorably you feel toward that group. The lower the number, the colder or less favorably you feel. If you feel neither warm nor cold toward them, rate them a five.

1. People of Middle Eastern or Arabic backgrounds?
2. People who are white?
3. People who are Islamic Fundamentalists?
4. People who are Hispanics or Latinos?
5. People who are Jewish?
6. People who are Christian fundamentalists?
7. People who are Black or African American?

Civil Liberties Abstract Question

I am now going to read you two statements. Please tell me which one you agree with most. To curb terrorism in this country, it will be necessary to give up some civil liberties. We should preserve our freedoms above all, even if there remains some risk of terrorism.

0. Necessary to give up some civil liberties (Security Response)
1. We should preserve our freedoms (Civil Liberties Response)

Civil Liberties Trade-Off Questions

1. Everyone should be required to carry a national identity card at all times to show to a police officer upon request. Being required to carry an identity card would violate people's freedom of association and right to privacy. Which statement do you agree with most?

    0. People required to carry national ID card (Security Response)
    1. ID cards violate freedom of association and right of privacy (Civil Liberties Response)
    2. Depends/Not sure/Don't know (If you had to choose, which opinion is closer to your own?)

2. Some people say it should be a crime for anyone to belong to or contribute money to any organization that supports international terrorism. Others say that people's guilt or innocence should not be determined only by who they associate with or the organizations to which they belong. Which of these opinions do you agree with most?

    0. Regarded as contributing to terrorism (Security Response)
    1. Guilt or innocence not determined by association (Civil Liberties Response)
    2. Depends/Not sure/Don't know (If you had to choose, which opinion is closer to your own?)

Experiment (If previous Security Response)

2a. Suppose, in doing this, people would be judged guilty by association rather than by a crime they may have personally committed. If that happened, would you be less likely to view such people as committing a crime, more likely to view them as committing a crime, or would it make no difference in your answer?

    1. Less likely (Civil Liberties Response)
    2. No difference
    3. More likely

Experiment (If previous Civil Liberties Response)

2b. Suppose people who contribute to these organizations actually are supporting the activities and goals of terrorist organizations. If that were true, would you be less likely to view them as innocent, more likely to view them as innocent, or would it make no difference in your answer?

1. Less likely
2. No difference
3. More likely (Civil Liberties Response)

3. Some people say the government should be able to arrest and detain a non-citizen indefinitely if that person is suspected of belonging to a terrorist organization. Others say nobody should be held for a long period of time without being formally charged with a crime. Which of these opinions do you agree with most?

    0. Detained as long at it takes
    1. Oppose detaining individuals
    2. Depends/Not sure/Don't know (If you had to choose, which opinion is closer to your own?)

Experiment (If Previous Civil Liberties Response)

3a. Suppose this means that many innocent people could be locked up for a long time without ever being charged with a crime. If that happened, would you be less likely to support such detention, more likely to support such detention, or would it make no difference in your answer?

    1. Less likely (Civil Liberties Response)
    2. No difference
    3. More likely

Experiment (If Previous Civil Liberties Response)

3b. Suppose there were strong suspicions that these people are terrorists and detaining them would prevent them from committing other crimes. If that happened, would you be less likely to oppose such detention, more likely to oppose it, or would it make no difference?

    1. Less likely
    2. No difference
    3. More likely (Civil Liberties Response)

4. Some people say that law enforcement should be able to stop or detain people of certain racial or ethnic backgrounds if these groups are thought to be more likely to commit crimes. This is called racial profiling. Others think racial profiling should not be done because it harasses many innocent people just because of their race or ethnicity. Which of these opinions do you agree with most?

0. Allow racial profiling

1. Oppose racial profiling (Civil Liberties Response)

2. Depends/Not sure/Don't know (If you had to choose, which opinion is closer to your own?)

Experiment (If Previous Civil Liberties Response)

4a. Suppose this means that racial profiling often leads to unequal treatment of people just because of their race or national origin. If this happened, would you be less likely to support racial profiling, more likely to support it, or would this not make any difference your answer?

1. Less likely (Civil Liberties Response)

2. No difference

3. More likely

Experiment (If Previous Civil Liberties Response)

4b. Suppose people from certain racial or ethnic backgrounds were actually more likely to commit crimes. If this were the case, would you be less likely to oppose racial profiling, more likely to oppose it, or would this not make any difference in your answer.

1. Less likely

2. No difference

3. More likely (Civil Liberties Response)

5. Some people say high school teachers have the right to criticize America's policies toward terrorism. Others say that all high school teachers should defend America's policies in order to promote loyalty to our country. Which of these opinions do you agree with most?

0. Help develop loyalty

1. Speak against policies (Civil Liberties Response)

2. Depends/Not sure/Don't know (If you had to choose, which opinion is closer to your own?)

6. Some people say that law enforcement should be free to search a property without a warrant solely on the suspicion that a crime or a terrorist act is being planned there. Others say that protection against searches without a warrant is a basic right that should not be given up for any reason. Which of these opinions do you agree with most?

0. Allow search without warrant
   1. Oppose searching without a warrant (Civil Liberties Response)
   2. Depends/Not sure/Don't know (If you had to choose, which opinion is closer to your own?)

7. Some people say that government should be allowed to record telephone calls and monitor email to prevent people from planning terrorist or criminal acts. Others say that people's conversations and email are private and should be protected by the constitution. Which of these opinions do you agree with most?
   0. Allow recording of conversations and emails
   1. Oppose recording of conversations and emails
   2. Depends/Not sure/Don't know (If you had to choose, which opinion is closer to your own?)

8. Some say that people who participate in nonviolent protests against the U.S. government should be investigated. Others say that people have the right to meet in public and express unpopular views as long as they are not violating the law. Which of these opinions do you agree with most?
   0. Investigate protesters
   1. Right to meet in public
   2. Depends/Not sure/Don't know (If you had to choose, which opinion is closer to your own?)

Partisanship

1. Generally speaking, do you think of yourself as a Republican, a Democrat, an Independent or something else?
   1. Democrat
   2. Independent
   3. Republican

2a. Would you call yourself a strong Republican or not a very strong Republican?
   1. Strong Republican
   2. Not a very strong Republican

2b. Would you call yourself a strong Democrat or not a very strong Democrat?

1. Strong Democrat
2. Not a very strong Democrat

3. If you are Independent, do you generally think of yourself as closer to the Democratic Party or the Republican Party?

1. Democratic
2. Neither
3. Republican

Self-Reported Ideology

1. Generally speaking, do you think of yourself as a conservative, a moderate, or a liberal?

1. Liberal
2. Moderate
3. Conservative

2a. Would you consider yourself very conservative or somewhat conservative?

1. Very conservative
2. Somewhat conservative

2b. Would you consider yourself to be very liberal or somewhat liberal?

1. Very liberal
2. Somewhat liberal

3. If you consider yourself moderate, do you generally think of yourself as closer to the conservative side or the liberal side?

1. Closer to the conservative side
2. In the middle
3. Closer to the liberal side

Political Interest

How interested are you in politics? Would you say you are very interested, somewhat interested, not very interested, or not interested at all?

1. Not interested at all
2. Not very interested
3. Somewhat interested
4. Very interested

Patriotism

How proud are you to be an American? Would you say very proud, proud, somewhat proud, not very proud, or not proud at all?

1. Not proud at all
2. Not very proud
3. Somewhat proud
4. Proud
5. Very proud

Qualities of a True American

1. To be a true American, how important is it to be born in America?
   1. Not important at all
   2. Not very important
   3. Somewhat important
   4. Very important

2. To be a true American, how important is it to be able to speak English?
   1. Not important at all
   2. Not very important
   3. Somewhat important
   4. Very important

3. To be a true American, how important is it to be a Christian?
   1. Not important at all
   2. Not very important
   3. Somewhat important
   4. Very important

4. To be a true American, how important is it to be white or Caucasian?
    1. Not important at all
    2. Not very important
    3. Somewhat important
    4. Very important

5. To be a true American, how important is it to be willing to serve the United States in times of war?
    1. Not important at all
    2. Not very important
    3. Somewhat important
    4. Very important

Root Causes of Terrorism

People have different opinion about the root causes of terrorism against the United States. As I list possible causes, please tell me whether you think it is very important, somewhat important, not very important, or not at all important.

1. The U.S. government's support of Israel
    1. Not at all important cause
    2. Not very important cause
    3. Somewhat important cause
    4. Very important cause

2. The United States not providing enough economic aid to poor countries.
    1. Not at all important cause
    2. Not very important cause
    3. Somewhat important cause
    4. Very important cause

3. The Islamic religion
    1. Not at all important cause.
    2. Not very important cause
    3. Somewhat important cause
    4. Very important cause

Appendix C   243

4. The United States pursuing only its own economic interests in its dealings with other countries
   1. Not at all important cause
   2. Not very important cause
   3. Somewhat important cause
   4. Very important cause

5. Terrorists believing that it is the only way that their grievances will be heard
   1. Not at all important cause
   2. Not very important cause
   3. Somewhat important cause
   4. Very important cause

6. The United States meddling too much in the affairs of other countries
   1. Not at all important cause
   2. Not very important cause
   3. Somewhat important cause
   4. Very important cause

7. Feelings of revenge by terrorists for harms done to their people
   1. Not at all important cause
   2. Not very important cause
   3. Somewhat important cause
   4. Very important cause

U.S. Responsibility

How much responsibility do you personally believe the United States bears for the hatred that led to the attacks of September 11?
   1. None at all
   2. A little
   3. Some
   4. A lot

Notes

Chapter 3

1. Before the September 11 attacks, my frame of reference for the clash of rights centered on public housing residents in Chicago, who were forced to sacrifice certain liberties for greater security from violent drug gangs. This has certainly shaped how I think about the trade-off decision, but more fundamentally, it shows that such values do not only clash in national crises.
2. What we later learned from Jackman (1972) was that the main difference between civic leaders over individual citizens was higher levels of education. Besides this, there was nothing intrinsically different about civic leaders. Sniderman and colleagues (1991) shows that while political elites were not protectors of democracy, as they were more likely than individual citizens to suspend civil liberties on several key issues (see also the work by Gibson and Bingham 1985).
3. This runs counter to research by James Kuklinski and his colleagues (1991) showing that greater reasoning and deliberation does not always produce greater tolerance.
4. However, not all trade-offs are equal, and may involve extremely difficult decisions. Fiske and Tetlock (1997) suggest that taboo trade-offs are very difficult, requiring mental operations that are unfamiliar or violate deeply held emotions.
5. An important distinction in my approach, compared to previous support for abstract democratic principles, is that my abstract support for civil liberties is phrased as tradeoff and value conflict as opposed to support for the specific principle (that is, support for freedom of speech, freedom of religion), which would elicit greater support.
6. An argument can be made that becauses they were not very useful in helping individuals structure their beliefs about civil liberties the three items that do not load highly on the first factor should be dropped from the index. Although I am sympathetic to such a viewpoint and doing so would result in a single factor with a higher explained variance and scale reliability, the correlation is quite high between an index using the full items and the reduced number of items ($r = .96$).
7. Respondents had to give valid responses to at least five of the eight civil liberties questions to be included. Lack of response was limited overall, in part

because of built-in probes. However, on the last three questions, a series of follow-up experiments led to somewhat larger numbers of respondents electing not to answer.
8. Race and ethnicity were measured with two questions. Ethnicity came first: "Are you of Hispanic, Latino, or Spanish origin?" Following this came race: "What is your race?" Respondents could have said they were white or Caucasian, African American or black, Arab or Middle Eastern, Hawaiian or other Pacific Islander, Asian or Asian American, or American Indian or Alaska Native. Because of the very small number of respondents, the analyses to follow rely on the whites, African Americans, and Latinos. For comparability across groups, only native-born Latinos are used in analyses. In several instances (chapter 4) Latino respondents are excluded from analysis because the smaller number of respondents would produce unreliable estimates.

Chapter 4

1. Portions of this chapter appeared in Darren Davis and Brian Silver (2004a).
2. A notable exception is Antonio Damasio (1994), who finds that threat does not interfere with cognitive processing; emotions are considered to help the decision-making process rather than hinder it. Likewise, research by Marcus and MacKuen (1993, 2001) suggest that a heightened level of anxiety is said to improve the quality of decisions by resulting in a more complete search for information. However, the context in which these studies were conducted—regarding presidential candidates that might appear as threatening—seem to tap into a different sense of anxiety than previous studies do.
3. A factor analysis of the personal threat items resulted in a single factor with an eigenvalue of 2.97. Each variable loaded very high on the first factor, with no loading below .72. Cronbach's alpha is .82. Instead of factor scores, I relied on an additive scale.
4. These data come from a survey that is part of the quarterly State of the State Surveys series in Michigan. The Office of Survey Research at Michigan State University conducted this survey from May 2005 to July 2005. The total number of respondents is 949 with a response rate of 46.4 percent, but the open-ended threat question was administered to a random half of respondents.
5. Seattle's Space Needle was speculated to be a target of terrorism, which compelled it to cancel its 2002 New Year's Eve festivities. Also, it was later reported that photos of the Space Needle were confiscated from computers in Afghanistan.
6. The trust measure is an additive index based on two items: "How much time do you think you can trust the government in Washington" and "Is the government run by a few big interests or it is run for the benefit of all people?" Because the "few big interests" item is a dichotomy, each value was transformed to either a 1 or a 4 and then added to the 4 response "trust government in Washington" to form a single index. Although it has been argued that the four-item scale captures different aspects of trust (Hethering-

ton 2005-6), analyses of it show that the trust item is more highly correlated with a trust dimension (Mason, House, and Martin 1985).
7. See note 6.
8. A factor analysis of the six dogmatism measures resulted in a single factor with an eigenvalue of 2.42. Each variable loaded very high on the first factor, with no loading below .57. Cronbach's alpha is .71. Instead of factor scores, I relied on an additive scale.
9. An increased sense of security is often among the primary reasons why some Hispanic groups migrate to the United States (Portes and Rumbaut 2001). Hilda Pantin and colleagues (2003) suggest that previous exposure to traumatic events in their homelands may render Latinos more sensitive to terrorist events. Because of heightened threat reactions, Latinos may be more supportive of the government and its efforts to combat terrorism.
10. Different Latino nationalities may respond differently to government. Research shows that it is problematic to treat Latinos as a monolithic group. Unfortunately, our data do not contain a sufficiently large sample of Latinos to examine differences by ancestry or country of origin. For comparability, only Latinos born in the United States are included in the analysis.
11. This argument may be time-bound given that the former Immigration and Naturalization Service (INS) began to question the status of Latinos and immigrant communities in the months following the attacks. Indiscriminant sweeps of workers in sensitive jobs, such as airports, border restrictions, and stringent visa checking, could also lead to greater resentment among the Latino community.
12. This nonrecursive model was examined using two-stage least squares approach. The coefficient for political trust was positive but statistically insignificant, and the two equations were not statistically significant. However, the coefficient for the civil liberties instrument was significant and positive. Sociotropic threat was also significant in each equation.

Chapter 5

1. A version of this chapter first appeared as a conference paper (Davis and Silver 2003).
2. It is possible that even after considering the implications and consequences, people may not find them particularly objectionable or worse than the alternative. Citizens who initially support civil liberties may have already fully processed the relevant information, and considered the ramifications of government efforts to protect citizens from terrorism.
3. Nonrandom assignment threatens the internal validity of the experiments as result that some unmeasured variable may be related to both the assignment (or initial opinion) and the dependent variable. Statistical tests are conducted to assess the extent of selection bias.
4. In all of the experiments, respondents who were initially undecided were randomly assigned to a counterargument for or against the civil liberties

position. Respondents who were coded as "don't know" in response to a counterargument were counted as saying "it makes no difference."
5. Because blacks and whites react very differently to the trade-off of civil liberties for security, there is a real threat that by including them in the same equation, they would cancel each other out and diminish the overall effect.
6. I tested the same model with whether people changed their responses at all due to the counterarguments as the dependent variable. Because none of the predictor variables consistently explained absolute change in responses, we are confident that our focus on the direction of change captures the most important aspect of the response to the counterarguments.
7. Because of possible selection effects in separating the analysis by respondents' initial responses, we combined the equations for each set of experiments and performed the same analysis. The substantive findings are consistent with our overall results.

Chapter 6

1. I do not assume that individual change will be reflected in aggregate change. It is quite possible that individuals can alter their preferences at a rate that would not be captured in aggregate analyses.
2. In addition to reports of prisoner abuse and torture in the Abu Ghraib prison in Iraq, there were reports of a memo in which President Bush asserted authority above the Geneva Conventions to deny protections to enemy combatants in the war in Afghanistan.
3. The survey design I used is equivalent to Campbell and Stanley's Posttest-Only Control Group Design.
4. The indefinite detention of Jose Padilla, a U.S. citizen suspected as a terrorist, is one example that brought a great deal of attention to the president's ability to detain a person on suspicion without bringing formal charges. Padilla was detained for three years on the suspicion that he was planning a dirty bomb attack on a major U.S. city.
5. With colleagues Brian Silver and Eric Raile (Davis, Silver, and Raile, 2005), we explored the extent to which the warnings raised people's concern about terrorism in the days immediately afterward. By disaggregating a series of surveys in Michigan by date of interview, we compared threat perceptions among respondents interviewed before an orange alert, six days immediately following the alert, and seven days after. The results suggest that the warnings almost invariably achieved the intended effect of increasing public alertness to the possibility of a terrorist attack. There was a significant increase in the level of public concern about terrorism within the six days of the alert period compared with the baseline period.
6. According to Gallup/CNN/USA Today poll conducted in September 2002, 79 percent of Americans supported "invading Iraq if other countries participated," but only 38 percent supported "invading Iraq is the U.S. had to do it alone." This is just one example of how perceptions of unilateralism affected perceptions of war with Iraq.
7. The question wording is not exact. The CNN/USA Today/ Gallup Poll used

the following question: "How likely do you think it is that there will be another terrorist attack in the United States within the next few months?" The Pew Research Center asked: "How worried are you that there will soon be another terrorist attack on the United States?" The CBS News asked: "How likely do you think it is that there will be another terrorist attack in the United States within the next few months?"
8. My use of such informed consent is a required by the Institutional Review Board at our university, and is in conformity with federal standards. The use of a more neutral or perhaps even deceptive statement of the purpose of the survey would have been inappropriate.

Chapter 7

1. The roots of the Democratic Party's civil libertarian position go back to President Truman's platform of support for civil rights and antisegregation during the 1948 Democratic National Convention. Although this position was solidified during the 1960s with Democratic Party support for the Civil Rights Act of 1964, it began a process that would eventually realign white southern Democrats.
2. Each conceptualization of party identification rests on the same seven-category response measure developed by the University of Michigan Survey Research Center (SRC). Survey respondents are asked whether they think of themselves as Republicans, Democrats, independents, or something else. A follow-up question gauges the strength of their initial response. Respondents who identified as independents are asked if they lean toward one of the parties. Responses to these three questions are combined to form a seven-category measure of party identification. We use this measure in our analyses.
3. Polarization is defined as an intensely felt affection for one political party, its candidates, and policy positions, along with an intensely felt disaffection for the opposing party (Campbell 2005).
4. My view is that individual analyses are probably more accurate than aggregate when both macro and micro data exist.
5. Unlike analyzing panel data, using cross-sectional analyses of macro-partisanship does not examine the same pool of respondents, but instead random representative samples assumed to approximate them. Sampling techniques, survey content, and interviewer characteristics may exacerbate changes in party identification. The party identification measures used to construct table 6.1 were taken from surveys of varying content, such as the war on terrorism, presidential performance, the invasion of Afghanistan, and the war in Iraq.
6. Southern Democrats were in this position for years, maintaining heterodox political views inconsistent with their attachments, until the identity of the Democratic Party began to change. This example underscores the stability of partisan attachment and the ability to maintain discordant political views. The actual process of change takes a long time.
7. Data from the ABC News/Washington Post poll support the finding that Democrats did not shift their affiliations in response to September 11. We

use Gallup data for this graph because of the number of polls conducted in each month with no missing months.

8. The 2000 presidential election was the fourth time in U.S. history that a candidate won the presidency and lost the popular vote. The others were 1824, 1876, and 1888. It was also the second-closest presidential election since states began choosing electors by popular vote.

9. I explored the relationship between threat and partisanship to determine whether there was a greater propensity among certain partisans to perceive a greater threat from the attacks. A body of literature suggests that political conservatives might be more prone to perceiving various threats than political liberals are. We did not find any direct relationship between partisanship and threat. Partisanship was unrelated to sociotropic threat in both bivariate and multivariate analyses. The relationship to personal threat is more complex. Although Democrats unexpectedly showed a greater propensity for personal threat in bivariate analyses, this relationship did not hold up controlling for gender in a multivariate analysis. Because women are more likely than men to be Democrats in our sample, and women tend to report higher levels of personal threat than men do, the significance of party identification in the bivariate case was capturing an aspect of gender.

10. In constructing a five-response category of party identification, I treat those leaning toward independent as independents. There is some disagreement over the meaning of independents and leaning independents. From one perspective, Keith and colleagues (1992) have argued that professed independents are almost as partisan as avowed Democrats and Republicans. Dennis (1992) also suggests that independents might be closet partisans. From a different perspective, Richard Niemi, David Reed, and Herbert Weisberg (1991) and Franco Mattei and Niemi (1991) reveal that leaners tend to think of themselves as nonpartisans, and their behavior reflect a certain sense of independence. Examining the differences in coding independents, we found very little difference and no change in our substantive conclusions.

11. I tested the same mode for Republicans, but the results indicated that the ideological discrepancy was essentially random. This is consistent with arguments that Republicans were not compelled to move as far ideologically as independents and Democrats were.

12. Nevertheless, we tested the ideological change model for Republicans, and as we expected, there were no significant explanations of ideological change. As result, we view the change among Republicans as random.

Chapter 8

1. A version of this chapter first appeared as a conference paper (Davis and Silver, 2004b).
2. As mentioned, different Latino nationalities may respond differently to government. Research shows that it is problematic to treat Latinos as a monolithic group. Unfortunately, our data do not contain a sufficiently large sample of Latinos to examine differences by ancestry or country of origin.
3. We tested for the simultaneous or nonrecursive relation between threat and

trust. Using a two-stage least squares approach, in which both ideology and presidential approval were instruments for political trust, the effects of trust on sociotropic threat for the combined model and for the model separately by race were not statistically significant. Though this confirmed our specification of a recursive model, the trust instrument was positive for blacks and negative for whites. Among whites, as threat increased, trust in government increased. Among blacks, as trust increased, government fear increased.

4. The democratic norms items revealed two underlying dimensions in an exploratory factor analysis (principal components). Confirming my suspicions about the influence of context on the measures, the treason item loaded lower on the first dimensions, while the remaining items loaded at least .52. The first factor had an explained variance of .31, and the second factor explained .20 of the variance (alpha = .59).
5. This analysis was conducted on dataset by James Gibson (1987b).
6. This is based on classifying the answers "very proud," "proud," and "somewhat proud" as "proud," and the answers "not very proud" and "not proud at all" as "not proud."
7. A factor analysis of these items resulted in a single factor with an eigenvalue of .34, explaining 47 percent of the variance. With the exceptions of the military service item (.59), all of the items loaded on the first factors with at least a .68 factor loading (Cronbach's alpha = .71).

Chapter 9

1. According to the Ford Foundation report, *Philanthropic Response to 9/11*, the September 11th Fund, which was established to respond to the needs of the victims and their families, collected $115 million in less than two weeks and $425 million within four months. By mid-October of the following year, more than $1 billion had been contributed to charities working in relief and recovery.
2. As a check on the validity of ten-point feeling thermometer ratings, we analyzed the 1989 American National Election Study, which included a split-ballot experiment using both ten-point and 100-point feeling thermometer ratings. Comparing the relative rankings of the various social groups on both scales shows incredible inconsistency.
3. Arabs, $r = .69$; whites, $r = .62$; Islamic fundamentalists, $r = .74$; Latinos, $r = .62$; Jews, $r = .64$; Christian fundamentalists, $r = .74$; African Americans, $r = .61$.
4. Islamic fundamentalists were intended to reflect the groups identified by the government and the media responsible for the terrorist attacks. This includes the Taliban, groups headed by Osama bin Laden, and groups sympathetic to the fundamentalist ideology (that is, Hamas, Hezbollah, Islamic Jihad). Islamic fundamentalism is distinguished from other forms of Islam by its strict, literal interpretations and belief in the infallibility of the Quran. It links the world's problems to secular influences, such as that of Western society.

References

Aberbach, Joel D., and Jack L. Walker. 1970. The Meanings of Black Power: A Comparison of White and Black Interpretations of a Political Slogan. *The American Political Science Review* 64(2): 367–88.

Abramowitz, Alan I., and Kyle L. Saunders. 1998. "Ideological Realignment in the U.S. Electorate." *Journal of Politics* 60(3): 634–52.

Abramson, Paul R. 1983. *Political Attitudes in America: Formation and Change*. San Francisco: W. H. Freeman.

Abramson, Paul R., and Ronald Inglehart. 1995. *Value Change in Global Perspective*. Ann Arbor: University of Michigan Press.

Abramson, Paul R., and Charles W. Ostrom. 1994. "Question Wording and Partisanship: Change and Continuity in Party Loyalties During the 1992 Election Campaign." *Public Opinion Quarterly* 58(1): 21–48.

Achen, Christopher H. 1975. "Mass Political Attitudes and the Survey Response." *The American Political Science Review* 69(4): 1218–31.

Adorno, Theodor W., Else Frenkel-Brunswik, Daniel J. Levinson, and R. Nevitt Sanford. 1950. *The Authoritarian Personality*. New York: Harper & Row.

Allen, Richard L. 2000. *The Concept of Self: A Study of Black Identity and Self-esteem*. African American Life Series. Detroit, Mich.: Wayne State University Press.

Allen, Richard L., and Richard P. Bagozzi. 2001. "Consequences of the Black Sense of Self." *Journal of Black Psychology* 27(1): 3–28.

Allen, Richard L., Michael C. Dawson, and Ronald E. Brown. 1989. "A Schema-Based Approach to Modeling an African-American Racial Belief System." *The American Political Science Review* 83(2): 421–41.

Altemeyer, Bob. 1996. *The Authoritarian Specter*. Cambridge, Mass.: Harvard University Press.

Altheide, David L. 2002. *Creating Fear: News and the Construction of Crisis, Social Problems and Social Issues*. New York: Aldine de Gruyter.

———. 2003. "Notes Toward a Politics of Fear." *Journal for Crime, Conflict, and the Media* 1(1): 37–54.

Alvarez, R. Michael, and John Brehm. 2002. *Hard Choices, Easy Answers: Values, Information, and American Public Opinion*. Princeton, N.J.: Princeton University Press.

Alwin, Duane F. 1997. "Feeling Thermometers Versus 7-Point Scales." *Sociological Methods and Research* 25(3): 318–40.

Arndt, Jamie, Jeff Greenberg, Jeff Schimel, Tom Pyszczynski, and Sheldon Solomon. 2002. "To Belong or Not to Belong, That Is the Question: Terror Management and Identification with Gender and Ethnicity." *Journal of Personality and Social Psychology* 83(1): 26–43.

Barlow, Kelly M., Donald M. Taylor, and Wallace E. Lambert. 2000. "Ethnicity in America and feeling 'American.'" *Journal of Psychology: Interdisciplinary and Applied* 134(6): 581–600.

Berlin, Isaiah. 1958. *Two Concepts of Liberty*. Oxford: Clarendon Press.

Bobo, Lawrence, and Frederick C. Licari. 1989. "Education and Political Tolerance: Testing the Effects of Cognitive Sophistication and Target Group Affect." *Public Opinion Quarterly* 53(3): 285–308.

Bolce, Louis, and Gerald de Maio. 1999. "The Anti-Christian Fundamentalist Factor in Contemporary Politics." *Public Opinion Quarterly* 63(4): 508–42.

Box-Steffensmeier, Janet M., and Suzanna DeBoef. 2001. "Macropartisanship and Macroideology in the Sophisticated Electorate." *Journal of Politics* 63(1): 232–48.

Brady, Henry E., and Paul M. Sniderman. 1985. "Attitude Attribution: A Group Basis for Political Reasoning." *The American Political Science Review* 79(4): 1061–78.

Brehm, Jack W. 1966. *A Theory of Psychological Reactance*. New York: Academic Press.

Brewer, Marilynn B. 1999. "The Psychology of Prejudice: Ingroup Love or Outgroup Hate?" *Journal of Social Issues* 55(3): 429–44.

Brown, Roger, and James Kulik. 1977. "Flashbulb Memories." *Cognition* 5(1): 73–99.

Butler, Gillian, and Andrew A. Mathews. 1983. "Cognitive Processes in Anxiety." *Advances in Behaviour Research and Therapy* 5: 51–62.

Campbell, Angus, Philip E. Converse, Warren E. Miller, and Donald E. Stokes. 1960. *The American Voter*. New York: John Wiley & Sons.

Campbell, Donald T., and Julian C. Stanley. 1963. *Experimental and Quasi-Experimental Designs for Research*. Boston, Mass.: Houghton Mifflin.

Campbell, James E. 2005. "Why Bush Won the Presidential Election of 2004: Incumbency, Ideology, Terrorism, and Turnout." *Political Science Quarterly* 120(2): 219–41.

Carmines, Edward G., and Michael Berkman. 1994. "Ethos, Ideology, and Partisanship: Exploring the Paradox of Conservative Democrats." *Political Behavior* 16(2): 203–18.

Carmines, Edward G., and James A. Stimson. 1981. "Issue Evolution, Population Replacement, and Normal Partisan Change." *The American Political Science Review* 75(1): 107–18.

Chang, Nancy. 2002. *Silencing Political Dissent: An Open Media Book*. New York: Seven Stories Press.

Chanley, Virginia A. 2002. "Trust in Government in the Aftermath of 9/11: Determinants and Consequences." *Political Psychology* 23(3): 469–83.

Chong, Dennis. 1993. "How People Think, Reason, and Feel about Rights and Liberties." *American Journal of Political Science* 37(3): 867–99.

Citrin, Jack. 1974. "Comment: The Political Relevance of Trust in Government." *The American Political Science Review* 68(3): 973–88.

Citrin, Jack, Ernst B. Haas, Christopher Muste, and Beth Reingold. 1994. "Is American Nationalism Changing? Implications for Foreign Policy." *International Studies Quarterly* 38(1): 1–31.

Citrin, Jack, Beth Reingold, and Donald P. Green. 1990. "American Identity and the Politics of Ethnic Change." *The Journal of Politics* 52(4): 1124–54.

Citrin, Jack, Beth Reingold, Evelyn Walters, and Donald P. Green. 1990. "The 'Official English' Movement and the Symbolic Politics of Language in the United States." *The Western Political Quarterly* 43(3): 535–59.

Citrin, Jack, Cara Wong, and Brian Duff. 2001. "The Meaning of American National Identity: Patterns of Ethnic Conflict and Consensus." In *Social Identity, Intergroup Conflict, and Conflict Reduction*, edited by Richard D. Ashmore, Lee Jussim, and David Wilder. Oxford: Oxford University Press.

Cole, David, and James X. Dempsey. 2002. *Terrorism and the Constitution: Sacrificing Civil Liberties in the Name of National Security*, 2nd ed. New York: New Press.

Converse, Philip E.. 1964. "The Nature of Belief Systems in Mass Publics." In *Ideology and Discontent*, edited by David E. Apter. New York: Free Press.

Converse, Philip E., and Gregory B. Markus. 1979. "Plus ca change...: The New CPS Election Study Panel." *The American Political Science Review* 73(1): 32–49.

Damasio, Antonio R. 1994. *Descartes' Error: Emotion, Reason, and the Brain*. New York: G. P. Putnam.

Davis, Darren W. 1995. "Exploring Black Political Intolerance." *Political Behavior* 17(1): 1–22.

———. 2000. "Individual Level Examination of Postmaterialism in the U. S.: Political Tolerance, Racial Attitudes, Environmentalism, and Participatory Norms." *Political Research Quarterly* 53(3): 455–75.

Davis, Darren W., and Christian Davenport. 1999. "Assessing the Validity of the Postmaterialism Index." *American Political Science Review* 93(3): 649–64.

Davis, Darren W., Moshe Haspel, and Brian D. Silver. 2005. "The Geography of Fear: Perceptions of Terrorism in the Urban Context." Paper read at the Annual Meeting of the Midwest Political Science Association. Chicago, Ill. (April 6–10, 2005).

Davis, Darren W., and Brian D. Silver. 2003. "Personal Security vs. Civil Liberties After 9/11: Some Sobering Evidence from Sober Second Thoughts." Presented to the Midwest Political Science Association. Chicago (April 2003).

———. 2004a. "Civil Liberties vs. Security in the Context of the Terrorist Attacks on America." *American Journal of Political Science* 48(1): 28–46.

———. 2004b. "One Nation Indivisible . . .: Racial Differences in Reactions to the Terrorist Attacks on America." Presented to Midwest Political Science Association. Chicago (April 2004).

Davis, Darren W., Brian D. Silver, and Eric D. Raile. 2005. "The Threat of Terrorism, Presidential Approval, and the 2004 Election." Paper read at Annual Meeting of the Midwest Political Science Association. Chicago, Ill. (April 6–10, 2005).

Davis, James A. 1975. "Communism, Conformity, Cohorts, and Categories: American Tolerance in 1954 and 1972–73." *American Journal of Sociology* 81(3): 491–513.

Dawson, Michael C. 1994. *Behind the Mule: Race and Class in African-American Politics*. Princeton, N.J.: Princeton University Press.

de la Garza, Rodolfo O. 1995. "The Effects of Ethnicity on Political Culture." In *Classifying by Race*, edited by Paul E. Peterson. Princeton, N.J.: Princeton University Press.

de la Garza, Rodolfo O., Angelo Falcon, and F. Chris Garcia. 1996. "Will The Real Americans Please Stand Up: Anglo and Mexican-American Support of Core American Political Values." *American Journal of Political Science* 40(2): 335–51.

Dennis, Jack. 1992. "Political Independence in America, III: In Search of Closet Partisans." *Political Behavior* 14(3): 261–96.

Devos, Thierry, and Mahzarin R. Banaji. 2005. "American = White?" *Journal of Personality and Social Psychology* 88(3): 447–66.

DiMaggio, Paul, John Evans, and Bethany Bryson. 1996. "Have American's Social Attitudes Become More Polarized?" *American Journal of Sociology* 102(3): 690–755.

Dreyer, Edward C. 1973. "Change and Stability in Party Identifications." *The Journal of Politics* 35(3): 712–22.

Du Bois, W.E.B. 1924/1970. *The Gift of Black Folk: The Negroes in the Making of America.* Knights of Columbus Racial Contribution Series. Boston, Mass.: The Stratford Co. Repr., New York: Washington Square Press.

Easton, David. 1965. *A Systems Analysis of Political Life.* New York: John Wiley & Sons.

———. 1975. "A Re-Assessment of the Concept of Political Support." *British Journal of Political Science* 5(4): 435–57.

Easton, David, and Jack Dennis. 1969. *Children in the Political System: Origins of Political Legitimacy.* Chicago: University of Chicago Press.

Entman, Robert M. 2004. *Projections of Power: Framing News, Public Opinion, and U.S. Foreign Policy.* Studies in Communication, Media, and Public Opinion. Chicago: University of Chicago Press.

Erikson, Robert S. 1979. "The SRC Panel Data and Mass Political Attitudes." *British Journal of Political Science* 9(1): 89–114.

Feldman, Stanley, and John Zaller. 1992. "The Political Culture of Ambivalence: Ideological Responses to the Welfare State." *American Journal of Political Science* 36(1): 268–307.

Finkenauer, Catrin, Lydia Gisle, and Olivier Luminet, eds. 1997. "When Individual Memories Are Socially Shaped: Flashbulb Memories of Sociopolitical Events." In *Collective Memory of Political Events: Social Psychological Perspectives*, edited by J. W. Pennebaker, D. Paez and B. Rime. Mahwah, N.J.: Lawrence Erlbaum.

Fiorina, Morris P. 1981. *Retrospective Voting in American National Elections.* New Haven, Conn.: Yale University Press.

Fiorina, Morris P., Samuel J. Abrams, and Jeremy Pope. 2005. *Culture War?: The Myth of a Polarized America,* 2nd ed. New York: Pearson Education.

Fiske, Alan P., and Phillip E. Tetlock. 1997. "Taboo Tradeoffs: Reactions to Transactions that Transgress Spheres of Exchange." *Journal of Political Psychology* 18: 255–97.

Fuchs, Lawrence H. 1990. *The American Kaleidoscope: Race, Ethnicity, and the Civic Culture.* Middletown, Conn.: Wesleyan University Press.

Garcia, John A. 1987. "The Political Integration of Mexican Immigrants: Examining Some Political Orientations." *International Migration Review* 21(2): 372–89.

Gibson, James L. 1987a. "Homosexuals and the Ku Klux Klan: A Contextual Analysis of Political Tolerance." *The Western Political Quarterly* 40(3): 427–48.

———. 1987b. *Freedom and Tolerance in the United States.* [Computer file]. Chicago, Ill.: University of Chicago, National Opinion Research Center [producer], 1987. Ann Arbor, Mich.: Inter-university Consortium for Political and Social Research [distributor], 1991.

———. 1988. "Political Intolerance and Political Repression During the McCarthy Red Scare." *The American Political Science Review* 82(2): 511–29.

---. 1989. "The Policy Consequences of Political Intolerance: Political Repression During the Vietnam War Era." *The Journal of Politics* 51(1): 13–35.

---. 1992. "The Political Consequences of Intolerance: Cultural Conformity and Political Freedom." *The American Political Science Review* 86(2): 338–56.

---.1993. "Perceived Political Freedom in the Soviet Union." *Journal of Politics* 55(4): 936–74.

---. 1995. "The Political Freedom of African-Americans: A Contextual Analysis of Racial Attitudes, Political Tolerance and Individual Liberty." *Political Geography* 14(6–7): 571–99.

---. 1996. "A Mile Wide But an Inch Deep(?): The Structure of Democratic Commitments in the Former USSR." *American Journal of Political Science* 40(2): 396–420.

---. 1998a. "Putting up with Fellow Russians: An Analysis of Political Tolerance in the Fledgling Russian Democracy." *Political Research Quarterly* 51(1): 37–68.

---. 1998b. "A Sober Second Thought: An Experiment in Persuading Russians to Tolerate." *American Journal of Political Science* 42(3): 819–50.

---. 2002. "Becoming Tolerant? Short-Term Changes in Russian Political Culture." *British Journal of Political Science* 32: 309–34.

---. 2004. *Overcoming Apartheid: Can Truth Reconcile a Divided Nation?* New York: Russell Sage Foundation.

---. 2006. "Enigmas of Intolerance: Fifty Years After Stouffer's Communism, Conformity, and Civil Liberties." *Perspectives on Politics* 4(1): 21–34.

Gibson, James L., and Richard D. Bingham. 1985. *Civil Liberties and Nazis: The Skokie Free-speech Controversy*. New York: Praeger.

Gibson, James L., Gregory A. Caldeira, and Lester Kenyatta Spence. 2002. "The Role of Theory in Experimental Design: Experiments Without Randomization." *Political Analysis* 10(4): 362–75.

Gibson, James L., Raymond M. Duch, and Kent L. Tedin. 1992. "Democratic Values and the Transformation of the Soviet Union." *Journal of Politics* 54(2): 329–71.

Gibson, James L., and Amanda Gouws. 2000. "Social Identities and Political Intolerance: Linkages within the South African Mass Public." *American Journal of Political Science* 44(2): 278–92.

---. 2003. *Overcoming Intolerance in South Africa: Experiments in Democratic Persuasion*. Cambridge Studies in Political Psychology and Public Opinion. New York: Cambridge University Press.

Gilmore, Brian. 2002. "Stand by the Man: Black America and the Dilemma of Patriotism." *The Progressive* 66(1): 24–27.

Glassner, Barry. 1999. *The Culture of Fear: Why Americans are Afraid of the Wrong Things*. New York: Basic Books.

Golebiowska, Ewa A. 1995. "Individual Value Priorities, Education, and Political Tolerance." *Political Behavior* 17(1): 23–48.

---. 1999. "Gender Gap in Political Tolerance." *Political Behavior* 21(1): 43–66.

Gomberg, Paul. 2002. "Patriotism is Like Racism." In *Patriotism*, edited by Igor Primoratz. Amherst, N.Y.: Humanity Books.

Green, Donald Philip. 1988. "On the Dimensionality of Public Sentiment toward Partisan and Ideological Groups." *American Journal of Political Science* 32(3): 758–80.

Green, Donald P., Bradley Palmquist, and Eric Schickler. 2002. *Partisan Hearts and Minds: Political Parties and the Social Identities of Voters*. Yale ISPS Series. New Haven, Conn.: Yale University Press.

Greenberg, Jeff, Tom Pyszczynski, Sheldon Solomon, Abram Rosenblatt, Mitchell Veeder, Shari Kirkland, and Deborah Lyon. 1990. "Evidence for Terror Management Theory II: The Effects of Mortality Salience on Reactions to Those Who Threaten or Bolster the Cultural Worldview." *Journal of Personality and Social Psychology* 58(2): 308–18.

Greenberg, Jeff, Sheldon Solomon, and Thomas A. Pyszczynski. 1997. "Terror Management Theory of Self-Esteem and Cultural Worldviews: Empirical Assessments and Conceptual Refinements." In *Advances in Experimental Social Psychology*, edited by M. P. Zanna. San Diego, Calif.: Academic Press.

Gurin, Patricia, Shirley Hatchett, and James S. Jackson. 1989. *Hope and Independence: Blacks' Response to Electoral and Party Politics*. New York: Russell Sage Foundation.

Hadari, Saguiv A. 1988. "Value Trade-off." *The Journal of Politics* 50(3): 655–76.

Hagner, Paul R., and John C. Pierce. 1984. "Racial Differences in Political Conceptualization." *The Western Political Quarterly* 37(2): 212–35.

Hetherington, Marc J. 2004. *Why Trust Matters: Declining Political Trust and the Demise of American Liberalism*. Princeton, N.J.: Princeton University Press.

———. 2005. *Why Trust Matters: Declining Political Trust and the Demise of American Liberalism*. Princeton, N.J.: Princeton University Press.

Hetherington, Marc J., and Michael Nelson. 2003. "Anatomy of a Rally Effect: George Bush and the War on Terrorism." *PS: Political Science and Politics* 36(1): 37–42.

Hochschild, Jennifer L. 1981. *What's Fair? American Beliefs About Distributive Justice*. Cambridge, Mass.: Harvard University Press.

Howell, Susan E., and Deborah Fagan. 1988. "Race and Trust in Government: Testing the Political Reality Model." *Public Opinion Quarterly* 52(3): 343–50.

Huckfeldt, R. Robert. 1984. "Political Loyalties and Social Class Ties: The Mechanisms of Contextual Influence." *American Journal of Political Science* 28(2): 399–417.

Huddy, Leonie, Stanley Feldman, Theresa Capelos, and Colin Provost. 2002. "The Consequences of Terrorism: Disentangling the Effects of Personal and National Threat." *Political Psychology* 23(3): 485–509.

Huddy, Leonie, Nadia Khatib, and Theresa Capelos. 2002. "The Polls–Trends: Reactions to the Terrorist Attacks of September 11, 2001." *Public Opinion Quarterly* 66(3): 418–51.

Hurwitz, Jon, and Mark Peffley. 1987. "How Are Foreign Policy Attitudes Structured? A Hierarchical Model." *The American Political Science Review* 81(4): 1099–1120.

———. 1990. "Public Images of the Soviet Union: The Impact on Foreign Policy Attitudes." *The Journal of Politics* 52(1): 3–28.

Hutcheson, John, David Domke, Andre Billeaudeaux, and Philip Garland. 2004. "U.S. National Identity, Political Elites, and a Patriotic Press Following September 11." *Political Communication* 21(1): 27–50.

Inglehart, Ronald, and Christian Welzel. 2005. *Modernization, Cultural Change, and Democracy: The Human Development Sequence*. New York: Cambridge University Press.

Jackman, Robert W. 1972. "Political Elites, Mass Publics, and Support for Democratic Principles." *Journal of Politics* 34(3): 753–73.

Jacobson, Gary C. 2005. "Polarized Politics and the 2004 Congressional and Presidential Elections." *Political Science Quarterly* 120(2): 199–218.

Janis, Irving L., and Seymour Feshbach. 1953. "Effects of Fear-Arousing Communications." *Journal of Abnormal & Social Psychology* 48: 78–92.

Jennings, M. Kent, and Gregory B. Markus. 1984. "Partisan Orientations over the Long Haul: Results from the Three-Wave Political Socialization Panel Study." *The American Political Science Review* 78(4): 1000–18.

Jones-Correa, Michael. 1998. *Between Two Nations : The Political Predicament of Latinos in New York City*. Ithaca, N.Y.: Cornell University Press.

Jost, John T., Jack Glaser, Arie W. Kruglanski, and Frank J. Sulloway. 2003. "Political Conservatism as Motivated Social Cognition." *Psychological Bulletin* 129(3): 339–75.

Keith, Bruce E. 1992. *The Myth of the Independent Voter*. Berkeley: University of California Press.

Keith, Bruce E., David B. Magleby, Candice J. Nelson, Elizabeth Orr, Mark C. Westlye, and Raymond E. Wolfinger. 1992. *The Myth of the Independent Voter*. Berkeley: University of California Press.

Kinder, Donald R., and Thomas R. Palfrey. 1993. *Experimental Foundations of Political Science*. Ann Arbor: University of Michigan Press.

Kinder, Donald R., and Lynn M. Sanders. 1990. "Mimicking Political Debate with Survey Questions: The Case of White Opinion on Affirmative Action for Blacks." *Social Cognition* 8: 73–103.

———. 1996. *Divided by Color: Racial Politics and Democratic Ideals, American Politics and Political Economy*. Chicago: University of Chicago Press.

Kluegel, James R., and Eliot R. Smith. 1986. *Beliefs about Inequality : Americans' Views of What Is and What Ought to Be, Social Institutions and Social Change*. New York: Aldine de Gruyter.

Knight, Kathleen. 1984. "The Dimensionality of Partisan and Ideological Affect." *American Politics Quarterly* 12: 305–34.

Kosterman, Rick, and Seymour Feshbach. 1989. "Toward a Measure of Patriotic and Nationalistic Attitudes." *Political Psychology* 10(2): 257–73.

Kramer, Gerald H. 1983. "The Ecological Fallacy Revisited: Aggregate- versus Individual-level Findings on Economics and Elections, and Sociotropic Voting." *The American Political Science Review* 77(1): 92–111.

Kuklinski, James H., Ellen Riggle, Victor Ottati, Norbert Schwarz, and Robert S. Wyer, Jr. 1991. "The Cognitive and Affective Bases of Political Tolerance Judgments." *American Journal of Political Science* 35(1): 1–27.

Lakoff, George. 2002. *Moral Politics: How Liberals and Conservatives Think*, 2nd ed. Chicago: University of Chicago Press.

Landau, Mark J., Sheldon Solomon, Jeff Greenberg, Florette Cohen, Tom Pyszczynski, Jamie Arndt, Claude H. Miller, Daniel M. Ogilvie, and Alison Cook. 2004. "Deliver Us from Evil: The Effects of Mortality Salience and Reminders of 9/11 on Support for President George W. Bush." *Personality and Social Psychology Bulletin* 30(9): 1136–50.

Lawrence, David G. 1976. "Procedural Norms and Tolerance: A Reassessment." *The American Political Science Review* 70(1): 80–100.

Layman, Geoffrey C., and Thomas M. Carsey. 2002. "Party Polarization and 'Conflict Extension' in the American Electorate." *American Journal of Political Science* 46(4): 786–802.

LeDoux, Joseph E. 1996. *The Emotional Brain: The Mysterious Underpinnings of Emotional Life*. London: Weidenfeld & Nicolson.

Leone, Richard C., and Greg Anrig. 2003. *The War on Our Freedoms: Civil Liberties in an Age of Terrorism*. New York: BBS PublicAffairs.

Lerner, Jennifer S., Roxana M. Gonzalez, Deborah A. Small, and Baruch Fischhoff. 2003. "Effects of Fear and Anger on Perceived Risks of Terrorism: A National Field Experiment." *Psychological Science* 14(2): 144–50.

Lerner, Jennifer S., and Dacher Keltner. 2000. "Beyond Valence: Toward a Model of Emotion-Specific Influences on Judgement and Choice." *Cognition and Emotion* 14(4): 473–93.

———. 2001. "Fear, Anger, and Risk." *Journal of Personality and Social Psychology* 81(1): 146–59.

Levitin, Teresa E., and Warren E. Miller. 1979. "Ideological Interpretations of Presidential Elections." *The American Political Science Review* 73(3): 751–71.

Li, Qiong, and Marilynn B. Brewer. 2004. "What Does It Mean to Be an American? Patriotism, Nationalism, and American Identity after 9/11." *Political Psychology* 25(5): 727–39.

Li, Xigen, and Ralph Izard. 2003. "9/11 Attack Coverage Reveals Similarities, Differences." *Newspaper Research Journal* 24(1): 204–19.

Locke, John. 1690/1980. *Second Treatise of Government*. Edited by C. B. Macpherson. Repr. Indianapolis, Ind.: Hackett Publishing.

Lule, Jack. 2002. "Myth and Terror on the Editorial Page: The New York Times Responds to September 11, 2001." *Journal and Mass Communication Quarterly* 79(Summer): 275–93.

Luskin, Robert C. 1990. "Explaining Political Sophistication." *Political Behavior* 12(4): 331–61.

MacKuen, Michael, and Courtney Brown. 1987. "Political Context and Attitude Change." *The American Political Science Review* 81(2): 471–90.

MacKuen, Michael B., Robert S. Erikson, and James A. Stimson. 1989. "Macropartisanship." *The American Political Science Review* 83(4): 1125–42.

Malveaux, Julianne, and Reginna A. Green. 2002. *The Paradox of Loyalty: An African American Response to the War on Terrorism*. Chicago: Third World Press.

Marcus, George E., and Michael B. MacKuen. 1993. "Anxiety, Enthusiasm, and the Vote: The Emotional Underpinnings of Learning and Involvement during Presidential Campaigns." *American Political Science Review* 87(3): 672–85.

———. 2001. "Emotions and Politics: The Dynamic Functions of Emotionality." In *Citizens and Politics: Perspectives from Political Psychology*, edited by James H. Kuklinski. New York: Cambridge University Press.

Marcus, George E., John L. Sullivan, Elizabeth Theiss-Morse, and Sandra L. Wood. 1995. *With Malice toward Some: How People Make Civil Liberties Judgments*. Cambridge Studies in Political Psychology and Public Opinion. New York: Cambridge University Press.

Maslow, Abraham H. 1954. *Motivation and Personality*. New York: Harper & Row.

Mason, William M., James S. House, and Steven S. Martin. 1985. "On the Dimensions of Political Alienation in America." *Sociological Methodology* 15:111–51.

Mathews, Andrew, and Colin MacLeod. 1986. "Discrimination of Threat Cues without Awareness in Anxiety States." *Journal of Abnormal Psychology* 95(2): 131–38.

Mattei, Franco, and Richard G. Niemi. 1991. "Unrealized Partisans, Realized Independents, and the Intergenerational Transmission of Partisan Identification." *The Journal of Politics* 53(1): 161–74.

McClosky, Herbert. 1958. "Conservatism and Personality." *The American Political Science Review* 52(1): 27–45.

———. 1964. "Consensus and Ideology in American Politics." *The American Political Science Review* 58(2): 361–82.

McClosky, Herbert, and Alida Brill. 1983. *Dimensions of Tolerance: What Americans Believe about Civil Liberties.* New York: Russell Sage Foundation.

McCutcheon, Allan L. 1985. "A Latent Class Analysis of Tolerance for Nonconformity in the American Public." *Public Opinion Quarterly* 49(4): 474–88.

Milburn, Michael A., and Sheree D. Conrad. 1996. *The Politics of Denial.* Cambridge, Mass.: MIT Press.

Miller, Arthur H. 1974. "Political Issues and Trust in Government: 1964–1970." *The American Political Science Review* 68(3): 951–72.

Myrdal, Gunnar, and Sissela Bok. 1996. *An American Dilemma: The Negro Problem and Modern Democracy*, 2 vols. New Brunswick, N.J.: Transaction Publishers.

Nacos, Brigitte Lebens. 2002. *Mass-Mediated Terrorism: The Central Role of the Media in Terrorism and Counterterrorism.* Lanham, Md.: Rowman & Littlefield.

Nelson, Thomas E. 1999. "Group Affect and Attribution in Social Policy Opinion." *Journal of Politics* 61(2): 331–62.

Nelson, Thomas E., and Donald R. Kinder. 1996. "Issue Frames and Group-Centrism in American Public Opinion." *Journal of Politics* 58(4): 1055–78.

Nie, Norman H., Sidney Verba, and John R. Petrocik. 1976. *The Changing American Voter.* Cambridge, Mass.: Harvard University Press.

Niemi, Richard G., David R. Reed, and Herbert F. Weisberg. 1991. "Partisan Commitment: A Research Note." *Political Behavior* 13(3): 213–21.

Noelle-Neumann, Elisabeth. 1993. *The Spiral of Silence: Public Opinion, Our Social Skin*, 2nd ed. Chicago: University of Chicago Press.

Norrander, Barbara, and Clyde Wilcox. 1993. "Rallying around the Flag and Partisan Change: The Case of the Persian Gulf War." *Political Research Quarterly* 46(4): 759–70.

Norris, Pippa. 1999. *Critical Citizens: Global Support for Democratic Government.* New York: Oxford University Press.

Nunn, Clyde Z., Harry J. Crockett, and J. Allen Williams. 1978. *Tolerance for nonconformity.* San Francisco: Jossey-Bass Publishers.

Office of the Press Secretary. 2001a. "Address to a Joint Session of Congress and the American People." Press Release (September 20). Available at: http://www.whitehouse.gov/news/releases/2001/09/20010920-8.html

———. 2001b. "Remarks by the President at Signing of the Patriot Act, Anti-Terrorism Legislation." Press release (October 26). Available at: http://www.whitehouse.gov/news/releases/2001/10/20011026-5.html.

———. 2003. "President George Bush Discusses Iraq in National Press Conference." Press release (March 6). Available at: http://www.whitehouse.gov/news/releases/2003/03/20030306-8.html.

O'Leary, Cecilia Elizabeth. 1999. *To Die For: The Paradox of American Patriotism.* Princeton, N.J.: Princeton University Press.

Oswald, Debra L. 2005. "Understanding Anti-Arab Reactions Post 9/11: The

Role of Threats, Social Categories, and Personal Ideologies." *Journal of Applied Social Psychology* 35(9): 1775–99.
Palmer, Douglas L., and Rudolf Kalin. 1985. "Dogmatic Responses to Belief Dissimilarity in the 'Bogus Stranger' Paradigm." *Journal of Personality and Social Psychology* 48(1): 171–79.
Pantin, Hilda H., Seth J. Schwartz, Prado Guillermo, and Daniel J. Feaster. 2003. "Posttraumatic Stress Disorder Symptoms in Hispanic Immigrants after the September 11th Attacks: Severity and Relationship to Previous Traumatic Exposure." *Hispanic Journal of Behavorial Sciences* 25: 56–72.
Pantoja, Adrian D., Ricardo Ramirez, and Gary M. Segura. 2001. "Citizens by Choice, Voters by Necessity: Patterns in Political Mobilization by Naturalized Latinos." *Political Research Quarterly* 54(4): 729–50.
Parker, Christopher S. 2003. "Shades of Patriotism: Group Identity, National Identity, and Democracy." In American Political Science Association. Philadelphia, Pennsylvania.
Peffley, Mark, Pia Knigge, and Jon Hurwitz. 2001. "A Multiple Values Model of Political Tolerance." *Political Research Quarterly* 54(2): 379–406.
Pew Hispanic Center/Kaiser Family Foundation. 2002. "National Survey of Latinos." December.
Portes, Alejandro, and Rubén G. Rumbaut. 2001. *Legacies: The Story of the Immigrant Second Generation*. Berkeley: University of California Press; New York: Russell Sage Foundation.
Price, Vincent, and Anca Romantan. 2004. "Confidence in Institutions Before, During, and After 'Indecision 2000.'" *Journal of Politics* 66(3): 939–56.
Prothro, James W., and Charles M. Grigg. 1960. "Fundamental Principles of Democracy: Bases of Agreement and Disagreement." *The Journal of Politics* 22(2): 276–94.
Pulcino, Tiffany, Sandro Galea, Jennifer Ahern, Heidi Resnick, Mary Foley, and David Vlahov. 2003. "Posttraumatic Stress in Women After the September 11 Terrorist Attacks in New York City." *Journal of Women's Health* 12(8): 809–20.
Pyszczynski, Tom, Jeff Greenberg, and Sheldon Solomon. 1997. "Why Do We Need What We Need? A Terror Management Perspective on the Roots of Human Social Motivation." *Psychological Inquiry* 8(1): 1–20.
———. 2003. *In the Wake of 9/11: The Psychology of Terror*. Washington, D.C.: American Psychological Association.
Rehnquist, William H. 1998. *All the Laws but One: Civil Liberties in Wartime*. New York: Alfred E. Knopf.
Rice, Tom W., and Tracey A. Hilton. 1996. "Partisanship over Time: A Comparison of United States Panel Data." *Political Research Quarterly* 49(1): 191–201.
Rokeach, Milton. 1960. *The Open and Closed Mind; Investigations into the Nature of Belief Systems and Personality Systems*. New York: Basic Books.
Schatz, Robert T., and Ervin Staub. 1996. "Manifestations of Blind and Constructive Patriotism: Personality Correlates and Individual-Group Relations." In *Patriotism: In the Lives of Individuals and Nations*, edited by Daniel Bar-Tal and Ervin Staub. Chicago: Nelson-Hall Publishers.
Schatz, Robert T., Ervin Staub, and Howard Lavine. 1999. "On the Varieties of National Attachment: Blind versus Constructive Patriotism." *Political Psychology* 20(1): 151–74.

Schneier, Bruce. 2003. *Beyond Fear: Thinking Sensibly about Security in an Uncertain World*. New York: Copernicus Books.

Schuster, Mark A, Bradley D. Stein, Lisa H. Jaycox, Rebecca L. Collins, Grant N. Marshall, Marc N. Elliott, Annie J. Zhou, David E. Kanouse, Janina L. Morrison, and Sandra H. Berry. 2001. "A National Survey of Stress Reactions After the September 11, 2001, Terrorist Attacks." *New England Journal of Medicine* 345(20): 1507–12.

Sears, David O., and John B. McConahay. 1973. *The Politics of Violence: The New Urban Blacks and the Watts Riot*. Boston, Mass.: Houghton Mifflin.

Sears, David O., Tom R. Tyler, Jack Citrin, and Donald R. Kinder. 1978. "Political System Support and Public Response to the Energy Crisis." *American Journal of Political Science* 22(1): 56–82.

Sharp, Carol, and Milton Lodge. 1985. "Partisan and Ideological Belief Systems: Do They Differ?" *Political Behavior* 7(2): 147–66.

Shaw, Daron, Rodolfo O. de la Garza, and Jongho Lee. 2000. "Examining Latino Turnout in 1996: A Three-State, Validated Survey Approach." *American Journal of Political Science* 44(2): 338–46.

Sherif, Muzafer. 1966. *In Common Predicament; Social Psychology of Intergroup Conflict and Cooperation*. Boston: Houghton Mifflin.

Sidanius, James, Felicia Pratto, and Lawrence Bobo. 1996. "Racism, Conservatism, Affirmative Action and Intellectual Sophistication: A Matter of Principled Conservatism or Group Dominance?" *Journal of Personality and Social Psychology* 70(3): 476–90.

Sidanius, Jim, Seymour Feshbach, Shana Levin, and Felicia Pratto. 1997. "The Interface Between Ethnic and National Attachment: Ethnic Pluralism or Ethnic Dominance?" *Public Opinion Quarterly* 61(1): 102–33.

Simmons, Martha J., and Frank A. Thomas. 2001. *9.11.01 : African American Leaders Respond to an American Tragedy*. Valley Forge, Pa.: Judson Press.

Smith, Rogers M. 1988. "The 'American Creed' and American Identity: The Limits of Liberal Citizenship in the United States." *The Western Political Quarterly* 41(2): 225–51.

Sniderman, Paul M., Joseph F. Fletcher, Peter H. Russell, and Philip E. Tetlock. 1996. *The Clash of Rights: Liberty, Equality, and Legitimacy in Pluralist Democracy*. New Haven, Conn.: Yale University Press.

Sniderman, Paul M., Joseph F. Fletcher, Peter H. Russell, Philip E. Tetlock, and Brian J. Gaines. 1991. "The Fallacy of Democratic Elitism: Elite Competition and Commitment to Civil Liberties." *British Journal of Political Science* 21(3): 349–70.

Sniderman, Paul M., and Douglas B. Grob. 1996. Innovations in Experimental Design in Attitude Surveys. *Annual Review of Sociology* 22: 377–99.

Sniderman, Paul M., and Thomas Piazza. 2002. *Black Pride and Black Prejudice*. Princeton, N.J.: Princeton University Press.

Stanford, Karen. 2002. "The War Within: African American Public Opinion on the War Against Terrorism." In *The Paradox of Loyalty: An African American Response to the War on Terrorism*, edited by Julianne Malveaux and Reginna A. Green. Chicago: Third World Press.

Stephan, Walter G., Oscar Ybarra, and Guy Bachman. 1999. "Prejudice Toward Immigrants." *Journal of Applied Social Psychhology* 29(11): 2221–37.

Stouffer, Samuel Andrew. 1955. *Communism, Conformity, and Civil Liberties: A Cross-Section of the Nation Speaks Its Mind.* Garden City, N.Y.: Doubleday.

Sullivan, John L., Amy Fried, and Mary G. Dietz. 1992. "Patriotism, Politics, and the Presidential Election of 1988." *American Journal of Political Science* 36(1): 200–34.

Sullivan, John L., George E. Marcus, Stanley Feldman, and James E. Piereson. 1981. "The Sources of Political Tolerance: A Multivariate Analysis." *The American Political Science Review* 75(1): 92–106.

Sullivan, John L., James Piereson, George E. Marcus. 1979. "An Alternative Conceptualization of Political Tolerance: Illusory Increases 1950s–1970s." *American Political Science Review* 73(3): 781–94.

———. 1982. *Political Tolerance and American Democracy.* Chicago: University of Chicago Press.

Sullivan, John L., Pat Walsh, Michal Shamir, David G. Barnum, and James L. Gibson. 1993. "Why Politicians Are More Tolerant: Selective Recruitment and Socialization among Political Elites in Britain, Israel, New Zealand and the United States." *British Journal of Political Science* 23(1): 51–76.

Tajfel, Henri. 1981. *Human Groups and Social Categories: Studies in Social Psychology.* Cambridge: Cambridge University Press.

Tajfel, Henri, and John C. Tuner. 1986. "The Social Identity Theory of Inter-group Behavior." In *Psychology of Intergroup Relations*, edited by Stephen Worchel and William G. Austin. Chicago: Nelson-Hall Publishers.

Tate, Katherine. 1994. *From Protest to politics : the new Black voters in American elections*, enlarged ed. New York: Russell Sage Foundation; Cambridge, Mass.: Harvard University Press.

Tetlock, Philip E. 1981. "Personality and Isolationism: Content Analysis of Senatorial Speeches." *Journal of Personality and Social Psychology* 41(4): 737–43.

———. 1983. "Cognitive Style and Political Ideology." *Journal of Personality and Social Psychology* 45(1): 118–26.

———. 1986. "A Value Pluralism Model of Ideological Reasoning." *Journal of Personality and Social Psychology* 50(4): 819–27.

———. 2000. "Coping With Trade-Offs: Psychological Constraints and Political Implications." In *Elements of Reason: Cognition, Choice, and the Bounds of Rationality*, edited by Arthur Lupia, Samuel L. Popkin, and Mathew D. McCubbins. Cambridge: Cambridge University Press.

Tetlock, Philip E., Kristen A. Hannum, and Patrick M. Micheletti. 1984. "Stability and Change in the Complexity of Senatorial Debate: Testing the Cognitive versus Rhetorical Style Hypotheses." *Journal of Personality and Social Psychology* 46(5): 979–90.

Thomas, Sandra P. 2003. "None of Us Will Ever be the Same Again." *Health Care for Women International* 24(10): 853–67.

Turner, John C. 1987. *Rediscovering the Social Group: Self-Categorization Theory.* Oxford: Blackwell Publishers.

Turner, Richard Brent. 2003. *Islam in the African-American Experience*, 2nd ed. Bloomington: Indiana University Press.

Weatherford, M. Stephen. 1987. "How Does Government Performance Influence Political Support?" *Political Behavior* 9(1): 5–28.

Wilcox, Clyde, Lee Sigelman, and Elizabeth Cook. 1989. "Some Like It Hot: Individual Differences in Responses to Group Feeling Thermometers." *Public Opinion Quarterly* 53(2): 246–57.

Wilson, Glenn D., ed. 1973. "The Temperamental Basis of Attitudes." In *The Psychology of Conservatism*. London: Academic Press.

World Views. 2002. *European Public Opinion & Foreign Policy*. Chicago: The Chicago Council on Foreign Relations and The German Marshall Fund of the United States. http://www.worldviews.org/

Zaller, John. 1992. *The Nature and Origins of Mass Opinion*. Cambridge and New York: Cambridge University Press.

Zaller, John, and Stanley Feldman. 1992. "A Simple Theory of the Survey Response: Answering Questions versus Revealing Preferences." *American Journal of Political Science* 36(3): 579–616.

Index

Boldface numbers refer to figures and tables.

ABC News polls, 26
ABC News/Washington Post polls, 148–52, 249n7
Abramowitz, A., 148
Abramson, P., 141, 142, 143
abstract-applied problems, 36
abstract survey questions, on civil liberties, 235
Abu Ghraib, 248n2
acculturation, 168
Achen, C., 93
acquiescence, political, 7–8, 9, 138
ACTA (American Council of Trustees and Alumni), 20
Adams administration, 2
Afghanistan War, 24–25, 34, 248n2
African Americans: American identity views, 181, 182, **183**; Bush approval ratings, 172–73; civil liberties, support of, 83, 111; civil liberties-national security trade-off, 55, 73–74, 80; in communities tolerant of racists, 35; counterarguments, 103, **105**; democratic norms, 175–78; feeling thermometer ratings, 200, 203, 207, 208, **209**, 210, 212; and Islam, 210–11; and Islamic fundamentalists, 205–6; party affiliation, 148, 154, 156; patriotism, 178–80; perceptions of threat, 66, 109–11; political trust, 74, 170–74; reaction to 9/11, 164, 166–68, 191; U.S. responsibility for 9/11, 185–86, 188, **189**; WWII perceptions, 167–68

age: civil liberties-national security trade-off, **55**, 57, 76, 80; perceptions of threat, **68**
aggregate change, 116, 137
airplanes, threat from flying on, **65, 123**
Alien and Sedition Acts, 2
alienation, political, 165–66, 167
al Qaeda, 24, 25, 121, 199
Altheide, D., 8
Alvarez, M., 38, 39, 93
ambivalence, 38–39
American Airlines: Flights 11, 77, and 175, 16–17
American citizenship, 180–84, 241–42
American Council of Trustees and Alumni (ACTA), 20
American National Election Study, 251n2
amygdala, 63
Anderson, L., 114
anthrax scare, 18, 64
anxiety, vs. fear, 60–61
Arab Americans: discrimination after 9/11, 195, 199; feeling thermometer ratings, 199, 206–7, **208, 209,** 212; intolerance for, 197; racial profiling, 19. *See also* Middle Eastern Americans
Arndt, J., 74
Ashcroft, J., 19, 21
assembly, freedom of, 46–47, 51
association, freedom of, 45–46, 49, 96
authoritarianism, 73

268   Index

Barlow, K., 182
Berlin, I., 5
Bingham, R., 33, 37
bioterrorism, 18, 64
Black Panther Party, 3
blacks. *See* African Americans
Bobo, L., 75, 204
Bolce, L., 202
boomerang effect, 95
Brady, H., 196
brain, fear response, 63
Brehm, J., 38, 39, 93
Brewer, M., 182, 193–94
Brill, A., 6, 37, 71
Bryson, B., 147
Bush (George W.) administration: approval ratings, 149–52, 172–73; election of 2000, 146–47, 167; electronic eavesdrop program, 43; on harassment of Middle Eastern Americans, 192; Iraq War, 25; on Islamic fundamentalists, 199; military tribunals, 24–25; nature of terrorism, 40; 9/11 response, 18–21; Patriot Act, 22; on terrorists' hatred of Americans, 187–88; on tolerance, 195–96; trust of, 127–31

Caldeira, G., 95
Campbell, A., 139
Campbell, D., 117
Canadian Charter of Rights, 35–36
Canadians, laws against written or spoken expressions of racial hatred, 90
Capelos, T., 48
Carmines, E., 148
CARNIVORE, 21, 43
Carsey, T., 148
CBS News/New York Times poll, 48
CBS News poll, 124–25
Challenger disaster, 10
Chanley, V., 70
Cheney, D., 3
Cheney, L., 20
Chicago Council on Foreign Relations, 185, 188
Chicago Tribune, 114

Chong, D., 36, 197
Christian fundamentalists, 199–200, 201–3, 207, **208, 209**
Christianity, as quality of true American, **183**
citizenship, definitions of and reactions to, 180–82, 241–42
Citrin, J., 69, 181
civil liberties: abstract survey question, 235; African Americans' support of, 83, 111; and context, 36; Latinos' support of, 83, 169; Patriot Act's perceived effect on, 135–36; persuasibility of, 88–93; and political ideology, 82–83; and political trust, 81–82, 84–85; support over time, 118–20; whites' support of, 83; women's support of, 76
civil liberties–national security tradeoff: African Americans, 55, 73–74, 80; and age, **55,** 57, 76, 80; changes over time, 118–20; counterarguments, 107–11; data sources, 12–13; decision, 6–7; and educational attainment, **55,** 57, 75, 80; and gender, **55,** 75–76, 80; under heightened vulnerability and threat, 3–4, 80–84; historical background, 2–3; and Iraq War, 25–26; Latinos, 55, 80; model of, 60, **61;** multivariate analysis, 76–80; and negative liberty, 5–6; Oklahoma City bombing, 48–49; and party identification, **56,** 57–58, 158–62, 222–23; and patriotism, **56,** 58, 79; political acquiescence, 7–8; and political affiliation, 158–62; and political ideology, **56,** 57, 79; and political interest, **56,** 58; and political trust, **56,** 58, 79, 132–33, 224; and promotion of fear by media, 8–10; racial-ethnic analyses, **55,** 73–75, 79–80, 221–22; regional analysis, **55;** research considerations, 4; sober second thought approach, 107–11; and sociotropic threat, **56,** 77, 126–27, 132, 134, 220–21; survey questions, 236–39; survey results, 49–58; theoretical considerations,

11–12; values conflict framework, 39–41; whites, 55
Civil War, 2
CNN/Gallup Poll, 25
CNN/USA Today/Gallup Poll, 124–25, 248–49n6–7
cognitive processing, 246n2
COINTELPRO, 3
Cold War, 9, 32
colleges and universities, professors' freedom of speech, 20, 45
Combating Terrorism Act (2001), 20–21
communists and communism, 2, 32–33, 158
conflict theory, 194
Conrad, S., 70
conservatives and conservatism: age effects, 57; anti-social welfare values, 38; civil liberties, support of, 82; civil liberties-national security trade-off, **56,** 57, 79; and counterarguments, 101; d prejudice, 204; intolerance, 210; patriotism, 72; political party identification, 153–54; worldview and values of, 70–71
context: change over time, 115–17; influence over political and social attitudes, 6
Contract with America, 148
Converse, P., 93, 141
cooperation, spirit of after 9/11, 147
counterarguments: survey questions, 96, 97–98; survey results, 98–107; use of, 94–95
crowds, threat from being in, **65, 123**
Cuban Americans, 182
cues, 196–97
cultural worldviews, 61–62
Curry, G., 191

Damasio, A., 246n2
data sources, 12–13, 228–29
decision making process, 246n2
de la Garza, R., 169
de Maio, G., 202
democracy, failure of, 3
democratic norms: abstract vs. specific, 48; and context, 6, 32–37; support by race and ethnicity, 175–78; survey questions, 233–35; trust of, 169–70
Democrats: affiliation with, 142–46; African Americans' support of, 148; civil liberties-national security trade-off, 57–58, 158–62; cooperation with Republican Party after 9/11, 147; depolarization and repolarization of, 149–52; disliked groups, 158; ideology, 153, 154, 156–58; patriotism of, 156; political acquiescence, 9, 138
Dennis, J., 250n10
depolarization, of Democratic Party, 149–52
deportation, 22, 23
detentions: at Guantánamo Bay, 24; indefinite, 96–97; material witness warrants, 20, 97; and Patriot Act, 21–22, 23, 96; public support for, 118; survey counterarguments, 97, **99,** 103; survey questions, 237–38; survey results, **49,** 51
Dietz, M., 72
DiMaggio, P., 147
discrepancy, partisan-ideological, 156–58
discrimination, 42–43, 195, 199. See also racial profiling
dogmatism, 72–73, 77, 100–101, **102,** 232–33
drinking water, safety of, **65, 123**
Dubois, W.E.B., 164

Easton, D., 169, 175
economic aid, lack of as root cause of terrorism, **189**
economy, partisan perceptions of Bush's handling of, 151–52
educational attainment: civil liberties-national security trade-off, **55,** 57, 75, 80; and feeling thermometer ratings, 204; perceptions of threat, 66, **68;** and political ideology, 156
egocentric threats, 63

270　Index

electronic surveillance. *See* surveillance
emotions, 10, 60–61, 91–92, 246*n*2
English language, importance to citizenship, 181, **183**
Entman, R., 8
equal protection, as democratic norm, **175**
Erikson, R., 93
ethnocentrism, 182
Evans, J., 147

Falwell, J., 199–200
Farrakhan, L., 201, 210
fatalism, 66
FBI (Federal Bureau of Investigation), 3, 21, 34, 43
fear: vs. anxiety, 60–61; brain response, 63; and civil liberties-national security trade-off, 4–5; media's promotion of, 8–9; of terrorism, 10, 62
Federal Bureau of Investigation (FBI), 3, 21, 34, 43
federalism, 2
feelings, 91
feeling thermometer ratings: groups, 198–200; before 9/11, 201–4; after 9/11, 205–16; and sociotropic threat, 207–11; survey questions, 235; use of, 198
Feinstein, D., 43
Feldman, S., 38, 63, 93
Feshbach, S., 63
Fiorina, M., 139–40, 148
First Amendment rights, 2–3
Fiske, A., 245*n*4
flashbulb memory, 10–11
food safety, **65, 123**
Ford Foundation, 251*n*1
foreign policy, 185, 188
Fourth Amendment, 46
freedom of assembly and protest, 46–47, 51
freedom of association, 45–46, 49, 96
freedom of press, 2
freedom of speech: in Canada, 90; historical background, 2; after 9/11, 44–45; restrictions, 51; in South Africa, 89–90; support for, **175**; survey question, 45
Fried, A., 72
fundamentalists, Christian, 199–200, 201–3, 207, **208, 209**
fundamentalists, Islamic. *See* Islamic fundamentalists

Gallup/CNN Poll, 25
Gallup/CNN/USA Today Poll, 124–25, 248–49*n*6–7
Gallup Poll, 24, **49,** 128, 141, 143
gender analyses: civil liberties-national security trade-off, **55,** 75–76, 80; perceptions of threat, 66, **68**
German Marshall Fund, 185, 188
Gibson, J., 33, 34, 35, 37, 63, 89, 90–91, 95, 115, 251*n*5
Gilmore, B., 166
Gingrich, N., 148
Glassner, B., 8
Golebiowska, E., 75, 76
Gouws, A., 63, 89
government: ability to ensure security, 28–29; individuals' view of, 12, **130;** response to 9/11, 18–21. *See also* political trust
Green, D., 140, 181
group behavior, 12. *See also* social group perceptions and reactions
Guantánamo Bay, Cuba, 24, 121

habeas corpus: survey question, 42; survey results, **49,** 51; suspension during Civil War, 2
Hadari, S., 38
Hatch, O., 43
Hetherington, M., 69
Hilton, T., 142
Hispanics. *See* Latinos
Hobbes, T., 5
Hochschild, J., 38
Homeland Security Department, 44, 121
homosexuality, 34, 201
Huddy, L., 48, 63
Hurwitz, J., 38, 72

Hussein, S., 25, 121, 144, 150
Hutcheson, J., 9
hypothetical threat, 12

identification cards, 44, **49**
identity, American, 180–84, 241–42
ideology, political. *See* political ideology
immigration: reasons for, 247n10; visa requirements and violations, 21, 22, 97, 169
Immigration and Naturalization Services (INS), 21, 169, 247n12
indefinite detentions, 96–97
independent political ideology, 153–54, 156–58, 250n10
individual change, 116, 120, 131–34, 137
individualism, 169
informed consent, 124–25
INS (Immigration and Naturalization Services), 21, 169, 247n12
Institute for Public Policy and Social Research (IPPSR), 228
integrated threat theory, 194–95
Iraq War: support for, 26, 34, 144, 150–51; and threat of terrorism, 25, 27–29; weapons of mass destruction as basis for, 25
Islam: African Americans' perception of, 210–11; harassment and violence toward followers of, 42–43; perception of before 9/11, 200–201; as root cause of terrorism, **189**; visas given to applicants from countries following, 21
Islamic fundamentalists: feeling thermometer ratings, 198–99, 205–6, 208, 212; groups included in, 251n4; intolerance of, 195, 197
Israel, U.S. policy, 188, **189**, 200

Jackman, R., 245n2
Janis, I., 63
Japanese Americans, internment of, 2
Jefferson, T., 2
Jennings, K., 141, 142
Jews: feeling thermometer ratings, 200, 203–4, 207, **208, 209**; intolerance toward after 9/11, 193; in Skokie, Illinois, 33
Jordan, V., 191
Justice Department, 21, 34

Keith, B., 250n10
Kennedy (John F.) assassination, 10
Khatib, N., 48
Kinder, D., 89
King (Martin Luther Jr.) assassination, 10
Knigge, P., 38
Knight, K., 198
Kuklinski, J., 40, 90–91, 92, 108, 245n3
Ku Klux Klan, 33, 34

Lakoff, G., 70
Lambert, W., 182
Latinos: American identity views, 181, **183**; Bush approval ratings, 172–73; civil liberties, support of, 83, 169; civil liberties-national security trade-off, 55, 80; counterarguments, 103, **105**; democratic norms, 175–78; feeling thermometer ratings, 200, 203, 207, 208, **209**, 210, 212; immigrants, 169, 247n10; party affiliation, 155–56; patriotism, 169, 178–80; perception of threat, 74; political trust, 74, 169, 170–73; reaction to 9/11, 168–69; U.S. responsibility for 9/11, 185, 186, 188, **189**
Lavine, H., 72
law enforcement, 21–25
Layman, G., 148
LeDoux, J., 63
Lee, B., 167
Li, Q., 182
liberals and liberalism: civil liberties-national security trade-off, **56**, 57, 79; and counterarguments, 101; political party identification, 153–54; support for civil liberties, 82; worldview and values of, 70–71
libraries, 23–24
Licari, F., 75
Lincoln administration, 2

Locke, J., 7
Los Angeles Times, 201
Los Angeles Times poll, 48, **49**
Luskin, R., 156

MacKuen, M., 246*n*2
mail, threat from opening, **65**, **123**
Marcus, G., 33, 91, 246*n*2
Markus, G., 141, 142
Maslow, A., 31
material witness warrants, 20, 97
Mattei, F., 250*n*10
McCarran Act (1950), 96
McCarthyism, 2, 32
McClosky, H., 6, 37, 71, 216
media: framing of terrorism, 40; freedom of, 2; promotion of fear, 8–9; research considerations, 8–9; role of, 8
memory, 10–11
methodology: changes in civil liberties-national security trade-off decision over time, 117–18; counterarguments, 94–95; party identification, 249*n*5
Mexican Americans. *See* Latinos
Middle Eastern Americans: feeling thermometer rates before and after 9/11, 199, 200–201, 205–6; harassment and violence toward, 192; racial profiling, 19, 97. *See also* Arab Americans
Milburn, M., 70
military service, **183**
military tribunals, 24–25
Miller, A., 69
moderates, 82, 101
Moussaoui, Z., 20
multivariate analysis, of civil liberties-national security trade-off, 76–80
Muslims. *See* Islam
Myrdal, G., 167

Nacos, B., 9
National Civil Liberties Survey: distribution of responses, 47–54; questions, 42–47, 231–43; time frame, 13. *See also* counterarguments

National Commission on Terrorist Attacks, 18
National Election Survey (NES), 142, 198, 201–4
national identification cards (NIDs), 44, **49**
national pride: civil liberties-national security trade-off, 79; after 9/11, 71–72; by race and ethnicity, 178–80
national security, Patriot Act's perceived effects, 135–36. *See also* civil liberties-national security trade-off
National Security Agency (NSA), 47
Nation of Islam, 201
nativism, 181
Nazis, in Skokie, Illinois, 33
negative liberty, definition of, 5–6
Nelson, M., 69
NES (National Election Survey), 142, 198, 201–4
"new normal," 114–15, 137, 219
Newsweek magazine, 9
New York Times, 45
New York Times/CBS News poll, 48
Niemi, R., 250*n*10
9/11/01. *See* September 11, 2001
9/11 Commission, 18
Nixon administration, 3
Noelle-Neumann, E., 7–8
nonattitudes, 36, 93
nonrecursive relationship, between civil liberties and political trust, 84–85
Norris, P., 170
NSA (National Security Agency), 47

Office of Survey Research (OSR), Michigan State University, 228, 246*n*4
Oklahoma City bombings, 1, 48–49, 199
Olympic Games, in Salt Lake City, 19
Osama bin Laden, 24, 25, 66, 121, 251*n*4
Ostrom, C., 141, 142, 143
Oswald, D., 195

Padilla, J., 248*n*4
Palmer Raids, 2

Palmquist, B., 140
Pantin, H., 247n10
Parker, C., 169
partisanship. *See* party identification
party identification: African Americans, 148, 154, 156; and civil liberties-national security trade-off, **56,** 57–58, 158–62, 222–23; and ideology, 153–58; methodology, 249n5; after 9/11, 142–46; and perception of threat, 250n9; research considerations, 138–39; revisionist conceptualization, 139–41; stability of, 140–46; survey questions, 239–40; traditional conceptualization, 139
party polarization, 146–52, 249n3
Patriot Act, 3, 21–23, 45–46, 96, 135–36
Patriot Act II, 23
patriotism: of African Americans, 178–80; and American citizenship views, 182; change over time, 131; civil liberties-national security trade-off, **56,** 58, 79; and conservatism, 72; of Democrats, 156; and intolerance, 210; of Latinos, 169, 178–80; measurement of, 72; after 9/11, 71–72; by race and ethnicity, 178–80; survey questions, 241; of whites, 178–80
Peffley, M., 38, 72, 91
Pentagon, attack on, 17
personal threat, 63–66, 77, 108, 122–23, 231–32
persuasibility, of civil liberties, 88–93. *See also* sober second thought approach
Pew Charitable Trust, 48
Pew Research Center, 11, 24, 124–25
Piazza, T., 210
Piereson, J., 33
polarization, of political parties, 146–52, 249n3
political acquiescence, 7–8, 9, 138
political alienation, 165–66, 167
political discussions, persuasibility arguments, 88–90
political elite, 34, 245n2

political identification. *See* party identification
political ideology: civil liberties-national security trade-off, **56,** 57, 79; and counterarguments, 101, **104;** after 9/11, 70–71; and political identification, 153–58; and support for civil liberties, 82–83; survey questions, 240
political interest, **56,** 58, 156, 240–41
political parties, polarization of, 146–52, 249n3. *See also* Democrats; party identification; Republicans
political partisanship. *See* party identification
political protests and demonstrations, 46–47, 51
political tolerance: Bush on, 195–96; for communists, 32–33; content-controlled measure, 33; and context, 6; nature of, 11–12, 218; after 9/11, 216; and political freedom of African Americans, 35; of Russians, 35, 89, 115; and social group perceptions, 196–97; and social identity, 193–96; of South Africans, 35, 89–90, 116; and threat, 197
political trust: of African Americans, 74, 170–74; change over time, 127–31; and civil liberties, support of, 81–82, 84–85; civil liberties-national security trade-off, **56,** 58, 79, 132–33, 224; dimensions of, 169–70; of Latinos, 74, 169, 170–73; measurement of, 246n6; model of, 170; after 9/11, 69–70; and presidential approval, 172–73; by race and ethnicity, 170–74; and sociotropic threat, 77, 170–71; of whites, 170–73
political values, 31, 37–41
posttraumatic stress disorder (PTSD), 220–21
Powell, C., 167
Pratto, F., 204
prejudice, 204
presidential approval ratings, 149–52, 172–73

presidential election of 2000, 146–47, 167, 250*n*8
presidents, popularity of and party affiliation, 141
press. *See* media
Princeton Research Associates, 48, **49**
privacy rights, 44, **49**, 51
profiling. *See* racial profiling
protests, political, 46–47, 51
psychological reactance theory, 95, 100
public opinion. *See* survey experiments
Puerto Ricans, 169. *See also* Latinos
Pyszczynski, T., 62

racial discrimination, 42–43, 195, 199
racial-ethnic analyses: American citizenship views, 180–84; civil liberties, support of, 83, 134; civil liberties-national security trade-off, **55**, 73–75, 79–80, 221–22; counterarguments, 103, **105**; democratic norms, 175–78; patriotism, 178–80; perceptions of threat, 66, **68**, 73–75; political alienation, 165–66; political ideology, 156; political system support, 169–70; political trust, 170–74; research considerations, 164–65; survey questions, 246*n*8; U.S. responsibility for 9/11, 184–90
racial profiling: after 9/11, 19; survey counterarguments, 97–98, **99**, 100; survey question, 42–43; survey results, **49**, 51
racism, 33, 34, 35
Raile, E., 248*n*5
random assignment, 94–95
reason, 92
Red Scare, 32, 34
Reed, D., 250*n*10
regional analysis: civil liberties-national security trade-off, **55**; perceptions of threat, 66, **68**
Reingold, B., 181
Republicans: affiliation with, 142–46; civil liberties-national security trade-off, 57–58, 158–62; Contract with America, 148; disliked groups, 158; ideology, 153, 154
research considerations: civil liberties-national security trade-off, 4; media, 8–9; party identification, 138–39; racial-ethnic analyses, 164–65; sober second thought approach, 87–88; social group perceptions and reactions, 193
revenge, as root cause of terrorism, **189**
Rice, T., 142
Rokeach, M., 73
Roosevelt (FDR), administration, 2
Rousseau, J., 5, 7
rural residents: civil liberties-national security trade-off, **55**; perceptions of threat, **68**
Russians, tolerance among, 35, 89, 115

sample attrition, 117–18
Sanders, L., 89
Saunders, K., 148
Schatz, R., 72
Schickler, E., 140
search and seizure, 22–23, 46, **49**, 51
Second Treatise of Government (Locke), 7
"Secret Wars" exhibit, in Houston, 20
self-categorization, 195
self-incrimination, right against, **175**
September 11, 2001: African Americans' reactions to, 164, 166–68, 191; conspiracy theories, 185; death toll, 17; government's response, 18–21; Latinos' reactions to, 168–69; media during, 9; Pentagon, attack on, 17; political ideology after, 70–71; political party identification after, 142–46; political trust after, 69–70; public's memory of, 10–11; spirit of cooperation after, 147; U.S. responsibility for, 184–90, 243; World Trade Center attack, 16–17
September 11 Fund, 251*n*1
Sidanius, J., 204
silence, spiral of, 7–8, 138
Silver, B., 248*n*5

Skokie, Illinois, 33
smallpox, 18
Smith, R., 181
Smith Act, 2
"sneak and peek" search warrants, 22–23, 46
Sniderman, P., 6, 35–36, 37, 88, 90, 196, 210, 245*n*2
sober second thought approach: civil liberties vs. national security trade-off decision, 107–11; counterarguments, 95–107; persuasibility experiments, 88–93; research considerations, 87–88; research methodology, 94–95
social contract, 7
Social Dominance Orientation (SDO), 195
social group perceptions and reactions: and group cues, 196–97; before 9/11, 200–205; after 9/11, 205–16; research considerations, 193; social identity theory, 193–96; by sociotropic threat, 207–11
social identity theory, 193–96, 207
sociotropic threat: and civil liberties-national security trade-off, **56, 77**, 126–27, 132, 134, 220–21; and counterarguments, 103, **106**, 108–11; definition of, 63; and political trust, 77, 170–71; and social group perceptions, 207–16; survey questions, 231; survey results, 63–69; survey results over time, 122, 123–27
South Africans, tolerance among, 35, 89–90, 116
Southern Christian Leadership Conference (SCLC), 3
southerners, party affiliation, 148
speech, freedom of. *See* freedom of speech
Spence, L., 95
SRC (Survey Research Center), 142, 249*n*2
stadiums, threat from being in, **65, 123**
Stanley, J., 117
state of nature, 6
Staub, E., 72

Stimson, J., 148
Stouffer, S., 32, 57, 76, 196, 218
suburbanites: civil liberties-national security trade-off, **55**; perceptions of threat, **68**
Sullivan, J., 33, 72, 158, 205
Sun, 18
surveillance: under Combating Terrorism Act, 21; NSA's secret spy program, 47; under Patriot Act, 21, 22; survey question, 43–44
survey experiments: persuasibility experiments, 88–90; response inconsistencies, 93–94; sample attrition, 117–18. *See also* National Civil Liberties Survey
Survey Research Center (SRC), 142, 249*n*2

Tajfel, H., 194
Taliban, 24, 199, 251*n*4
tall buildings, threat from going into, **65, 123**
Taylor, D., 182
teachers, freedom of speech, 51, 118, 120
Terror Alert System, 10, 121
terrorism: event timeline, 225–27; fear of, 10, 62; framing by Bush administration, 40; perceived threat of, 25, 27–29, 65–66; root causes of, **189**, 242–43; targets of, 246*n*6; war against, 150. *See also* September 11, 2001
terrorist organizations: crime to belong to, 95–96, **99**; financial support of, 45, 96
terrorists: hatred of Americans, 187–88; identification of, 22; of 9/11, 17–18
terror management theory (TMT), 61–62, 197
Tetlock, P., 39, 245*n*4
Thomas, S., 76
threat: measurement of, 63; perceptions of, 60–69; perceptions over time, 120–27, 219; personal form of, 63–66, 77, 108, 122–23, 231–32; and

tolerance, 197. *See also* sociotropic threat
Time magazine, 9
TMT (terror management theory), 61–62, 197
tolerance. *See* political tolerance
trade-offs, 39–40. *See also* civil liberties-national security trade-off
Transportation Department, 44
treason, bail for those committing, **175**
Treasury Department, 45
trust, in government. *See* political trust
Turner, J., 194

United Airlines, Flight 93, 17
United Nations, 25, 167
urban residents: civil liberties-national security trade-off, **55**, 57; perceptions of threat, 66, **68**
USA Patriot Act, 3, 21–23, 45–46, 96, 135–36
USA Today, 17, 137
USA Today poll, 124–25, 248–49n6–7

value conflict, 31, 37–41
value pluralism, 39–40
value trade-off reasoning, 39
Vietnam War, 3, 34
visa violations, 21, 22, 97
voting rights, 181
vulnerability: and civil liberties-national security trade-off, 3–4, 80–84; feelings after 9/11, 10; reasons for, 65–66

warrants, search, 20, 22–23, 46, 97
Washington Post, 26, 147
Washington Post/ABC News polls, 148–52, 249n7
weapons of mass destruction, 25
Weisberg, H., 250n10
welfare, 38
whiteness, 182, **183**
whites: American identity views, 181, 182, 183–84; Bush approval ratings, 172–73; civil liberties, support of, 83; civil liberties-national security trade-off, 55; counterarguments, 103, **105**; democratic norms, 175–78; feeling thermometer ratings, 200, 204, 207, 208, 210, 212; party affiliation, 155, 156; patriotism, 178–80; political trust, 170–73; U.S. responsibility for 9/11, 185, **186**, 188, **189**
Wilcox, C., 198
Winter Olympics, in Salt Lake City, 19
wiretaps, 23, 43, **49**
women, 76. *See also* gender analyses
World Trade Center: attack on, 16–17; collapse of, 17
worldviews, 61–62, 70–71
World War I, 2, 19
World War II, 2, 167–68

Zaller, J., 38, 93